TOUCHING
MY FATHER'S
SOUL

TOUCHING MY FATHER'S SOUL

A Sherpa's Journey to the Top of Everest

JAMLING TENZING NORGAY
WITH BROUGHTON COBURN

HarperOne
An Imprint of HarperCollinsPublishers

HarperOne

HarperCollins books may be purchased for educational, business, or sales promotional use. For information, please e-mail the Special Markets Department at SPsales@harpercollins.com.

HarperCollins Web site: http://www.harpercollins.com
HarperCollins®, ☁®, and HarperOne™
are trademarks of HarperCollins Publishers.

Back cover photograph of baby Jamling with his father is from the Tenzing Collection.
Map illustration by Paul J. Pugliese, General Cartography Inc.

Designed by Joseph Rutt

Library of Congress Cataloging-in-Publication Data
Norgay, Jamling Tenzing.
Touching my father's soul : a Sherpa's journey to the top of Everest /
Jamling Tenzing Norgay with Broughton Coburn.—1st ed.
p. cm.
ISBN: 978-0-06-251688-6
1. Norgay, Jamling Tenzing. 2. Mountaineers—India—Biography.
3. MacGillivray Freeman IMAX/IWERKS Expedition (1996 : Mount Everest).
I. Coburn, Broughton. II. Title.
GV199.92 .N65 2001
796.52'2'092—dc21   00—068723

19 20 LSC(H) 15 14 13 12

For my late parents; my wife, Soyang; and the Sherpa people.

—J. T. N.

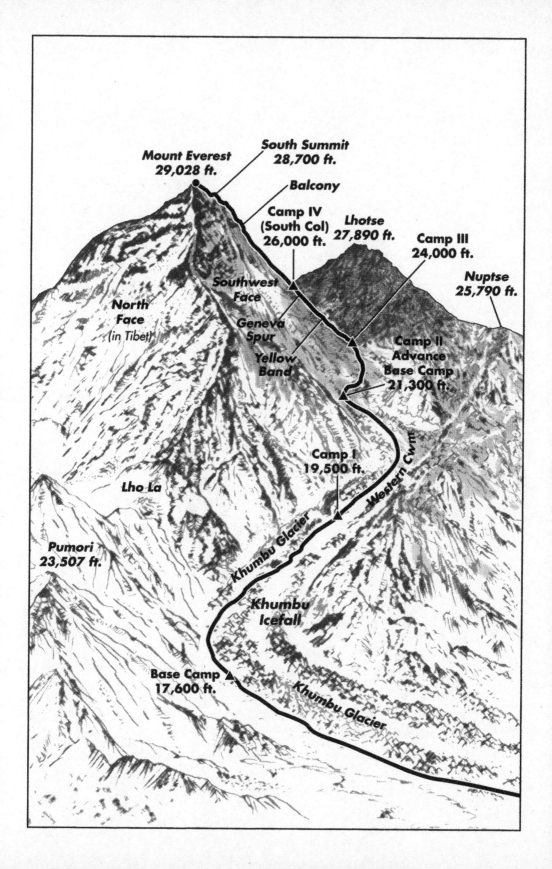

Mount Everest
29,028 ft.

South Summit
28,700 ft.

Balcony

Camp IV
(South Col)
26,000 ft.

Lhotse
27,890 ft.

Camp III
24,000 ft.

Nuptse
25,790 ft.

Southwest
Face

North
Face
(in Tibet)

Geneva
Spur

Yellow
Band

Camp II
Advance
Base Camp
21,300 ft.

Camp I
19,500 ft.

Western Cwm

Lho La

Khumbu Glacier

Pumori
23,507 ft.

Khumbu
Icefall

Base Camp
17,600 ft.

Khumbu Glacier

contents

Contents

foreword

THE DALAI LAMA

J amling Tenzing Norgay is the son of Tenzing Norgay, who, with Sir Edmund Hillary, was the first man to reach the summit of Mount Everest, or Jomolungma, as we call it in Tibetan. In this book he tells the story of his participation in the successful ascent of Everest in 1996. Although generally Tibetans do not attempt to scale the peaks of mountains, being content to cross the passes that characterize journeys in Tibet, Jamling Tenzing Norgay takes a very Tibetan view of the enterprise—he regards it as a pilgrimage. It is a pilgrimage on the one hand in tribute to his renowned and courageous father, but also because of the traditional Tibetan sense that such mountains are the abodes of divine beings.

Of course, pilgrimage is often regarded as a physical counterpart to the spiritual way of life. Both require a special attitude, careful preparation, a determination not to give up whatever the cost, courage to overcome whatever obstacles get in the way, and caution in the face of danger. Members of mountaineering teams become acutely aware of their dependence on their companions and at the same time their own responsibility towards them.

I congratulate Jamling Tenzing Norgay both on his safe and successful climb of the world's highest mountain and on writing a book that I am sure will be a source of positive inspiration for many readers.

The Dalai Lama
December 2000

introduction

Nearly five years have passed since the disturbing cascade of events that has come to be known as the 1996 Mount Everest disaster. Hundreds of thousands of words on the subject have been committed to print in the interim. The most recent account of the tragedy, *Touching My Father's Soul*, by Jamling Tenzing Norgay, is, by my rough calculation, the seventeenth book to be published about it. A half-decade after the fact, one would be forgiven for wondering why anybody other than the most obsessive Everest fanatic should bother reading yet another account of that infamous season on the world's highest mountain.

But Jamling's book should be read—it is in fact among the best of the bunch. There is much to marvel at in these pages. It taught me a great deal.

Jamling was the Climbing Leader of the 1996 expedition that made the hugely popular IMAX film *Everest*. Although most of the other accounts of the Everest disaster were written by men and women who, like Jamling, witnessed the catastrophe first-hand, this is the only one authored by a Sherpa—the Buddhist people whose homeland surrounds Mount Everest, and who have played a singular, utterly crucial role in the great peak's mountaineering history since the British first ventured onto its flanks in 1921.

Climbing Everest has always been an exceedingly hazardous undertaking, and the toll in Sherpa lives has from the beginning been disproportionately high—in large part because the non-Sherpa climbers responsible for hiring them have routinely subjected their Sherpa employees to significantly greater risks than they have taken themselves. Nevertheless, this is just the second book about Himalayan mountaineering written from a Sherpa's point of view. The only other, published thirty-seven years ago, has long been out of print and is now difficult to find. That book, as it happens, is the autobiography of Jamling's father, the late, world-renowned Tenzing Norgay.

On May 29, 1953, it was Tenzing who, in the company of a New Zealand beekeeper, name of Ed Hillary, made the first ascent of Everest. The 1996 tragedy provides the narrative architecture that gives shape to *Touching My Father's Soul*, but, as this title suggests, Jamling's book is to no small degree about his larger-than-life father and the complicated, emotionally charged bond they shared. Its publication seems especially propitious now that Tenzing's autobiography, *Tiger of the Snows*, has vanished from bookstore shelves.

In the heady months that followed his 1953 Everest climb, Tenzing was catapulted to the loftiest reaches of celebrity. He was lionized around the globe as one of the preeminent heroes of the post–World War II era. The newly crowned queen of England awarded the thirty-nine-year-old Sherpa the George Medal, the greatest honor that could be bestowed on a non-citizen of the United Kingdom. Feted throughout the world, he was befriended by the Indian prime minister Jawaharlal Nehru.

Throngs of adoring Hindus, convinced that Tenzing was a living embodiment of the deity Shiva, made pilgrimages to the Norgay home. Born in Tibet, raised in Nepal, and a resident of India since the age of nineteen, he had become a symbol of hope and inspiration for millions of caste-bound Indians, poverty-stricken Nepalese, and politically oppressed Tibetans—all of whom regarded him as a countryman.

Thirteen years after Tenzing stood atop Everest, Jamling was born in Darjeeling. According to Jamling, the relationship between father and son was "old-fashioned—he was strict and disciplined." Jamling also reports that he and his siblings came to understand at a very tender age that their father wasn't "an ordinary dad." By this time Tenzing's celebrity had long since become a burden, yet he considered fulfilling its obligations a duty that could not be shirked. Toward that end, he traveled prodigiously until his death in 1986, and his presence in the household was missed acutely by young Jamling. Tenzing left his family alone "for months at a time," recalls Jamling. "His absence was what I resented when I was a boy—a boy who wanted to join him and be with him."

As the son of such an eminent figure, Jamling, like his two brothers, was sent to one of India's most elite private boarding schools, Saint Paul's. Everest loomed large in Jamling's imagination as he was growing up, and he decided when still young that he would one day emulate his father by climbing it. When he was eighteen, with graduation from high school approaching, Jamling had an opportunity to join an Indian Everest expedition if he could convince his father to pull the necessary strings. Tenzing refused, sternly explaining, "I climbed Everest so that you wouldn't have to." Jamling was crushed.

Upon graduating from Saint Paul's, he traveled to the United States to attend Northland College, in Wisconsin, which had given his father an honorary degree many years earlier. Jamling would spend the next ten years in America, much of it in the flat suburban sprawl of New Jersey—virtually as far from the Himalaya as one can travel—but his dream of climbing Everest never vacated his thoughts. On May 9, 1986, while Jamling was still enrolled at Northland, he received word that his father had abruptly collapsed and died. It was a severe blow to the entire Norgay family, but, Jamling writes, "after my father's death, my desire to climb Everest only intensified."

Ten years later, Jamling was finally given an opportunity to fulfill this long-deferred aspiration. The eminent mountaineer and filmmaker David Breashears invited him to join the 1996 IMAX expedition, and Jamling accepted. His account of the ensuing events, including the disaster, is enthralling to read, largely because Jamling observes the behavior of his fellow climbers from a rare, inimitable perspective: He was intimately acquainted with both of the profoundly disparate cultures that met—and more than occasionally clashed—on the slopes of Everest that unfortunate spring: the Sherpas' on the one hand, and on the other that of the wealthy "white eyes," or *mikaru* (as the Sherpas called us), who hired them to risk their lives on our behalf.

The extent to which Jamling's life has straddled these two wildly incongruent worlds is reinforced by passages in the book that delineate his religious beliefs. Like most Sherpas, he was raised as a practicing Buddhist, but throughout his adolescence and young adulthood, Jamling writes, "I felt that stringing prayer flags was little more than a superstitious gesture. . . . Buddhism hadn't fully captured my heart. It wasn't a subject taught at

Saint Paul's, and my father was off climbing and traveling too much to teach me." He admits to feeling "cynical," and "unsure of my belief in Buddhism—skeptical, in fact," right up until the eve of the 1996 expedition. But then, arriving at the foot of Everest, he found himself drawn with surprising power by the traditions of his Buddhist ancestors.

The notorious storm that enveloped the peak on May 10, leaving nine dead climbers in its wake, played no small role in Jamling's religious transformation. "[O]nce I arrived in the lap of the mountain," he writes, "surrounded by Sherpas who believed, and confronted by a rich history of death—and death itself—I could no longer remain cynical."

Touching My Father's Soul is thus a story of spiritual evolution, with its concurrent struggles, failings, and irreconcilable contradictions. But more than that, it is the story of a son's quest to make things right with a father who was both a living legend and a painfully fleeting presence, and who died when the son was still teetering on the cusp of adulthood. Probing his own heart, Jamling asks, "What, honestly, was my motivation to climb [Everest]? For my teammates the expedition was somewhere between a job and a personal challenge, and these forces were drawing me, too. But I was driven primarily by a need for understanding. I felt that only by following my father up the mountain, by standing where he had stood, by climbing where he had climbed, could I truly learn about him. I wanted to know what it was that drove him and what it was he had learned. Only then would I be able to assemble all the missing parts of a father's life that a young man envisions and longs for but never formally inherits."

Jon Krakauer
February 2001

In the spring of 1996, I went for an audience with Geshé Rinchen Sonam Rimpoche. It was fortunate that his divination about the coming climbing season diverged slightly from an earlier reading. Rimpoche passed away in the summer of 1996.

1

AN
OMINOUS
FORECAST

1

AN OMINOUS FORECAST

Rimpoche bunched his *mala* rosary into his cupped hands and blew on it sharply. He withdrew the string of beads slowly and inspected it, turning his head slightly and squinting, as if trying to peer inside each individual bead. He looked up at me.

"Conditions do not look favorable. There is something malevolent about the mountain this coming season."

I felt as if I had been punched in the stomach—a feeling that surprised me considering that I was nothing of a devout Buddhist.

Rimpoche sat on a wide, flat cushion, and he adjusted his robe and began to rock back and forth as if he, too, had been surprised by the divination. He clapped his hand loudly to call the attendant monk. His clap broke the silence the way a guru's clap in a Buddhist teaching is meant to trigger awakening to the nature of emptiness, sparking a flash of recognition that all life is impermanent, containing no inherent existence. I experienced a narrow, momentary space of calmness, a millisecond of emptiness, then felt my stomach again.

A monk padded in quietly and served us tea, gently lifting the filigree silver cover from Rimpoche's jade teacup, which sat on a silver stand. The monk then offered me some fried breads from a woven bamboo tray. I declined, then accepted after the third offer. Such trays are always kept heaping full, and I had to concentrate to avoid knocking off the other pieces. My hand was shaking.

◆————————◆

IN EARLY JANUARY 1996, I had traveled here to Siliguri, West Bengal, for an audience with Chatral Rimpoche, a respected but reclusive lama of the Nyingma, or "ancient lineage," of Tibetan Buddhism. His principal monastery was located in Darjeeling, where I lived with my wife, but Rimpoche's patrons and supporters had built him a small monastic center in the northern plains of India, several hours away by jeep. The West Bengal landscape is relentlessly flat, far from the remote monasteries that the Nyingmapas established, beginning a millennium ago, across the Himalaya. I felt fortunate to have been born on the south side of the Himalaya, safe from the Chinese invasion of Tibet. Since the late 1950s, Tibetans have been crossing their border into India, Sikkim, and Nepal seeking refuge. Partly as a result of their unerring devotion, Tibetan Buddhism continues to flourish along the south side of the Himalaya, including among my people, the Sherpa.

Rimpoche's chapel and quarters are painted in the bright primary and earthen colors of Himalayan monasteries. Accented by the tall prayer flags on the roof, the compound looked invitingly familiar across a landscape of banana trees, Tata trucks, and blowing dust. It hardly seemed like a place to get a technical reading on the advisability of attempting to climb the world's tallest peak, Mount Everest.

I told Rimpoche that I was there to request a divination, then cautiously asked him about the coming season on the mountain.

I wondered how accurate such divinations really are, statistically speaking. The ability of some lamas to see into the future is remarkable, my parents always said, and their words can be frightening for some. Indeed, fear of prior knowledge of events is one reason why many Sherpas are careful about requesting divinations—and one reason why lamas often shroud their counsel in generalities and aphorisms. The truth, especially when presented in advance, can be too much for some people to accept graciously. They tend to become angry or to deny it, only further exhibiting the "afflictive emotions" of anger and ignorance. Many lamas feel that laypeople don't use knowledge of the future properly. Seldom do people apply it to further their self-understanding or to aid noble causes. Again and again, people hope vainly to control events that have yet to occur, events that never seem to play out in the way they imagined.

Raised in a religious family, I was aware of the danger of asking questions of lamas. "When you request a divination, you must always be prepared to abide by the answer," my father, Tenzing Norgay Sherpa, had cautioned me. Fine, as long as it was a positive answer or even neutral. But this divination was unequivocally bad.

I was already firmly—inextricably—committed to climbing Mount Everest. Should I tell my teammates on the Everest IMAX Filming Expedition about Rimpoche's ominous forecast?

How could I? I was the Climbing Leader. Were I to drop out, and only three months before the start of the climb, it would cast a long shadow over the expedition and, I felt, over my father's name and my family legacy. My wife, Soyang, was the reason I was here. She is a young and educated Tibetan woman, yet traditional and reserved. She was against my plan to climb Everest unless a lama pronounced it safe.

A week earlier the veteran Himalayan mountaineer David Breashears had phoned me from the United States. He said that a modified IMAX movie camera had been successfully field-tested and that funding had been secured for an expedition that would try to haul the cumbersome forty-two-pound device to the summit. An extraordinarily ambitious goal. "I need you, Jamling," he told me. "Your story, your father's story, and the story of the Sherpas will be important to the film. But I first wanted to make sure you haven't committed to another climb for this spring. If not, then welcome to the team. Let's talk details soon."

Soyang overheard the phone call. She had been uneasily quiet all afternoon. That night, lying in our bed at home in Darjeeling, she sat up and looked at me sternly. In a determined voice, she said that we had better talk about my Everest plans.

"You don't simply say you're going to climb Everest in the manner that you say you're going to see a movie." Her tone was imploring, but not entirely dissuasive. She knew that I'd been dreaming of Everest for years and that if I didn't go I would regret it for the rest of my life. Ever since I was a boy I had heard stories of my father's historic climb of Everest with Edmund Hillary in 1953. I had always wanted to join my father on the summit. When I became an adult, and after my father's death, my desire to climb Everest only intensified. I wanted to preserve the family name, which was being eclipsed by a new era of climbing. My father and Hillary's first ascent was approaching the limits of living people's memories.

But other forces were also driving me. I had to learn what it was that had driven my father and what he had found on the mountain. Our relationship had been old-fashioned—he was strict and disciplined—and when he died, much had been left unsaid. I was twenty-one years old at the time, and I knew that there was so much more for him to teach me and so much more for me to learn.

Soyang rolled over and was quiet again, then got up to nurse our young daughter. When she returned, she said that if I first had a *mo*, a divination, done by a high lama, and if his forecast was favorable, she would relent. As I lay in bed, I thought of the effort it had taken me to get this far, and I knew the timing would never be perfect. I had already missed two chances, and I felt that this, the lucky third time, had been prescribed by fate, or karma.

While I was growing up in Darjeeling, my father directed the Himalayan Mountaineering Institute, India's foremost mountaineering school, which provided training for the citizens and armed forces of several South Asian countries, and for Sherpas and Tibetans. In 1983, during my last year of high school, I heard that an Indian expedition was planning to attempt Everest. I desperately wanted to join them and knew that getting selected for the team at my young age would require my father's influence. I wanted to be the youngest person to climb Everest.

I cut classes one day to meet him at our family home and found him in the sitting room with his secretary, Mr. Dewan. He dispatched Mr. Dewan so we could speak. I put on my most assertive, adult face, secure in the knowledge that, for Sherpa families in Darjeeling, it was understood and expected that children would follow in their father's footsteps. For me this was no problem, because I loved climbing. And I felt a duty to make my father proud by upholding his reputation. But my trepidation was clearly showing.

I asked him.

"You aren't ready," he answered abruptly—too abruptly, I felt.

Had he thought about it? Might he want some time to consider?

"I can't help you with it," he continued. "I'd like for you to finish school and go to college."

I groped for a response, for words that would casually deflect his reply, but his fatherly conviction told me he had made a decision.

As I picked up my rucksack and headed for the door, I noticed that my hands were trembling. My body felt stiff and awkward. I could see blown snow drifting into and filling the footsteps he had made for me up the mountain, leaving only a powdery, seamless expanse of white.

"I climbed Everest so that you wouldn't have to," he said as I stood near the doorway. "You can't see the entire world from the top of Everest, Jamling. The view from there only reminds you how big the world is and how much more there is to see and learn."

Instead of returning to school, I walked up the street to the house of my uncle, Tenzing Lotay, to ask him what I should do.

Uncle Tenzing was equally abrupt. "You have no experience, Jamling, and you need it to join that team. Those guys are very proficient climbers."

"But it's not a matter of experience," I countered. "It's a matter of desire and motivation and strength." I was Jamling, derived from *Jambuling Nyandrak*, the full name given to me by a high Buddhist lama. It means "world renowned."

My logical mind, trying vainly to speak over the din of my emotions, told me that my father and uncle were right. I would need age and experience.

It wasn't until 1995 that I came close, for the second time, to getting a shot at the mountain. An American had invited me to join his team if I could raise $20,000, my share of the costs. I was working in New Jersey at the time, and America was a more likely place to find sponsors than India, so I stayed there to work and raise funds.

I sent out hundreds of requests but got nothing. No money, no sponsors. As consolation, the leader invited me to trek to Base Camp with them anyway. He even asked me to guide part of the expedition: the group of volunteers who had signed on to clean up litter along the approach route. It was a ticket to Everest, and I took it, though I was disappointed—humiliated, in fact—to be a simple trekker on an expedition to Everest and a garbage collector, Asia's lowliest occupation. I bore no ill will toward the American team, but it was then that I vowed to redeem my family's name and my father's legacy.

BOWING TOWARD CHATRAL RIMPOCHE, hands together, I respectfully backed out of his reception room and stepped into the claustrophobic heat of the Indian plains. I felt I was walking through a dungeon, chewing on the distasteful words that Rimpoche had thrown me. He was said to be able to divine the intentions of those who came to him for blessings. Half-hearted Buddhist that I was, I wondered if my motivation was entirely pure. My mother had told me that the poorest of people would dress like nobility in borrowed clothes, and approach him with offerings of whatever paltry sums of money they had saved. He could easily spot them, and always sent them away with their offerings.

I returned to Darjeeling with troubled thoughts, which began to invade my dreams. Soyang slept poorly, too. I told her that Chatral Rimpoche didn't have much to say about the mountain this season, but she saw right through me, just as I felt Rimpoche had.

Not only would I be defying my wife if I chose to climb, but in disregarding the lama's words I'd be going against my family and religious heritage. I knew what my mother would have thought had she been alive. The last time she defied the cautious directive of a divination, she died.

Like many traditional Sherpas, my mother, Daku, became more religious and devout as she aged. In the years before her death, she grew single-mindedly attentive to Chatral Rimpoche, donating grains, sugar, and other staples to his monasteries in Darjeeling and Siliguri. She commissioned the painting of *thangkas* (religious scroll paintings) for the assembly halls, and paid for the construction of monks' quarters.

Daku was outgoing and social. She often traveled with my father when he was invited overseas to give lectures, and she never suffered culture shock. Typically, they were VIP guests of local dignitaries, but she always took her Himalayan trinkets along with her and spread them out on a blanket on the steps of their hotels to sell to passersby. From that beginning, she built a small trading business, expanded into the travel trade, and opened an office in the Darjeeling bazaar.

Her sole motivation was to send her three sons to Saint Paul's, one of India's most expensive and elite private schools, located on a ridge just fifteen minutes' walk from our home, and to send her daughter to the Loretto Convent. When my youngest brother, Dhamey, began attending Saint Paul's as a boarding student, my mother had largely completed what we regard as the second stage of life. She had fulfilled her obligations and duties as a householder. She remained as busy as always, but her face and body movements told me she was anticipating the final phase of life, the religious phase, when she could devote herself to spiritual matters and preparation for death. She was only in her late forties, but one cannot begin spiritual practice too soon. Years before at the stupa of Boudhanath in Kathmandu, it had surprised me to see her prostrate by body lengths around the stupa. Wearing a heavy apron over her street clothes, she would stretch out on the stone walkway, reach out with her hands as far as she could, place her forehead on the pavement, then rise and step forward to begin her next prostration at the furthest point her fingers had touched.

After my father died in 1986, she began to dream of going on pilgrimage to Pema Cave, in the remote region of Pema-kö, high in the hills of southern Tibet and the Indian states of Arunachal Pradesh and Assam. She knew that pilgrimage is an excellent way to gain merit. And if the pilgrimage site is holy and powerful enough, one can gain direct transmission of wisdom simply by appearing before the deities present there and bathing in their sacred blessings.

Pema-kö, however, is legendary for its unfriendly hill tribes that are believed to poison strangers, and the area is restricted even to Indians from outside the region. It took a year for my mother to gain permission to visit this site. Before departing, she sought Chatral Rimpoche's blessings, and then she set out from Darjeeling with two of his monks. The trail was long and torturous, and the journey took them over a month.

At the time, my brother Norbu was living in California, and when he phoned me in New Jersey, he was disturbed and frightened. He had received a call from Darjeeling saying that Mom was in Siliguri, after having been evacuated from a remote part of Arunachal, and that she was very sick. Little else was known about her condition.

She had reached Pema Cave, at which point the more devout pilgrims must circumambulate three sacred mountains. While circling the nearest mountain, she took ill with undefined internal problems and decided to retreat to the town of Tuting to recover. She remained there for eight days, yet her sickness worsened. The doctors were unable to identify her ailment, so they put her on a plane to Gauhati and then Bagdogra, and from there the monks took her by car to a hospital in Siliguri. Medical staff in underequipped rural hospitals sometimes prefer to send difficult cases to larger hospitals to sidestep blame if the patient dies on their watch. Indeed, for many on the subcontinent, hospitals are known as places where people go to die.

At the hospital, my mother lost her appetite entirely and grew weaker. She asked continually about her family. My brother Dhamey and sister Deki were also in the United States, and just before we caught flights to India, I received another phone call. The barely audible voice on the phone informed me that she had died. It was September 22, 1992. She was fifty-two years old.

We returned to Darjeeling with her body for the cremation. I was distraught, but the monk who had accompanied my mother reminded me that most people are born with a time of death already prescribed by their karma and astrological alignment, and that whatever time they die is the right time. I'm not sure I believed that; it sounded like a rationalization. Then he told me that it was remarkable that her body gave off no odor, which Buddhists claim is a very good omen and a sign of a great practitioner. For me, it was little consolation.

At her memorial service, another monk from Chatral Rimpoche's monastery approached me, saddened that the community had lost "Neela," as they referred to her, the familiar but respectful term for "aunt."

"Ever since her death, it's as if our hands have been bound," he said. "When she visited our *gompa*, she brought with her an aura of serenity and compassion. We all felt it. Once, after a long absence, she viewed the statues in the assembly hall and said to us, 'These deities are crying, they are sweating and writhing, due to your negligence in cleaning them!' She sponsored many repaintings and regilding of the statues, but many times the painter, witnessing the sincerity and depth of her devotion, refused to accept payment from her."

The day after her funeral, I saw the monk again, and he told me that Neela had turned down an offer to be evacuated by helicopter from Tuting; he also suggested that she may have been poisoned by the Pema-kö people or that she could have sustained the bite of a poisonous spider or inadvertently eaten a poisonous plant. For countless events that transpire in India, it seems, it is difficult to identify causes or assign blame.

He then told me that Rimpoche had done a divination for Neela, and he foresaw that this particular journey to Pema-kö looked extremely unfavorable. He advised her not to go. "Stay here in Siliguri. I will give you some land, and you can build a house on it and practice *dharma*," Rimpoche had offered.

I was shocked to hear this, but somehow I could understand my mother's reasoning. She was torn between her devotion to Rimpoche and her desire for merit and blessings from this holy site. She knew that it was not Rimpoche she would defy by going on pilgrimage. It was her own planetary alignment, her own fate she was tempting—a risk she was willing to take for the sake of additional merit. That her motive was a spiritual one did little to assuage my grief. It seemed unusual, and perhaps prescient, that she had already bought many of the wedding gifts and other items for her children, though only Norbu was planning to marry at the time she died.

My mother had not heeded Chatral Rimpoche's premonition. I was beginning to think that I should. For one thing, I was still firmly planted in the householder stage of life, with a wife, young daughter, and thoughts of more children. Because I had an obligation to care for them, I had an obligation to care for myself. As the Buddhists say, I had been granted a "precious human rebirth," which should not be squandered.

I was unsure of my belief in Buddhism, however—skeptical, in fact. Nonetheless, it would have been as excruciating to defy our family's religion as to abandon my hopes for climbing. Fortunately, there was still one other possibility. We were going to Kathmandu, Nepal, shortly, where I would be able to seek a second opinion about the coming season on Everest. It would have to be favorable.

Soyang urged me to visit Geshé Rimpoche, her family's guru, a learned lama I had met some years before. He was living in Kathmandu and was known for his accurate divinations. Even foreigners posted at some of the embassies sought him out for advice.

We had planned to spend the spring of 1996 with Soyang's parents, who lived in a Tibetan community just south of Kathmandu. They were refugees, wealthy by local standards, and their house would be a good place to prepare for the Everest IMAX Filming Expedition. And to prepare for another divination.

The day before we left Darjeeling for Nepal, I stepped out the back door and hiked through the trees above our house.

Intersecting the ridge, I followed it to the top of Tiger Hill, Darjeeling's highest point, a good place to string prayer flags. *Lungta* they are called—windhorses. With each flap of the flag, my mother would say, the horse depicted on the cotton print gallops off into the wind with prayers, circling the globe, benefiting all sentient beings. I tied several lengths of them together, climbed two nearby pine trees, and hung them in a smiling arc across the clearing at the top of Tiger Hill.

In fact, my mother had explained to me, the lungta horse bears a deity carrying wish-fulfilling gems, which we need in order to thrive. But lungta also represents the degree of positive spiritual energy and awareness that propels people—their level of divine inner support. Sherpas say that if their lungta is high, they can survive almost any difficult situation, and if it is low, they can die even while resting on a grassy slope like Tiger Hill. One's lungta can be cultivated through meditation and through awareness and right actions. Indeed, for those with a high lungta, the lamas say, only the karma generated in previous lifetimes that has "ripened" can bring misfortune.

But at the time, I felt that stringing prayer flags was little more than a superstitious gesture, done only out of respect for my parents. Buddhism hadn't fully captured my heart. It wasn't a subject taught at Saint Paul's, and my father was off climbing and traveling too much to teach me. Perhaps I needed to learn more about it.

From Tiger Hill I looked north across the green valleys of Sikkim and followed the line where the dark blue sky encounters a jagged horizon of black and white—the eastern Himalaya. Kangchenjunga, the "Five Treasures of the Great Snows," stood above the others at the intersecting borders of Sikkim, Nepal, and Tibet. Kangchenjunga, the world's third-highest peak at 28,146 feet, wasn't climbed until 1955, well after Everest's successful ascent—though not for lack of trying. Climbers were killed on virtually all of the early attempts on this peak, beginning with the first try in 1905.

From Tiger Hill, the Himalaya seem to bow upward in the middle, dipping slightly at the far ends, as if spanning a visible arc of the earth's curvature. Jhomolhari and other peaks in Bhutan capture the northeast skyline. Panning back to Nepal in the northwest, I could see the massive giant of Makalu, over 8,000 meters (26,250 feet) tall, and behind it Lhotse and Nuptse. And behind them all stood an incongruous peak, its solid black triangular pyramid seeming to anchor and support the others. A narrow plume of clouds streaked from its summit like a *kata* blessing scarf. It was named Chomolungma, "Unshakable Good Elephant Woman," abode of the beneficent and protective goddess Miyolangsangma. Mount Everest. I wondered why anyone would want to rename a mountain as sacred and majestic as Chomolungma after a human.

From the moment he arrived in Darjeeling as a young man, my father remained homesick for Khumbu, the homeland of the Sherpas, where he grew up in the shadow of Chomolungma. But the view of the mountain from Tiger Hill reminded him that he had not moved far. It continued to uplift him, then it came to dominate his imagination. He had come to Darjeeling partly in search of work, but mainly to consummate his destiny with this peak.

Far below me lay the hamlet of Alu Bari, or "Potato Field," where my father first found lodging. In 1932, after sneaking away from his home in the Khumbu village of Thame, he trekked two weeks over high ridges and into deep valleys to Nepal's western border with India. There, a Tibetan trader gave him work for several weeks cutting firewood, then eventually took him to Darjeeling on the steam-powered "Toy Train," where he found him a job tending cows.

Before 1951, when Nepal opened to the outside world for the first time, Everest expeditions were staged out of Darjeeling, a town that was created in the mid-1800s by the British raj as a hill station. Beginning in the 1920s, the British approached Everest from the Tibet side. On their way northward through Darjeeling, they picked up Sherpas who had moved there from Nepal looking for work.

Many of the early Darjeeling Sherpas, or "Bhotias" (Tibetans), as they were first referred to, settled in the poor hamlet of Toong Soong Busti, just beyond the bazaar on the back side of the ridge. They lived semi-communally in clusters of shacks braced against one another on the steep hillside as if in defiance of gravity. In the mid-1930s my father moved into a tin-roofed structure owned by Ang Tharkay, a prominent Sherpa *sirdar*, or expedition foreman, who had been awarded a "Tiger of the Snows" medal by the Himalayan Club for his climbing prowess. He would go on to be sirdar for the French on Annapurna in 1950. Even today many Sherpas, including some of my relatives, continue to live in Toong Soong.

My father was a simple boy from the hills, and the upper, wealthy part of Darjeeling town fascinated him. Here were the houses built by the British, modeled on English country homes with high ceilings and spiral, red-carpeted staircases graced by smooth, polished banisters. After he climbed Everest, a prominent Indian newspaper offered him the house we now live in, though he paid for most of it, he said, so they wouldn't someday find an excuse to take it away. During the winters now, we close off much of the house to conserve heat. Only the British colonials could have afforded the labor to cut the wood required to keep its seven fireplaces fully stoked.

After independence in 1947, wealthy Indians bought most of these luxurious homes. Some have been converted into guest lodges that house the waves of Indian tourists who ascend the seven-thousand-foot rise to Darjeeling, like thermal convection, to beat the summer heat. After 1953, Indians from West Bengal especially were on a pilgrimage to our door, hoping for a glimpse of the famous "Sherpa Tenzing." Hindus believe—or used to, anyway—that any human who could stand on the summit of Everest must be an incarnation of Shiva, the wrathful destroyer deity of the Hindu trinity. My father made no such claims, of course, and he quickly grew tired of the obsessive adoration.

The Planters' Club—until 1947 a social venue for British only—still presides over the middle of town. Sitting in the shade on Tiger Hill, I pictured the early days of the Sherpas. Ragtag groups of them in long braided hair would line up on the terrace below the club's veranda, shoulders tensed, hands stiff at their sides, to be scrutinized by British in pith helmets and puttees, busy consulting their expedition conscription lists. Working for the obsessed and often eccentric foreign climbers was sometimes difficult, but the pay was respectable considering that the Sherpas were coming from a subsistence, barter economy. And, especially for my father, climbing was an adventure.

In the early thirties my father carried milk from his landlord's cows past the Planters' Club to sell in the bazaar. One of his customers was my late stepmother, his second wife, Ang Lhamu. She later came to visit him when he worked as a laborer on the reconstruction of the Saint Paul's School chapel, following the Great Bihar Earthquake of 1934. She brought milk for him to drink, the first of many generous deeds that culminated, I learned from a respected lama, in her contribution to his success on Chomolungma.

THE FOLLOWING MORNING, Soyang and our daughter and I departed Darjeeling for Nepal. Riding in a succession of cars and rickshaws and a small commercial plane, we arrived in Kathmandu that evening.

It was comfortable visiting with Soyang's parents, but I was anxious to see Geshé Rimpoche, the family lama. Soyang wanted to join me, no doubt to hear and interpret the words of the divination herself. We took a taxi to the Great Stupa of Boudhanath.

This ancient reliquary, on the northeast side of Kathmandu, is the spiritual nerve center of Nepal's Tibetan and Sherpa community. The stupa's mandala-shaped stone skirt is worn smooth by countless circuits of murmuring, devout Buddhists, the soles of their buffalo hide boots and Chinese sneakers scuffing through a thin layer of dust. Motorized traffic, now blocked from entry, growls and shrieks impatiently outside the gates.

We did a circumambulation of the stupa and then peeled off to a small monastery located just off the busy pilgrims' circuit. Standing in the courtyard garden, walled in on three sides by two-story monks' quarters, we prepared our offerings of fruit, money, and kata scarves. A monk greeted us and guided us to Geshé Rimpoche's quarters. I was surprised that his room was little more than a simple monk's cubicle on the bottom floor, uncharacteristic of lamas' quarters, which are usually situated above the others or in a separate building.

The monk drew back the door curtain, and Soyang and I entered. Rimpoche was old, wrinkled, and thin, and his head was nearly bald, but his chin sprouted long, white hair. I felt a chill. *What a simple person,* I thought. I could see that he had his bed, his attendant, his texts, and nothing else. I envied him his simplicity, for in it he had clearly found peace, which seemed to radiate from him not in glorious waves but rather in a childlike naturalness. I immediately felt burdened and confused, by contrast, and ashamed for these feelings.

We presented Rimpoche with kata blessing scarves, in which I enclosed some rupee notes. Without speaking, he placed the rupees on his prayer table, unfurled the scarves, and draped them around our necks, as a blessing in return; then he motioned us to sit. He told the attendant to bring tea, which arrived in cups and saucers.

Rimpoche sat cross-legged on his daybed, and I found myself looking mostly at the simple stitching on his maroon and brocade robes, as if, were our eyes to meet, he would see too far into me. We talked about family and marriage and my deceased parents. Then I told him about the Everest expedition.

Rimpoche may have sensed my anticipation, or Soyang's nervousness, and I broached my reason for being there by expressing concern about conditions for the coming season on the mountain. Then I asked him for a divination.

"Why do you want to do this thing anyway?" he asked loudly, with a tone of urgency above the level of our prior conversation.

The question of why is difficult enough when asked by a stranger, but now my wife's lama was grilling me. Rimpoche may have been aware of the deaths on the mountain—the more than 150 who have died attempting to climb it, or about one for every five who have reached the summit. Many Sherpas have been killed there, including my own cousin Lobsang Tsering. Because of our precious human rebirth, Buddhists consider it irresponsible to voluntarily place oneself in harm's way unless the act is motivated by need or compassion. For the Sherpas who grew up in Everest's shadow, carrying loads up the mountain is a job, a justifiable necessity. For most foreigners, it is a form of recreation.

Ethnically I am a Sherpa, but I would also be a full climbing member of the IMAX expedition. What, honestly, was my motivation to climb? For my teammates the expedition was somewhere between a job and a personal challange, and these forces were drawing me, too. But I was driven primarily by a need for understanding. I felt that only by following my father up the mountain, by standing where he had stood, by climbing where he had climbed, could I truly learn about him. I wanted to know what it was that drove him and what it was he had learned. Only then would I be able to assemble all the missing parts of a father's life that a young man envisions and longs for but never formally inherits.

"I guess I *have* to," I said, groping. "There's something about my father, and I feel a family connection to the mountain. I think it was written on my forehead at birth."

If only my father had been a carpenter or a plumber, I thought, I wouldn't have been looking up at Mount Everest with such a passion to climb it.

"And also," I added, reaching for something to further bolster my purpose, "I've been asked by a team of foreigners to help carry a big movie camera to the top."

The last reason drew a brief puzzled look from Rimpoche. He was unsure of the motives of most people these days, the great mass of humanity distracted by the trappings and fabricated urgency of modern life. I then added what I really meant to say, which was that perhaps through my involvement with the film the world would learn more about Sherpas, Sherpa beliefs, and Buddhism.

Rimpoche nodded. "This is good," he said. He knew my family history, and my quest seemed to satisfy him. Ultimately, the Buddhist teachings say, misfortune happens less often to those whose motives are pure.

Then Rimpoche shifted farther back on his seat and half-closed his eyes. Mouthing a mantra, he slowly pulled a small, well-worn leather pouch from the folds of his robe. The pouch was oiled with grease from his hands, which in turn were oiled by the butter from votive lamps and the butterfat rime on his wooden teacup. He withdrew three Tibetan dice from the pouch, and placed them between his cupped palms. He seemed to go into deep concentration. Vigorously, he blew on the dice inside his hands, then one by one he rolled them onto the prayer table. He picked up the dice and repeated the process twice more while looking at me, or rather *through* me, it seemed.

He raised his head and was about to speak, then paused. I held my breath, hoping his pause was merely for effect.

"There are obstacles. . . . The mountain will see some difficulties this year." He looked at me quizzically, as if I, better than he, might be able to interpret what that meant. Momentarily stunned, I waited for him to say more. "The season looks bad . . . but not entirely unfavorable." I waited quietly for more. Anything more.

"What can I do about the obstacles?" I asked.

"Offerings and rituals. And prayers. You should have some

obstacle-removal rituals done, and make offerings at the stupa of Boudhanath, especially. To prepare yourself sufficiently will require some perseverance from you, I think. And patience."

I sat for a moment, thinking hard, then leaned forward. He poured some blessed water from a *bhumpa* ceremonial urn into my outstretched palm as I cupped my other hand respectfully beneath it. I lifted my palm to my mouth, sipped half of it, then rubbed the remainder in my hair.

Rimpoche smiled politely as we stood to leave. His sympathetic look conveyed that he had found more in his rosary than he had told me about but decided it would be best not to say more.

As we were leaving, he added an afterthought. "I can also see that many people will hear about you and the events of this coming season—as much as they heard about your father, Tenzing, after his climb."

Palms together in front of us, Soyang and I backed our way out through the curtained doorway.

Outside, we drew deep, simultaneous breaths and looked at each other, trying to imagine what his closing words meant or what would have to transpire for his words to be fulfilled. Few people outside my family and my neighbors even knew that I was planning to attempt Everest. Sherpas believe that to advertise one's resolutions is to invite misfortune.

My assignment was clear: I would have to begin dislodging obstacles on the path to Everest, preferably without alerting people to the divination and its unfavorable forecast. I didn't think that expedition leader David Breashears was superstitious, but he might be spooked by a judgment coming from a high lama. The Sherpas on the expedition definitely would be.

◆————◆

IN LATE MARCH the IMAX team arrived in Kathmandu, most of them on the same Thai Airways flight from Bangkok. Aside from Breashears, I had met none of them before, but I was impressed by their formidable climbing résumés.

Late that afternoon the members settled at the Hotel Yak and Yeti, and we gathered in the lobby. They were all strong, fresh, and youthful, I remarked to myself, products of superior training and nutrition. The plush leather seats of the sitting area seemed to make them physically uncomfortable.

Araceli Segarra of Lleida, Catalonia, had a beguiling smile, and her impeccable posture nicely matched her occupation of physiotherapist. She was a versatile ice, rock, and alpine climber and had climbed the South Face of Shishapangma (26,273 feet) in Tibet in lightweight alpine style. In 1995 she attempted the North Face of Everest, reaching within 3,000 feet of the summit. If she made it this time, Araceli would be the first Catalonian woman, and the first Spanish woman, to climb the mountain.

She had come to mountaineering by way of spelunking. Once, while she and her partners were resting on a ledge deep within a cave, water flooded the exit passageways above them and filled the cavern below, subsiding only twelve hours later. Her transition to Himalayan mountaineering seemed a conservative move.

Sumiyo Tsuzuki had been on Everest twice before, reaching 23,000 feet by way of the North Col in 1995. Only one Japanese woman had reached Everest's summit, twenty years earlier, and Sumiyo hoped to repeat the feat.

Ed Viesturs, the Deputy Leader, was hoping to climb Everest

a fourth time—his second without supplemental oxygen. But this trip up Everest was merely a detour on his mission to be the first American to climb all fourteen of the peaks higher than 8,000 meters (26,250 feet) without oxygen. He had climbed Mount Rainier in the state of Washington 187 times and had earned the nickname "Steady Ed" for his professional and mature manner.

Ed's wife, Paula, was joining us as Base Camp manager, and she would provide logistical support while we were on the mountain. Ed and Paula had been married in Mexico only three weeks before their trip to Everest.

Robert Schauer of Graz, Austria, an accomplished cinematographer, brought the extra talent and experience needed to operate the IMAX camera at 26,000 feet. He had climbed five of the world's eight-thousand-meter peaks and had been the first Austrian to reach Everest's summit, eighteen years earlier. The climb he was proudest of was the alpine-style (unsupported and without fixed ropes) first ascent of the West Face of Gasherbrum IV in Pakistan, a feat that has yet to be repeated. He had trained for that ascent by climbing the north face of the Eiger, in the Swiss Alps, in winter.

As Climbing Leader, I was in charge of the Sherpas and the load-carrying logistics high on the mountain. We were taking as much film equipment as food and climbing gear, quadrupling the strategic headaches compared to those of a normal climbing expedition. Yaks and *zopkios*—yak-cow crossbreeds—would carry our loads on the approach to Base Camp, with help from porters, generally of the Rai, Limbu, and Tamang ethnic groups of southeast Nepal. Porters hang out at airstrips and roadheads looking for loads to carry, especially expedition loads, and the few dollars a day they earn is decent pay by local standards.

By comparison, the high-altitude Sherpas are skilled labor and are paid according to the weight they carry, their experience, and the altitudes they reach. In order to avoid jealousy, defections, and strikes, climbing Sherpas' wages would be set at a general meeting of all the expeditions at Base Camp. If some Sherpas perform exceptionally well, they may be paid a bonus under the table. Climbing Sherpas can earn more than $1,500 in a season, several times what most Nepalese make in a year. Still, only the top sirdars and those with access to investment capital own houses and businesses in Kathmandu—where land prices exceed those of most upscale American residential communities.

Breashears was the obvious choice for team leader and director. He was the first American to summit Everest twice, and he had directed or worked on eight films shot on the mountain. Hauling an unwieldy IMAX camera to the summit was not something he thought entirely possible at first, but David was inspired by the dream of seeing Everest projected onto screens ninety feet high.

Because IMAX films generally have a science focus, we were also joined by advisers. Roger Bilham, professor of geology at the University of Colorado, arrived with suitcases loaded with tools, superglue, transistors, batteries, a laptop computer, and duct tape—which I think he used mainly on his suitcases. Roger had already been working with Nepal's Department of Mines on setting up a network of GPS (global positioning system) satellite receivers to measure movements of the tectonic plates beneath the Himalaya. He would be continuing this work along the approach route, which follows the dynamic suture line of the Eurasian and Indian continents, landmasses that are still converging. Eventually, the information gained might contribute to the forecasting of earthquakes, though Roger emphasized that the prospect of doing this in a practical manner is a long way off.

The climbing historian Audrey Salkeld also joined us. She had written a book about George Mallory and Andrew "Sandy" Irvine, the British pair who disappeared high on Everest in 1924. In 1953 my father and Ed Hillary had looked for traces of them on the top but found nothing. In 1999, seventy-five years later almost to the day, Conrad Anker and members of the Mallory-Irvine Research Expedition would find Mallory's body two thousand feet below the summit. Apparently he had been killed in a fall. The camera he was carrying with him was not found, but if it can be recovered—perhaps from Irvine's still-missing body—and the film developed, it might determine whether they reached the summit. If they did, however, it would not affect the stature of Hillary's and my father's climb. First ascents are generally recognized as successful only when the climbers return alive.

As we lounged in the Yak and Yeti lobby, Ed summarized his approach to mountaineering, which had served him well in the Himalaya: "Getting to the top is optional; getting down is mandatory." The climbers became quiet for a moment. I swallowed hard, hoping it didn't show.

Most of the thirty-five Sherpas hired for the IMAX expedition had hiked to Kathmandu from Khumbu, Solu, and Rolwaling, the valleys along and near the approach route to Base Camp. As always, they brought with them their customary unrestrained humor and playfulness, and I immediately felt comfortable with them. On this expedition I was a "member," not a "Sherpa," in the term's specific sense of high-altitude climbing porter. Ethnically, however, I'm a Sherpa, and I intended to do much of the repetitive load-carrying to high camps, partly to show solidarity with the other Sherpas and partly because I enjoyed their company.

While living in America, I had adopted the genial and humorous mannerisms common in the West, yet they sometimes felt forced and calculated. Simply holding a conversation in Sherpa or Nepali with my Sherpa friends made me feel lighter, and effortlessly cleansed my complicated modern thoughts; in their company the mountains felt even more like home. The main difference between me and the other Sherpas was economic: I had traveled more and been educated in a private school, but I was still one of them.

Even before I arrived in Kathmandu from Darjeeling, Wongchu Sherpa, our sirdar in charge of logistics, had been locked in frustrating battle over the climbing permit process with officials of the government of Nepal. He termed one of their ponderous, poorly attended offices the "Garbage Ministry," decrying the time and attention they give to each expedition's litter deposits. His joking banter, quick wit, and pockets full of rupees helped him prevail in most of these exchanges. It was unfortunate that, just as the government of Nepal had neglected to pay much attention to my father after his Everest ascent in 1953, the country didn't grasp the potential of an IMAX film for boosting tourism. Few people are aware that our climb coincided with the government's launching of "Visit Nepal Year," an expensive tourism promotion campaign that never seriously addressed the problems, such as pollution, that were keeping tourists away in the first place.

The bureaucracy was arguably more challenging than climbing. Mountaineering takes nerve and persistence, but its goals are generally reachable. I was proud of Wongchu for his tenacity in fighting the near-insurmountable government regulations and recalcitrance. One enduring obstacle was the "incentives" demanded by officials before they would process the paperwork on incoming supplies. On one expedition, Wongchu discovered some of the team's equipment under piles of lost baggage in a Kathmandu customs warehouse long after they had already purchased replacement gear. Wongchu tooled around town in a sport utility vehicle, talking on his mobile phone, and he liked to tell me that some of the Sherpas he was now hiring had hired him as a cookboy, ten years earlier. He had also climbed Everest, twice.

AS WE MADE preparations for the climb, I thought more about Geshé Rimpoche's advice on the importance of obstacle-removal rituals. The lighting of butter lamps at the Great Stupa of Boudhanath is one of the more propitious offerings one can make, and I wanted to sponsor such a lighting. Most important, it would be an offering for the safe passage of the entire expedition. One must always dedicate to others any merit or blessings that accrue from offerings.

On a day selected by Soyang's family astrologer, the IMAX team members and twenty Sherpas twisted cotton wicks and gathered shallow pottery cups for use as lamps, and we arranged them along the outline of the three main tiers of the stupa. We had prepared 25,000 by the time sunset approached. It wasn't the optimum number of 100,000 lamps, but it would still be a respectable offering.

The afternoon light faded, and the Sherpas—along with scores of mostly Tibetan volunteer bystanders—began lighting the rows of lamps. The Tibetans topped up the lamps with their own melted butter, which they had brought in vacuum flasks. To sacrifice consumption of a valuable commodity such as butter demonstrates that one is willing to nourish the gods before oneself.

A slight breeze can make it impossible to light the butter lamps or to keep them lit. I had visited the stupa the two previous afternoons to arrange for the offering. Sitting now on a rickety bench in the tiny office adjacent to the stupa, listening to the pleasant clang of the votive bells, I chatted with the caretakers. They said that every evening of the past week had been too windy to even consider a butter lamp offering.

Patience. Just what Geshé Rimpoche had spoken about. I watched several Tibetans pass, their handheld prayer wheels revolving smoothly, consistently, as if turning under their own power. My reverie was broken by a Sherpa woman who stepped up to the northern cardinal point of the stupa. She grabbed an oversized prayer wheel attached to the wall and gave it a focused, sharp thrust, as if sending a message to the gods that she meant business and expected a prompt response. Best not to be impatient, I thought.

The lamps could be lit only by huddling protectively over each one, and when the last one sprang to life, we climbed a narrow stairway to the roof of an adjacent building. The blazing sunset and the golden glow of butter lamps reflected off our faces, and for a moment I felt infused with a sense of calm and warmth and proximity to Guru Rimpoche—Padmasambhava, the founder of the stupa and the most important saint for Sherpas and Himalayan Buddhists. Venus sat twinkling serenely above the sunset, winking back at the lights of landing airplanes.

A Buddhist nun approached me with a broad smile. She bowed her head slightly in gratitude and said that although the entire afternoon had been quite windy, it was fortunate that the wind had stopped.

"Perhaps the gods are looking favorably on our offering?" I suggested.

"At the least, the butter lamps will bless all who behold them," she replied.

A FEW DAYS before our departure for the mountain, I visited Geshé Rimpoche again. He placed in my hand a packet of sacred relics, in the form of brown, spherical pills containing minute quantities of the hair and fingernails of high lamas, mixed with hundreds of herbs. He told me to place them on the summit if I reached it. He also handed me some *sungdis,* blessing strings made of thin braided nylon to wear around my neck and to tie onto the key climbing equipment, such as my harness, ice ax, and cram-pons, for protection. He also gave me a small pouch of what looked like sand, and indeed it had been collected from intricate sand mandalas created during lengthy rituals in his monastery. This was mixed with blessed grains of rice to make a protective mixture called *chaane.* He told me to sprinkle this on dangerous stretches, or wherever I felt scared, such as in avalanche-prone areas and the Khumbu Icefall.

Rimpoche also presented me with a protective *sungwa* amulet, a piece of handmade paper inscribed with astrological designs and religious symbols and mantras. As I watched, he folded it precisely and bound it in a crosshatch pattern of colored threads. He told me to wrap the amulet in plastic, to protect it from sweat and dirt. I made a mental note to have it sewn into a silk brocade bag, too.

Geshé Rimpoche then turned on his cushion and reached behind him into a stack of texts wrapped in saffron-colored cloth. "I was waiting for your return visit," he said as he opened the texts and began flipping over folios on the prayer table in front of him. "I wanted to read something to you from a text by the eighteenth-century scholar Jigme Lingpa, *Treasury of Precious Qualities*":

> *When the eagle soars up, high above the earth,*
> *Its shadow for the while is nowhere to be seen;*
> *Yet bird and shadow still are linked. So too our actions:*
> *When conditions come together, their effects are clearly seen.*[1]

He read on, selecting passages that seemed to have been written especially for me, addressing my own personal dilemma. I marveled at the depth of memory it took to simply remember all these references and where to find them. My Western education seemed a jumble, a misguided detour from such simple yet detailed thought.

Rimpoche then pulled me toward him and whispered some mantras in my ear. He told me to repeat them in audible tones while on the mountain, especially in hazardous places.

I left Geshé Rimpoche's feeling protected and prepared but

---

[1] Requoted from Patrul Rinpoche, *The Words of My Perfect Teacher* (Boston: Shambhala, 1998), p. 119.

mildly anxious. Whether the butter lamps at the stupa and blessed threads and mantras would work or not, I didn't know. But I was beginning to feel that the healthy skepticism I learned in America would have its useful limits. I was headed for a dangerous mountain and would need all the help I could find.

The Tengboche monastery, at 12,800 feet on the approach route to Base Camp. Our team was blessed here, as was my father and the 1953 British expedition.

2

FLYING INTO THE UNKNOWN

2

FLYING INTO THE UNKNOWN

Three tons of expedition equipment and supplies had been shipped from the United States and were sitting in wax-coated boxes in a compound in Kathmandu: 57 crates of food, 20 loads of climbing hardware, 40 tents, 3,000 feet of rope, 75 bottles of oxygen, 200 rolls of toilet paper, 47 tins of Spam, and endless loads of film and filming gear. Adding the food and supplies that the IMAX team's Sherpas and I had purchased in Kathmandu, the final count came to 230 boxes, bags, duffels, and plastic drums that would have to be transported to Everest Base Camp.

One-third of this total was film and film equipment, yet we still had 120 fewer loads to keep track of than my father did in 1953. I figured that part of the additional burden of the earlier expedition came from the heavier gear they used and the supplies they needed during the nearly monthlong approach march. In 1953 Nepal had virtually no roads, and the British expedition began walking just outside the capital city, two hundred miles from the mountain. Their porters were dispatched in two separate groups, a day apart, to alleviate congestion on the trail and at campsites.

I was grateful that we were flying most of the way to Everest and in only forty minutes would bypass the relentlessly steep up-and-down trek route. And I was equally grateful for a budget that relieved us of the hassle of fighting to save every rupee, even though that is a skill at which Sherpas excel. Our resourcefulness is born out of living in a subsistence economy, and in some cases out of desperation.

At the domestic terminal in Kathmandu, I watched the sirdar for a trek group check his gunny bags for the flight to Lukla, the staging point for Everest treks and expeditions.

"Isn't this a lot of baggage?" the staff at the check-in counter queried, in the same manner he had queried the Sherpa before him.

"Oh, it's nothing really," the sirdar ventured confidently, while hefting two 50-pound sacks of milk powder and his personal possessions onto the scale: 160 pounds—somewhat over the domestic airline weight limit of 33 pounds.

Our team had chartered an ancient, or at least well-used, Russian Mi-17 military transport helicopter, operated by a Sherpa-owned airline. One flight had already ferried a load of our supplies to Lukla. When it returned to Kathmandu, we climbed aboard and strapped ourselves in like paratroopers, sitting against the windows on long seats made from aluminum tubes with canvas strung between them. One of the Russian pilots turned to look in on us. He pointed his finger toward Lukla, then gave a buoyant thumbs-up and a wag of his head, as if proud and surprised that the previous flight had actually made it. The Russian pilots were generally on the rough side, as one travel agent described them, but had trained themselves to fly straight after a hard night of drinking.

The vibration on liftoff made my vision flutter and blur. I squinted through the dirty windows, saddened by the oppressive pollution of the city. But as we rose above the haze, a chorus line of Himalayan giants gradually took center stage. The purity of the mountain slopes, white with snow, and the mystery of their forested high valleys beckoned seductively: angular Dorje Lhakpa, Shishapangma (in Tibet), and Gauri Shankar, the sacred summit of which lies exactly on the meridian to which Nepal has fixed its clocks, fifteen minutes off the hour. Then Karyolung, Numbur, Cho Oyu, Gyachung Khang, and Makalu. Far to the northwest I could make out Darjeeling's sentinel and siren, Kangchenjunga. Above them all stood Chomolungma—its triumphant pennant of snow blowing from the summit.

IT WAS EXHILARATING enough simply to have left the city behind. When I first visited Kathmandu with my father in the early 1970s, we rode bicycles across town and encountered only a handful of motor vehicles—old Toyota and Ambassador taxis mostly, orange, toylike cars painted with black tiger stripes and grimacing eyebrows above the headlights to scare newly arrived villagers out of their path. I remember watching two villagers perched nervously on the sidewalk, one coaching the other on how to cross the street: "Run as fast as you can, and just be sure to look only straight ahead—if you glance right or left, you'll only become confused."

My father first visited Kathmandu in the late 1920s, more than twenty years before the country opened its frontier to the outside world. At that time the city's few luxury cars, owned by the ruling Rana oligarchy, had been carried by porters one hundred miles over forested passes that switchbacked into the valley from the south, and they were carried back to India for repairs. Even then, the city seemed modern and strange to my father. He was impressed by the sense of civilization and culture in the crowded, narrow bazaars and the statues and intricate carvings of the Hindu and Buddhist temples. There were no hotels in the almost medieval city, but he was welcomed at a Buddhist monastery near the Boudhanath stupa.

Nepal's capital city is now gridlocked with cars, trucks, buses, motorcycles, scooters, three-wheelers, pushcarts, and rickshaws. Foreign aid projects and wealthy Tibetan carpet factory owners have discovered sport utility vehicles, and government officials have become attached to them, too. Cars are driven primarily for status, not transportation, and motorized traffic has slowed to the point that bicycling across the city is faster than driving. Distressingly, the temples have lost their battle with billboards and neon signs. For centuries the culture of the Kathmandu valley emphasized the importance of achieving as much spiritual progress as possible during one's short lifetime. In little more than three decades, this tradition has been superseded by a fixation on achieving material progress. One by-product of this shift has been the disappearance of statuettes and other antiquities from the temples and sacred sites of the valley; indeed, some galleries in the West have more impressive collections of "portable" Nepalese art than what one now finds in Kathmandu.

Nonetheless, the valley is still home to ancient power spots—geomantic focal points of divine energy that confer blessings on those who visit them. The stupa of Swayambhunath is one of these. *Swayambhu* means "self-arisen," and according to legend, the hilltop on which the stupa is perched spontaneously emerged from the lakebed that is now the Kathmandu valley. The stupa's spired dome balances on the hill like a mythical launching pad, primed to dispatch mankind into the next era, the next Hindu-Buddhist cycle of the multi-millennial ages. Lamas and pundits say we are now approaching the end of the fourth and last age of this era—the Kali Yug, or Black Age—in which human societies are in a downward spiral that will climax in destruction and oblivion. The good news is that a new era will then begin afresh, characterized (at the start at least) by long, joyful lives led in idyllic surroundings. But we still must pass through many human lifetimes, they say, before the cataclysm comes.

A daily stream of supplicants—both Hindu and Buddhist—climb the endless stairs to the Swayambhu stupa to pray and throw grain to the rhesus monkeys and pigeons that have claimed Swayambhu as their own. The team members joined me in spinning prayer wheels and burning incense. Then we "burned some film." One saddhu, a mendicant holy man, agreed to be filmed, but each time Breashears called for "Action!" the saddhu would simply stand there and look at me. I told David that *Ek chin!* is the Nepali imperative for "Wait a minute!"

I immersed myself in the energy and excitement, the filming work, and the opportunity to make offerings. Each evening I told Soyang about the preparations for the expedition, and slowly she began to warm up to the idea of the adventure. Each morning she prayed and filled the seven water bowls on the altar at her parents' home. Water is free (bottled water notwithstanding), and it is something we can offer without the least feeling of attachment or expectation of something in return, Soyang reminded me. She also burned incense on the terrace on the top floor, for purification, before turning to cook meals and endless pots of tea for the monks who arrived to perform protection and long-life rituals. Slowly, her sense of respect for my mission grew. Or maybe it was her fear that was growing, her fear of the high stakes involved.

While organizing gear one day, Wongchu alerted me that our climbing season fell within an inauspicious black year, the second and most dangerous year in a recurring cycle of nine years. But a black year can also be a powerful time, and its negative influences can be transmuted to good, so the astrologers say, and was therefore not unavoidably bad. I wondered why the lamas hadn't alerted me, although I know that they tend to overlook astrological predictions, preferring that people focus on spiritual thought and practice. In any event, the planetary alignment for the year would change favorably on May 15, according to Wongchu, and most Everest summit climbs are made after this date. Nonetheless, I hoped Soyang wouldn't find out about the year's questionable astrology.

TEN YEARS EARLIER I had made my first trip to Lukla on an eighteen-passenger Twin Otter, a STOL plane used widely in the Canadian bush. When I'd glimpsed the tiny airstrip laid at an eight-degree upward angle through the middle of the village's potato fields, I figured there was no way we could land there. The plane hit hard and bounced a couple of times, then needed full power to taxi uphill to the parking area.

This time the Mi-17 landed at the top end of the airstrip in a glorious cloud of dust and aviation fuel exhaust—to the Nepalese, a wonderful sign of progress. Stepping from the helicopter door, I was reminded that clear, unpolluted mountain air has a strong, refreshing smell and taste, almost biting, like fine Scotch whiskey. We busily unloaded the helicopter, then closed the door and patted the side. A siren alerted the gawkers and livestock on the runway, and it lifted off. Nearby, two Twin Otters took on orderly lines of sun- and windburned trekkers headed for Kathmandu. A prim, city-bred stewardess seemed grateful to be leaving behind Lukla's gravel airstrip, an awkward surface for high-heeled shoes. She stepped in last and closed the door behind her.

When it was constructed in 1964 to bring in building materials for a hospital, few people had expected this airstrip would become the gateway for thousands of tourists. Now scores of lodges and shops crowd the main route leading out of town. Lukla Sherpas—all relatively recent settlers—have successfully rallied to halt the growing Mi-17 helicopter traffic to the Syangboche airstrip. Two days north of Lukla at twelve thousand feet, it had threatened to take business away from this lucrative trailhead.

Wongchu and I, along with the high-altitude sirdar Jangbu Sherpa, spent the day organizing the lowland porters who had gathered at the airstrip in response to our radio message, and we dispatched them with loads. The porters marched off on bare feet the color and texture of elephant hide, feet that had reached their carrying capacity for dust and dirt, blending in with the trail. We followed them, walking on flagstones worn into smooth dish shapes by years of bare feet, sneakers, and climbing boots. Base Camp was only sixty miles away by footpath, but we would take nearly three weeks to get there to allow for filming and acclimatization en route.

We skirted barley fields and hiked through pine forests, following the Dudh Kosi ("Milk River") to its confluence with the Bhote Kosi, a river that begins near the Tibet border. Climbing sharply 2,000 vertical feet, we arrived at Namche Bazaar, Khumbu's largest village, at 11,400 feet. This was the heart of Sherpa country, the area our ancestors settled after migrating over the Himalaya from eastern Tibet over 450 years ago.

The Sherpas maintained close economic and cultural ties with Tibet over that period, and our religion is basically Tibetan Buddhist. Sherpa language and some local practices have evolved and diverged, just as they have in many remote areas of Tibet itself. Most of the visible changes within Khumbu Sherpa society have occurred within the past thirty years, a by-product of expeditions and tourism.

Mixed in with Namche's hundred-plus houses are nearly twenty lodges, some of them four stories tall, topped by picture-window restaurants and one cyber-café. Other commercial and goodwill ventures have found their way to this remote but bustling trading post, and most Namche houses now have telephones and running water. The town runs on electricity from a small hydroelectric station located a ten-minute walk from the house where my father grew up. At a dental clinic established with aid from the American Himalayan Foundation, two young Western-trained Sherpas do fillings and other dental work. Khumbu villagers are fond of gold tooth caps, but these are discouraged in favor of more basic dental care.

The town is different from the Namche my father knew well from growing up in the nearby village of Thame. In 1952, when he returned to Khumbu from Darjeeling with the Swiss, the Namche people quickly closed their doors and shutters, not so much out of fear of the foreigners themselves as for worry about the *nerpa*, the bad luck associated with malignant spirits that outsiders might bring to the community. My father saw few changes between 1933 and 1952, other than the construction of a one-room schoolhouse by the government.

Now, Namche Sherpas good-naturedly drag foreign trekkers

into their hotels and shops—many of them converted from the same houses that existed in 1952.

We parked our loads in the center of town at the Khumbu Lodge, where Jimmy Carter, Robert Redford, and other celebrities had taken lodging some years earlier. As a result of exposure to expeditions and trekking groups from a variety of countries, Namche residents can often identify travelers' country of origin by their appearance and accent and speak a few of their words. Young Sherpas have better command of English than many European trekkers. In 1952 few Sherpas even knew Nepali, the national language. Now all of them are bilingual.

The secondhand items for sale in the Namche trek shops reflect Everest's international character. One early Catalan expedition sold off cases of marinated trout and rabbit, brought down from Base Camp, and the Russian national expedition left behind plastic barrels filled with large glass dishes of Black Sea caviar. "Fish eggs—can you believe it?" their Sherpa sirdar remarked, disgusted that anyone would want to eat something so sacrilegious. Sherpas and Tibetans avoid eating fish partly because they lay so many eggs, each one with the potential to beget another living sentient being.

The Sherpas' own culturally prescribed hospitality has been good for business and public relations. Trekkers are delighted and sometimes startled to be invited so enthusiastically into our homes and lives. For many foreigners, it is during their outing in the Himalaya that they form friendships for the first time with people markedly poorer than themselves. This experience brings on feelings of guilt and a yearning to give their hosts something in return.

"What can we do for you?" some of them generously offer, usually near the end of a trek when the tips are dispensed. Typically, the trekkers have already noted that Sherpas along the Everest route aren't living in abject poverty, and that many of their houses are overflowing with high-quality trekking and mountaineering equipment inherited from generations of climbers.

"We are poor but happy," many Sherpas respond. "Life in our hills is tough—we lose our sons on the mountain in climbing accidents, and we lose our livestock to predators and storms and crevasses. But we wouldn't trade our lifestyle for anything else." And then the clincher: "We do regret, however, not having better educational opportunities for our children, as are available in Kathmandu and overseas." That's when the trekkers, a husband and wife for instance, nod to each other and often reach for their checkbooks. Sponsors who can afford to send the Sherpa children overseas or to India are desirable, but Kathmandu will also do.

I have to commend the Khumbu Sherpas on their skill at eliciting such support, but I feel the time has come to focus more on the opportunities they have within their own community. The Khumjung School, established by Sir Edmund Hillary and the Himalayan Trust, not only is academically comparable to many of the private schools in Kathmandu but provides a superior learning environment, free from the pollution and dubious cultural influences of the capital. Many Sherpas admit that their children begin to lose their native Sherpa tongue and customs after studying only a few years in Kathmandu. But many Khumbu Sherpas want to live in Kathmandu themselves, close to the business opportunities.

It is natural for people to want to have a positive personal impact on others. Generosity is a natural and noble character trait. I feel, however, that the best way to help the Sherpas is through community-level projects that benefit all villagers more or less equally, such as building schools, health posts, or dental clinics. Private investment is another way, though that is a longer-term commitment. The foreigners who have invested in the tourism industry, for instance, have hired, trained, and supported many Sherpas, providing opportunities at which the smart and hardworking excel. That legacy is alive today in the many successful businesses that Sherpas have established in Khumbu and Kathmandu.

On an earlier trip the mayor of Namche told me that he wasn't sure that tourism and prosperity have been universally good for the Sherpa community, because of the social upheaval and divisiveness that accompany them. For instance, when two brothers go trekking with different groups and one of them returns with a foreign sponsorship for his child and the other doesn't, the seed of family and clan division is planted. The have-nots have been turned into the haves overnight. That's fine in terms of equality and redistribution of wealth, which people in the West speak about so much. Foreigners' charity is not always based on merit or performance, however, and the often arbitrary and excessive nature of these changes can upset a social balance that has developed over centuries.

Disagreements and feuds arrive on the Namche mayor's doorstep on an almost daily basis. The troubled parties sit on benches along the perimeter of his expansive living area while his wife serves tea. He nods and makes suggestions. Making decisions is a more difficult matter.

At the least, the new prosperity has made cashing travelers' checks easier. Some Sherpas will take deutsche marks, Japanese yen, or personal checks—a far cry from the days of the 1953 expedition when five porter loads, accompanied by two armed guards, were needed to carry the strongboxes of Nepalese silver rupee coins. These were literally the only coin of the realm, owing to the general distrust of paper money.

"*Mikaru* ['white eyes,' or Westerners] are much like cattle," a Sherpa woman told me in Namche as we discussed the Sherpas' success in the tourism industry. "They are happy wandering about aimlessly all day long . . . , they are constantly getting sick . . . , and you have to lead them by the nose over difficult terrain or they'll fall off the trail. . . . But if you feed them well, they'll produce a lot of rich milk for you." Her words were more empathetic than judgmental.

Poorer villages, sequestered in drainages away from the main trek route, are home for a number of Sherpas who have engaged in informal trade between Nepal, Hong Kong, and Singapore. Some of them have been imprisoned for carrying contraband, but one Sherpa told me that prison isn't so bad—they get free lodging and all they can eat, and by the time they are released, generally within two or three years, they speak excellent colloquial English. One could speculate that their fate drove them to it, living as they do in relative poverty only because their villages are a few miles away from the tourist flow. Sherpas trying to keep up with the Sherpas.

By the 1990s Khumbu Sherpas had, by and large, gained enough economic independence to be able to retire from high-altitude mountaineering work. Nowadays most of the climbing Sherpas come from remote areas like the Rolwaling valley, reached from Khumbu over a difficult and dangerous pass. Rolwaling provides a glimpse of how Khumbu would look in the absence of trekking and mountaineering, because these villages look exactly like the Khumbu of forty years ago: hand-hewn wood shutters on the houses instead of glass windows, potato pancakes and *tsampa* (roasted barley flour) on the table instead of yak meat stew and rice. Rolwaling is quaint and scenic from a trekker's point of view, I imagine, but offers little to young Sherpas longing to chase their dreams.

MY FATHER FIRST left his boyhood hamlet of Thame in 1932, at age eighteen, to look for challenges, excitement, and income—any diversion from his life of herding yaks and growing potatoes and grains. He was part of an early wave of Khumbu Sherpas to strike out from the East in search of the West, and they found it in Darjeeling. Something more than diversion and opportunities was drawing my father, however—something in a triangular shape, the shape of a mountain.

My father returned to Khumbu and Thame to visit his parents on occasion, but when he passed through Namche with the British in 1953, his father and mother walked down from Thame to send him off, loaded with gifts and food. There, my grandmother Kinzom met the expedition's leader, Colonel John Hunt, and she blessed him and the team members. Grandmother worried greatly that my father had risked his life on Everest too many times—six times already—and she begged him to be careful. This was precisely what my father's second wife, Ang Lhamu, had told him before he left Darjeeling, and what my wife, Soyang, had told me. When I think of my mother's and Soyang's love and concern—the same feelings that Grandmother

Kinzom and Ang Lhamu felt for my father—it is hard not to think twice about the danger of climbing Everest, as I'm sure my father did. He had almost decided against joining the '53 expedition, and I too nearly declined in '96.

The village of Thame was also my mother's natal home. Thame symbolized familial sanction and support; it was my connection to Khumbu. As we sat in Namche, I felt an irresistible force drawing me there, the way a holy pilgrimage site demands an appearance before one can reasonably continue on an important mission.

Of all my relatives in Thame, only my maternal grandfather remained; he was in his late eighties and in failing health. A Thame woman visiting in Namche reminded me how much he would be thrilled to see me. Unless I detoured from the expedition and hiked the three hours to Thame, I might never see him again.

I left Namche shortly before sunrise. Gaga, as we called him, lived at the northern edge of Thame, in the first settlement that Tibetans encounter when coming over the Nangpa La pass from Tibet. For the past three decades he had become more accustomed to housing pilgrims, traders, and refugees than his own family, most of whom had moved to Darjeeling, Kathmandu, or the United States.

His house, too, has shutters instead of glass in the windows, and a traditional low doorway. Ghosts of dead relatives are unable to bend over and thus can't get back inside to cause trouble for the household.

Hunching over, I found my way through the dark bottom floor, past old wooden plows, dirt-encrusted mattocks, and globes of yak skin packed with butter. Here the yaks and zopkios were stabled, and the animals' body heat warmed the kitchen and sitting room on the floor above. To reach the second floor, I scrambled up a log with notches carved into it.

Sitting near the window, Gaga appeared frail, but his kindly patriarchal demeanor was still robust. He looked up and smiled without surprise, as if he'd been expecting me. He offered me a wooden bowl of *chang*, thick barley beer, and I declined. Gaga had been alone for years until he took in a young orphan girl, Ang Nimi, who helped him with the herding and cooking. They still fried their potato pancakes on a stone slate rather than in a metal frying pan.

As Ang Nimi slowly prepared a pancake, Gaga told me about how, beginning in 1959, he had been providing shelter to Tibetan refugees escaping from the Chinese. They continued to arrive in Nepal over the nineteen-thousand-foot Nangpa La pass, desperate and in tatters, and some suffering severe frostbite. He said that he never asked for money.

He maintained a sizable herd of yaks, and his eldest son, one of my uncles, still crosses the Nangpa La, mainly to breed the animals in Tibet. Gaga had visited Kathmandu only once or twice in his life, preferring to remain in the village to pray and practice Buddhism. He had already given much of what he owned to the Thame monastery. One grandson of his had climbed Everest once, another one twice, and yet another one four times. One of them, Pemba Norbu, is married to the sister of Apa Sherpa, who by the spring of 2000 had climbed Everest eleven times, more than any other human.

He was disappointed that his sons hadn't visited him, mainly because they were far away. My mother was his favorite, he said, so my visit was just as good as a visit from a son.

"Why do you want to stay here alone?" I asked him. "We'll give you a place to stay in Darjeeling, and you can bring Ang Nimi, too."

"I'm happy here and don't know anything else," he responded. "I simply wish that my youngest son would come to take over the farm and property."

I didn't tell him of my Everest plans, because I knew he would worry, and he didn't need more to worry about at his age. In a strange way, I felt bathed in his generous and compassionate energy—the blessing that older people impart simply by their presence.

I ARRIVED BACK in Namche just before Wongchu walked into the bunkroom of the Khumbu Lodge with the unfortunate news that our team member Sumiyo was in trouble. The Namche police had recognized her as the person who had climbed and filmed on Ama Dablam without permission three years earlier, and they were rescinding her Everest permit. Defeatedly, she sat down on one of the bunks. She admitted they had told her she wouldn't be allowed to climb in Nepal for five years.

David paced around the dormitory, desperately searching for a solution to this unexpected problem. We needed Sumiyo. She had already been filmed with the team in Kathmandu, and those scenes would have to be refilmed if she had to drop out.

All official decisions, and some reversals of decisions, I speculated, are formalized in writing. Paperwork is what initiates the bureaucratic process (which consists of more paperwork). David and I sat down, and he drafted a letter in English while I drafted one in Nepali, asking the government to be lenient toward Sumiyo for this particular climb. We pointed out that HMG

(His Majesty's Government—retained as the formal name despite the advent of a multi-party democracy) had already accepted a royalty fee of $10,000 for her inclusion on the team, and we suggested that the government restrict her or punish her later, after the expedition. We hoped that HMG, which thrives on decrying the country's poverty in its pleas for foreign aid, wouldn't overlook the value of an IMAX film for tourism promotion.

Sumiyo left for Kathmandu with the letters, assuring us that she would call on the satellite phone with any news.

THE NEXT DAY we climbed to the village of Khumjung, one thousand feet and one hour above Namche. Khumbi Yül Lha, the "country-god" of Khumbu, a scraggy peak of dark-colored granite eighteen thousand feet high, presides over the village and protects its inhabitants and livestock. This peak and village had remained vivid in my memory from stories of yeti, the abominable snowman that my father had told me of when I first visited here. In his boyhood, when he and his friends had herded yaks together on Khumbi Yül Lha's flanks, they believed that a yeti lived behind the peak and came out when dispatched by the god who controlled the village's fortunes. In those days, whenever I trekked through Khumbu, and around Khumjung especially, I was petrified to step outside at night to take a leak, certain that this gargantuan, reeking beast with its feet on backward would carry me off.

For several nights we stayed at the house of a successful mountaineering sirdar, Nima Tenzing, and his wife, Pema Chamji. Their large sitting room acted as a communal bedroom for the expedition, quickly filling with wet clothes and camera equipment.

Hospitality can't be refused in a Sherpa house, and Pema Chamji served endless cups of Tibetan tea that had been noisily blended with butter and salt in a tall churn. In the afternoons she held bowls of chang in front of each of us until we accepted, and Sherpa custom dictates that every bowl must be refilled at least twice. Sherpas are so used to this that, even when we don't care to drink, we would feel uneasy if some beverage weren't urged upon us.

Charging money for food and lodging is a new custom. When foreigners first visited Khumbu, it would have been an insult to demand money for something that cost only one's time and labor to produce. That remains true today with wild vegetables: for instance, when bamboo shoots emerge in the late spring, they are made into a curry, a tasty surprise for guests who show up during shoot season. Since the shoots require no human effort to grow, we feel it would be improper to accept remuneration for them.

To place phone calls, the team hiked up to the "Om Lhasa," the Sherpa nickname for the Hotel Everest View, a Japanese-built megalith perched on a ridge at 12,700 feet. The place operates like a ship. A pressurized room was built there for use as a hyperbaric chamber to treat high-altitude sickness, which commonly affects those flying in directly from Kathmandu, at only 4,600 feet. I was told that one patron suffered a heart attack on the front steps. The hotel has never made a profit, but its Japanese investors continue to run and maintain it as a matter of pride.

The hotel depends entirely on reliable air service to the nearby Syangboche airstrip. I remember waiting on the grassy strip with trekkers and friends in earlier years, and I once halted an excited conversation because I thought I heard the arriving plane. Listening intently, we picked up the low celestial drone of an elderly Sherpa who was standing five yards away, spinning his prayer wheel, and chanting *Om Mane Padme Hum* in a run-on mantra. We broke into laughter. When you're desperate to leave, anything sounds like an arriving airplane.

When the six-seater Pilatus Porter STOL plane finally sets down at Syangboche, the props beating at the thin crystal air drop in tone as they change their pitch, sounding like a grateful sigh, "I made it." For years the Pilatus, which was designed for mountain flying, was flown by Emil Wick, the Swiss pilot appointed by the Pilatus factory to fly and maintain the plane in Nepal. His favorite stunt was to buzz within a few feet of the Tengboche monastery, only moments after turning to his terrified passengers and saying that he wanted to "spin a few prayer wheels." I was intrigued when Wick said that the sound of the prop can set off an avalanche if he flies tightly next to a snow-encased cliff face.

In 1997 the veteran pilot A. G. Sherpa was killed while piloting the Pilatus Porter. Shortly after lifting off from the airstrip, he made a turn in the fog and smashed into the side of Kwangde. This tragic accident and the later crash of a larger Twin Otter operated by a Sherpa-owned airline put a dent in the Sherpas' collective pride. Nonetheless, Sherpas continue to fly. Ang Zangbu, from a village below Namche, is taking training on a Boeing 747. As a boy, he hiked barefoot each day nearly three thousand vertical feet to attend the Khumjung School. In his teens, while carrying loads for trekkers, one of his American clients, a senior executive at Boeing, recognized Ang Zangbu's unusual motivation and intelligence.

"What would you like to do most when you're older?" the executive asked him.

"Fly airplanes," Zangbu responded, as if on cue. Like many Sherpas, he had dreamed of flying planes since his boyhood days of chasing the family's yaks across high Khumbu pastures, from where he watched distant aircraft approach the Lukla airstrip.

Zangbu's English skills and school grades were good enough to qualify him for flying school, and the executive offered to help him. At age seventeen, he hiked to Kathmandu, where he saw a motor vehicle for the first time. Three years later he had married a German woman and was enrolled in flying school in Seattle. By the age of twenty-two, he had his commercial pilot's license and was piloting Twin Otters into Lukla—to the elation of the Sherpas, who lined the taxiway on his maiden voyage to greet him with kata scarves. Soon he was flying jets for the Royal Nepal Airlines Corporation (RNAC—or "Really Not Altogether Certain"). But flying in the Himalaya is nerve-racking. The tiny country of Nepal sees more crashes each year than the average annual number of commercial airline crashes in the United States.

On the morning of March 24, as we departed Khumjung, David filmed me in the village gompa lighting the same brass-receptacle butter lamps that my father had lit when he came through the village on his way to Everest.

We continued on to the Tengboche gompa, Khumbu's most prominent monastery. Descending first to the bottom of the Imja Khola gorge, we passed young Sherpa women carrying seventy-pound loads of firewood suspended from their foreheads by a tumpline, which freed their hands to knit while they sang and chewed gum. "Multi-tasking" they called it where I worked in New Jersey.

In the trees near the river, I took out my camera to photograph a boy's healthy, burly-looking yaks, in slick black coats.

When he waved his arms and told me not to, I realized that the wood strapped to the yaks' backs was green firewood, the removal of which is illegal. He thought I was busting him.

The Tengboche Lama and the National Park staff are distressed by the random and excessive cutting of green wood in the forests below the monastery. The army guards designated as the Protection Unit repeatedly inform the Sherpas that they have orders to shoot anyone seen cutting green wood, despite the grave sacrilege of harming someone in the vicinity of the monastery. Even this warning is little deterrent. The firewood cutters are too desperate, and the army's threats too hollow. Intense card games keep the guards busy full-time anyway.

We switchbacked uphill through a fir forest and emerged onto a colorful hillside of blooming rhododendrons, forming an arborway to the monastery. Finally we could see a corner of the main structure, balanced on a sandy, glacial moraine, two thousand vertical feet above the Imja Khola. Nearing the monastery grounds, we passed through the *kani*, a tunnel-like entryway. To deter evil spirits from following them in, the ceiling's wood panels are painted with a pantheon of Buddhist and local deities, meditating and levitating. The paintings are also meant to imbue a sense of philosophical reflection in those who visit the monastery.

An ancient Tibetan Buddhist text says that one of the great early lamas of Khumbu, Lama Sangwa Dorje, enraptured by devotion to Guru Rimpoche, flew to the grassy pasture that is now Tengboche. He landed on a boulder there, leaving a footprint that is visible today. Years later, in 1916, Tengboche was established as the first celibate gompa in Khumbu, and it now houses forty monks, a record number that is partially attributable to the Sherpas' new tourism-derived prosperity.

Larger incomes have allowed more families to offer an able-bodied son to the monastery, generally the third son, and to support him there.

I was grateful to be a householder and not a monk, though a householder is burdened with worry and attachment. Already I missed Soyang and our young daughter Deki. The expedition had gone beyond the last land-based telephone, and future calls on the expensive satellite phone would have to be limited. Instead of phoning, I thought and worried about them—as much as I worried about the mountain. I could blame only myself if I were injured, regardless of the circumstances, and when frightening images of the mountain arose, I felt guilty in advance.

THE TENGBOCHE LAMA had been in strict meditative retreat for the past three months, so I requested a protection ceremony from the monastery's *Lopon* ("Diamond Master"), the head monk.

Araceli, Ed, and I climbed the stairs and crossed the courtyard to the main assembly hall as the drone of horns and drums intensified, the low vibration as palpable as it was audible. We halted outside the immense, colorfully painted wooden doors to the hall, removed our shoes, and stepped over the threshold.

I took three steps forward and viewed the massive interior. Before me at the north end of the hall sat an imposing statue of Buddha Sakyamuni, the "Buddha of the Present," over fifteen feet high in seated posture. His gilded shoulders and head extended through an opening in the second floor—as if the building had been altered after construction to accommodate his miraculous, boundless growth. In the foreground, smaller gilded figures stood in attendance: the bodhisattvas Chenrezig and

Jambayang, and the disciples Shariputra and Mangalputra, who possess miraculous powers. Eight Tatagathas, fully enlightened Buddhas, seemed to levitate behind Sakyamuni and soar about within the floor-to-ceiling nimbus behind the statue.

I stood inside the main door for several minutes, hands together, praying. Then I prostrated three times, lowering myself, extending prone, placing my forehead on the floor, and rising again.

Sitting in rows facing a center aisle, a dozen or more monks recited from long texts opened on low prayer tables. Some read aloud, rocking back and forth slowly, while those who had committed the text to memory chanted along while they studied the three of us with detached interest.

Just as my father had done forty-three years earlier, I approached the altar, then turned to silently present a long silk kata scarf to the Lopon, who was sitting on a thronelike platform. I handed him the roll of prayer flags that I planned to unfurl on the summit.

Continuing to chant in unison with the monks, the Lopon touched a bhumpa urn and a *dorje* ritual thunderbolt to the bundle, then dribbled some blessed barley grains from his hand into the bundle's folds. Then he paused to meditate intensely, transferring blessings directly to the flags. Buddhists say that through intense concentration that is possible only after years of training, accomplished lamas can visualize the deities as inseparable from their objects of meditation.

When my father passed through Tengboche en route to Everest in 1953, the Tengboche Lama, then only seventeen years old, was absent. My father was also blessed by the lopon. Now I could feel my father's presence beside me, but somehow the year was 1953, not 1996, and it was I who was standing beside him, joining him on his mission. His mission felt the same as my own, and ultimately it was a mission of self-awareness, a beginning point for understanding. We had a long way to go, or at least I did.

I placed a kata at the base of the Sakyamuni statue, lit some butter lamps, and walked three clockwise circuits around the interior perimeter of the assembly hall. Then I departed.

I wrote a note to the Tengboche Lama, and it was delivered by an attendant monk. When the monk later found me at our tent sites in the pasture, he handed me some carefully wrapped blessed objects that Rimpoche had wanted me to have. Rimpoche's handwritten reply said that he would recite prayers on our behalf. Wrapped in rice paper were protective sungdi blessing strings that he had included for all the team members. I passed them around, and we immediately tied them around our necks. David tied one to the IMAX camera, as well.

ONE YEAR EARLIER at Tengboche, Bob Hoffman, the leader of my cleanup group, had introduced me to David Breashears. David was returning from Base Camp, where he had been testing the first of two modified IMAX cameras that we were now using. I was headed toward Base Camp, collecting litter with some wealthy Americans.

"It was because of your father that I started my own climbing career," David told me as we sat on a boulder on the margin of Tengboche's yak pasture. "I was eleven years old when I first saw the photo of Tenzing standing on top of Everest. I was spellbound. I couldn't fathom that a human could climb such a high mountain, and I often studied the image, wanting to know everything about the equipment he used, the clothes he wore, and the mountain he stood atop. Especially now, having climbed Everest twice, I look at that photo and marvel at the cumbersome oxygen system, at the flags and ice ax held aloft, and at the triumph and fatigue so apparent in his heroic pose. I view it as perhaps the greatest moment in mountaineering history."

David looked at me sincerely and warmly. He had met my father in Lhasa in 1981, and told me that I was much like him in appearance and manner. "That mountain belongs to you and your father," he said simply. Then he said that he might have something in mind for me and asked whether I had plans for the following spring.

The image of Miyolangsangma, the protector goddess who resides on Everest, leaped to mind. My father believed that Miyolangsangma was the deity who had guided him and granted him safe passage up the mountain. Her thangka scroll painting dominates the chapel of our family home in Darjeeling, her radiant figure riding comfortably on a lactating female tiger, her hair studded with wish-fulfilling gems. A cornucopia of divine fruit in her left hand represents an offering of good fortune, wealth, and abundance—including supernatural powers—while her right hand is held in a gesture of giving. Miyolangsangma is inseparable from, and is indeed synonymous with, her abode, Chomolungma. The Buddhist texts say that Miyolangsangma is one of the "Five Long-Life Sisters" who provide protection and spiritual nourishment to Khumbu and nearby valleys. Originally, Miyolangsangma and her sisters, who reside on nearby peaks, were pre-Buddhist demonesses, but they were subdued and converted to a Buddhist path of beneficence by Padmasambhava, the great "lotus born" saint known as Guru Rimpoche.

My father worshiped Miyolangsangma. As a child, I would stand in the chapel doorway and watch him prostrating before her as she peered down upon him with quiet grace. Now I could see her serene, all-powerful form quietly stepping down from her tiger mount and extending her hand to take me, too, as she had my father.

I was humbled and encouraged by David's Everest offer but wanted to be sure he wouldn't regret it. "I've taught rock climbing and ice climbing and am strong," I told him. "But I'm not greatly experienced at high altitudes."

Somehow Breashears sensed—and an Everest veteran might perceive this better than I—that I would be able to climb the mountain. My father had done it, and I was a Sherpa. Mostly he could see my desire. He had faith in me.

I gratefully accepted, then wondered whether Breashears was inviting me simply because I was Tenzing's son and could serve as some kind of prop for the IMAX film. That would simply mean that I would have to prove I could make it not only to my father, but to Breashears and the other team members, too.

Remaining hopeful, I sent him a short letter expressing my interest—then worried that it might have sounded too self-assertive. Apparently it didn't. At two o'clock in the morning on November 16, 1995, he phoned me in Darjeeling with the news that the film's producers had raised most of the production money and the expedition was moving forward. Finally he was able to extend a formal invitation to me to join the team.

BREASHEARS ALSO WANTED me to act as liaison with the Sherpas and to make sure that all went smoothly. This vital function, which my father had also performed, is not easy on a large and complicated expedition. My father had told me that he almost deferred joining the 1953 expedition not so much out of concern for his safety, but because of the trouble he encountered in negotiating wages for the Sherpas and Nepalese porters on the Swiss expeditions in the spring and fall of 1952. But the British stressed that his ability to "handle the men" was precisely why it was essential that he go.

Something about our IMAX expedition was reminding me of 1953. Colonel Sah'b—as the Sherpas referred to John Hunt, the leader—had run the 1953 expedition in a quasi-militaristic way, yet he was considerate and fair. Making a large-format film requires a similar commitment to organization, discipline, and fairness, and Breashears shared many of Hunt's qualities. Perhaps more than in 1953, however, we were a cohesive team, Sherpas and Westerners together—the collective outgrowth of several decades of Himalayan mountaineering and cultural understanding.

Araceli's good cheer set the tone for the approach march. I felt like an elder brother to her, solicitous for her welfare, but needlessly so. Bouncier than the rest of us, she plugged her Catalan music into her headset and literally danced up the mountain, humming and singing to herself, sometimes loudly and out of tune, her mudra-like hand movements directing a world of her own. As she danced, we followed her into the powerful arms of the omniscient, bountiful goddess of Everest, Miyolangsangma.

Ice axes and other climbing equipment are placed on the altar of the Base Camp lhap-so, where they are blessed, providing us with an extra level of protection on the mountain.

3

STANDING
BEFORE THE
GODDESS

We departed Tengboche in the early morning, gazing up respectfully at the double-humped peak of Ama Dablam, "Mother's Amulet Box," and the distinctive hanging glacier below the summit that formed the charm box itself.

Near the trail beyond Tengboche on a shelf above the Imja Khola, the river that drains Everest, lies a grove of ancient junipers growing in Zen garden–like tranquillity. Interspersed among the contorted trees sit stone houses that look more abandoned than not. The roofs are patched and leaking, and the traditional Sherpa whitewash is little more than a memory. This is the nunnery of Dewoche, where eleven aging nuns live in the shadow of the better-endowed and better-attended Tengboche monastery.

Three-quarters of a century ago, one of my father's elder sisters, Lhamu Kipa, left the village of Thame to become a nun at Dewoche. She had been a second mother to my father, raising him as much as his own mother did, and whenever he passed through Dewoche, he brought food for her. Eventually, she met a Tengboche monk there, and they resigned from their cloisters and married—a not uncommon occurrence in view of the nunnery's proximity to the monastery. They continued to practice dharma as laypeople and later moved to Darjeeling with their children. One of Lhamu Kipa's sons is my cousin Gombu, who at age eighteen joined up with the 1953 Everest expedition as a climbing Sherpa and went on to become the first person to climb Everest twice. Amazingly, during the summers Gombu still guides on Mount Rainier, in Washington State, though he must be close to sixty-five years old.

I took a side trip from the team to make a donation to the nuns. Standing amid the trees facing Dewoche's small chapel courtyard, I felt a calmness that I hadn't experienced since my last visit, a year earlier. The tiny compound was perfectly quiet, but wisps of smoke filtered from the kitchen doorway. Silently, Ngawang Doka, the head nun, appeared. I told her that I wanted to see the assembly hall. She pulled a large key from the folds of her robe, bent at the waist, and fumbled to undo the massive lock that secured the door panels to the threshold.

The heavy doors opened with loud, timeworn *krrrriks,* each spasm of the panels denoting a decade. Shafts of light from the small skylight illuminated airborne dust motes so thick that the altar was momentarily obscured. As my eyes adjusted, I watched the deities, including the loving and peaceful Miyolangsangma, come to life on the walls. They spoke from another age.

No wonder Miyolangsangma and the bounty of fruit and precious gems she offered weren't conferring wealth on the nunnery—she was locked up inside, concealed by darkness and dust. If my mother had been here, she would have torn the rotting curtains from the skylight, dragged out the sitting cushions for an airing, and begun cleaning.

Nuns do not traditionally receive the support from families and the community that monks do, and without a resident lama to provide teachings, Dewoche has devolved into a halfway house between dharma practice and the next life. The nuns' average age is over sixty, and only some of them have the money or strength to make seasonal treks to take teachings with the highly respected Trulshig Rimpoche, who lives in a hillside monastery in Solu, the Sherpa region that is a three-day walk to the south of Khumbu. Outside support has helped the nuns further their education, and the American Himalayan Foundation—whose development director is my brother Norbu—has provided modest stipends and a local teacher for them.

Only five minutes earlier I had been chatting with David about solar electric panels and satellite phones. I marveled at how far away I could go, culturally speaking, within a few instants of time. And I wondered whether I had become swept up in the busy-ness of the expedition and had been overly distracted by modern, temporal affairs—empty activities that could hinder any spiritual evolution to which I might aspire. At the same time I worried that Dewoche might have been trapped in time. In an earlier era it sufficed to sit and simply observe and perpetuate the cycles of life, to pray and to practice, to eat and to sleep. But by the terms of the modern age, to practice such a routine was only to move backward.

Before leaving to rejoin the team, I spun the nunnery's giant prayer wheel, which occupied its own room. It is said that these wheels, packed with prayers and mantras block-printed on hundreds of rice paper scrolls, release the written invocations heavenward with each revolution.

ONE YEAR EARLIER during his test shoot, David wanted to film Ama Dablam from a point near the Pangboche bridge, an undulating walkway suspended eighty feet above the Imja Khola river. "The shots don't come to you," he told us as we peered into the steep-walled gorge. He then recounted how the IMAX camera was lowered on ropes, to get the best camera angle for a shot of the bridge, the gorge, and Ama Dablam.

David and the Sherpas prepared anchors high on each bank of the river. From a tree on the far side, the Sherpas threw across a line, and David tied into it. The Sherpas lowered him using a system of belay devices, then eased the camera alongside. Using another rope, the Sherpas on the far side then pulled David to a point above the river and held him there in a dangerous-looking "V." If that rope had been released, David would have swung eighty feet like a pendulum, finally smashing on to the walls of the gorge like a ripe tomato.

This year, he wanted yaks in the shot. By walkie-talkie, David and I coordinated the timing of a yak train that would cross the bridge, followed by climbers. I knew well that yaks usually stop as they approach a bridge, and at least one always turns and bolts. The height doesn't scare them, but if they have ever snagged a load in the wire mesh of the bridge, they don't want a replay of the event; in their terror, yaks frequently injure themselves and damage the bridge and their loads. In one account I had heard, a square cage strapped to the side of a yak, containing more than a gross of eggs, became hooked on this bridge. Subsequently, the bridge was slippery and yellow for days.

With the precious IMAX film rolling, it took several takes, and vigorous waving and shouting from David, before they all made it across; yaks are not natural actors.

The bridge was a fine place for prayer flags. The dependably strong winds funneling through the gorge would easily carry the prayers aloft. I unraveled a roll of the five-colored muslin flags and strung them along the rail of the bridge, tying them to scores of other tattered windhorses.

I peered up at Ama Dablam, a mountain that many consider to be the most beautiful in the world. It was first climbed in 1961 by two New Zealanders, a Brit, and the American Barry Bishop, who went on to climb Everest, along with my cousin Gombu, on the first American expedition in 1963. At the base of Ama Dablam's massive west-facing wall, I could see the ledge where Sir Edmund Hillary and other New Zealanders and Brits had worked with Sherpas on digging and clearing Khumbu's first airstrip. At more than fifteen thousand feet, it was one of the highest landing fields in the world. The strip was conceived by the Swiss Red Cross in the early 1960s as a way to fly in grain, clothing, and relief supplies for the Tibetan refugees who were escaping into Nepal after the Chinese occupation of Tibet.

The Sherpas applied their customary ingenuity to the effort: when confronted by a massive boulder of several tons, they simply dug a wide, deep hole next to it and rolled it in. Leveling the airfield was even easier. They drank pitchers of chang, then linked arms for hours of traditional Sherpa line dancing—which to the uninitiated looks like synchronized foot-stamping. They wove back and forth across the field, flattening away.

Fog rolled over us, and we meandered around simple stone houses and wind-stunted junipers, until the vegetation gave way to rocks and lichens. We passed to the left of *mani* walls, piles of stone tablets incised with *Om Mane Padme Hum*, the mantra of Avalokitesvara, the Bodhisattva of Compassion. These mani walls act as reminders of attentiveness, and seem to have been placed on the trail at just the intervals at which the mind tends to wander off into grasping, self-centered samsaric thought.

Yaks can trigger alertness, too. At one point, Araceli was pushed—or scared—from a steep portion of the trail after she failed to get up-slope from one of the shaggy beasts. Yaks and zopkios rarely charge, but their horns tend to sweep about menacingly at waist level as they saunter down the trail.

We took a side trip to the yak pastures of Dingboche, a hamlet of summer herders' huts that had been remodeled into solar-powered trekking lodges, with private rooms and two-page menus. The luxury was pleasant, but I was concerned that the National Park had been doing little to prevent random, unplanned hotel construction in remote parts of Khumbu. When asked of his thoughts on commercial overdevelopment, the Tengboche Lama said, "You people in the tourism industry may have caused this: you establish campsites and surround them with rocks, and trekkers use the sites year after year. The campsites become sanctified. It is only natural that someone eventually covers them with a makeshift roof, which becomes a house, and then a hotel." It was true that the underpaid staff of the National Park, recruited from outside the area, would never be powerful enough to face down wealthy lodge owners. This has led to sporadic enforcement of regulations, when they are enforced at all.

It was easy to understand the reason for all the lodge construction: there are few trustworthy investment vehicles in Nepal, such as a booming stock market, and the Nepalese rupee is not accepted as currency in other countries. The Nepalese quickly convert any rupee income from tourism into hard assets such as buildings and real estate.

Spending a few days here in Dingboche at 14,000 feet would help the team better acclimatize for the two-day ascent to Base Camp at 17,600 feet. Trekkers are advised not to ascend more than 1,000 vertical feet a day, but because of our filming we were climbing at an even slower rate. It would take us a month at Base Camp to reach maximum acclimatization, where we could expect to recover about 90 percent of our sea-level capacity to exert. Above Base Camp that percentage would only decrease.

People acclimatize at different rates and to different maximum altitudes. It's not easy to predict in advance how one will respond, but physiologists believe that Sherpas and Tibetans may possess a gene that allows for more efficient oxygen delivery at high elevations. "Sherpa sea level" is around 6,000 or 7,000 feet, in effect, and Sherpas have a head start over most lowlanders. Nonetheless, I'm amazed that humans can adjust to altitude to the degree that they do. Suddenly taking someone who lives at sea level to 20,000 feet, without bottled oxygen, would cause them to collapse within half an hour, and they probably would die soon afterward. The available oxygen at Everest's summit is one-third that of sea level.

From Dingboche, Ed Viesturs, Jangbu, and I went ahead of the team to check the condition of the trail. Reports had reached us that fresh snow had fallen between the settlement of Lobuche and Base Camp, making the final leg of the route impassable for yaks. The yak drivers were refusing to lead their animals through the deep drifts. Hazard pay can tempt the Sherpas, but they won't risk their yaks for any price. We had nearly one hundred of the animals, but the loads would have to be carried by porters.

Except that there weren't any. While Ed forged on toward Base Camp to establish a campsite, Jangbu and I remained in Lobuche to look for porters, although above the highest permanent villages at 13,000 feet it is hard to recruit porters even in the best conditions. We brought wool sweaters and additional clothing for them, but the sudden demand for transport by all the expeditions had made the porters more interested in money than in goods. I was impressed by how the handful of porters at Lobuche kept straight faces as they went bargaining from camp to camp, clearly enjoying the game of playing one expedition off another. Their wages quickly ratcheted upward.

Two Rai porters, their thigh and calf muscles bulging beneath their worn and dingy skirts, entered our lodge in Lobuche to negotiate with us. They were careful to step over the doormat to keep dirt off it. For a high premium, we secured them, and a few of their friends, which would help in moving the urgent loads forward. It struck me that in my father's day all the loads were carried by Sherpas (and a handful of yaks), but within a generation our ethnic group has climbed a full rung higher on the socioeconomic ladder. Most of the loads are now carried by Rai and Tamang porters. These Tibetanoid tribes, natives of Himalayan valleys to the east and west of Khumbu, had cultural histories not unlike that of the Sherpas—but without our history of mountaineering and the prosperity it has brought us.

Early the next morning I took a group of Sherpas and porters toward Base Camp. We chipped enough of a route through the snow and ice with our ice axes to make it passable for porters and eventually, we hoped, yaks. Over the next three days I made several trips, Jangbu made twelve circuits, and the other Sherpas jumped in and carried. We shouldered our loads alongside the porters, exhorting them lightheartedly, hoping some of our good cheer would rub off, though porters are eternally recalcitrant.

The porters had insisted that the loads weigh no more than

thirty kilograms. After we agreed, some of them promptly doubled up their loads, earning a good week's wages in a morning. They had asked for an advance to cover their food along the trail, but I knew from experience to not give them too much before the loads were delivered or they might spirit the loads around a corner, drop them, and disappear.

THE TRIAL OF Everest had begun. The unseasonable snowfall would at least improve the climbing conditions because it is easier to climb rock that is covered with snow. But it would also heighten the risk of avalanches. I recalled the tragic snow slides that had killed more than sixty people the previous November, when a cyclone in the Bay of Bengal diverted north to the Himalaya, dumping ten feet of snow in less than two days. In the nearby valley of Gokyo, a trekkers' destination known for its turquoise lakes and stunning views, an avalanche of wet snow had entombed a teahouse, killing thirteen Japanese trekkers and their Sherpa guides and kitchen crew, a total of twenty-six people. Across the southern slope of the range, helicopters had rescued more than five hundred stranded trekkers and villagers.

By the time we reached Lobuche, most of our team members and some of the Sherpas had developed a bronchitis-like cough; but the good news was that Sumiyo had caught up with us. She had been granted a reprieve by His Majesty's Government for the time being and could rejoin the team.

After all the time spent in preparation, it was exhilarating to finally arrive at Base Camp, and I stood and beheld the curious jumble of quartzite blocks and rubble scattered across the edge of the glacier. This would be our principal home for the next two months. For my father's expedition, this was the site of their Camp I. In 1953 the British established their Base Camp a couple hours' walk farther down the same side of the Khumbu Glacier at a place called Gorak Shep, which now hosts a small cluster of tea shops and simple lodges.

The porters dumped their last loads onto a growing pile, then lined up to be paid. Using the stamp pad that I always carried with me, they applied their thumbprints to my handwritten receipts. I wondered where I would have to go to find a thumbprint expert, and what they could actually do for me. Probably not much, considering that the porters tended to forcefully mash and rotate their thumbs on the paper when they left their prints. And it was always after they had signed and accepted their pay that they would tell me what else I owed them. This feature of Himalayan travel hasn't changed since my father's day.

I set my tent up some distance from the kitchen tent and the other climbers, knowing that Base Camp can get fairly noisy at times. Porters and trekkers were quickly adding to the population of Sherpas, climbers, and liaison officers. I prepared a rock platform for my tent and made sure it was oriented so that I wouldn't be sleeping with my feet pointed toward the mountain—to do so would be disrespectful and unlucky.

It would take a week of sorting gear and filming around Base Camp before we could head up the mountain. Our first step would take us into the dreaded Khumbu Icefall—the Khumbu Glacier's twisted mass of unstable ice that protrudes menacingly from the high valley between Lhotse and Everest. I stood at the edge of the looming beast and quietly surveyed it, wondering about the condition of this year's route through it.

Yak herders had seen the Khumbu Icefall for centuries, surely never imagining that humans would attempt to climb through it. Simply living at the vegetation line was hard enough—why choose to make it harder? Even the first foreigners who finally viewed the Icefall from a good vantage point on the south side, in 1950, predicted that this approach would be very dangerous and difficult, if not impossible.

My father was not the only one who felt, at first, that the southern route was too hazardous to attempt. Ang Tharkay, his landlord in Darjeeling and one of the great "Tigers of the Snows," had been the sirdar for Eric Shipton's British reconnaissance in 1951. Even Ang Tharkay had refused to join the first serious south side attempt, made by the Swiss in the spring of 1952. He bet my father twenty rupees that the Swiss, like Shipton and his team, would never get through the Khumbu Icefall and across the enormous crevasse at its crest; in those days a single crevasse spanned the glacier from rock wall to rock wall.

Aluminum ladders and improvements in mountaineering equipment since then have helped in the task of establishing a route through the Icefall. Front-point crampons allow climbers to ascend near-vertical ice barriers. Russian-made, high-pressure, refillable oxygen bottles provide several hours' more oxygen, at a quarter of the weight of the earlier bottles. Reasonably accurate weather forecasts can be made from data collected by satellites and then communicated quickly to climbers on the mountain. These developments, combined with down clothing, polypropylene underwear, and lightweight tents, food, and radios, make Everest today a different and in some ways easier mountain than my father faced.

Nevertheless, getting even this far, to the foot of the mountain, had been a long journey, and in the larger picture it may have been the hardest part, mentally if not physically.

THE TENTS OF five expeditions were already erected within this uninviting landscape, and seven more groups were due to arrive. Some of these were commercial, guided expeditions, for which clients had to cough up $30,000 to $65,000 or more. The cost of a large expedition can run to more than half a million dollars, and so climbers, who are perennially short of funds, take on clients as a way of financing their climbing obsession.

By the spring of 1993 the number of expedition permits granted on the south side of Everest had grown to a record of seventeen. That's when HMG jacked up the royalty to $50,000 per expedition, with additional fees for extra members, liaison officers, conservation officers, and garbage collection. Climbing royalties have boosted Nepal's mountaineering revenues and become a minor cash cow for the Treasury: $800,000 a year from Mount Everest alone is not a small sum for a developing country. But it bothers me that only a nominal portion of these funds has been returned to benefit the local people or used to promote mountain safety and environmental conservation. And the Chinese authorities in Tibet must be colluding with the Nepalese government: on the north side, the royalties and local expenses involved in climbing are comparable to those on the Nepal side. In Tibet, too, the government has done little with the revenue from these fees to improve the lives of the people or the environment. These two governments are shrewdly selling the climbers' holy grail to the highest bidders and pocketing the proceeds.

The social dynamic at Base Camp reminded me of college. This makeshift city on the side of a sometimes hostile mountain was like a boot camp without a drill sergeant, or a boomtown without a mayor. I couldn't understand why the Western climbers needed to surround themselves with so many material comforts. Each expedition's camp was laid out with restaurant-sized kitchens, dining hall tents, communications tents with evening videos, and cleared landing areas for helicopters.

Once the ten other teams had established themselves at Base Camp, the population swelled to more than four hundred people. It dawned on me that we were all shooting for the same narrow window of stable weather that usually opens up each spring, for a few days around mid-May. The two largest groups alone, those led by the American Scott Fischer and the New Zealander Rob Hall, would be sending twenty-two guides and clients, and nearly as many high-altitude Sherpas, on a single route up the mountain.

I felt uncomfortable when I overheard foreign climbers talking about the summit and what it would mean to them when they reached it, as if their success was a foregone conclusion. And those who spoke most about it tended to be those who were working the least and were the least prepared. Sherpas say that people who brag or become rich overnight are prone to a reversal of fortune—like the couple from the village of Pheriche who became suddenly wealthy, then one of them promptly died of syphilis. Never gloat over good fortune, we say, for it will certainly be lost one day. The ripening of karma is sometimes predictable, but generally it is not, and the exact manner in which it ripens never is.

The more I witnessed the garish displays of ego and individualism in some of the foreign teams, the more I felt they were inviting misfortune. I distanced myself from them. Sherpas, including my father, have always spoken about approaching

Everest with an attitude of respect, awareness, humility, and devotion. Perhaps if these foreign climbers had a better understanding of the cultures, history, values, and beliefs of the people who have lived in Everest's shadow for centuries, they would not encounter so much hardship on the climbs. Their desire for the summit—at all costs—consumes their energy and eclipses their good luck.

So what motivates these foreigners to climb? Why were they here? For the commercial guides—like the Sherpas—it is a business. Some of them come for the personal challenge, wanting to test themselves on the mountain, though this motive may be a surrogate for the more enigmatic task of hurling themselves against their inner demons. Those who climb because they want to prove something to someone, or to gain recognition, tend to be arrogant, and the Sherpas tend not to like them. Many others have reasons that are more complex and subtle; they are on a path, searching for something beyond the physical challenge and the glory. Most of these climbers, myself included, don't know what we will find during our journey, other than a brief glimpse of impermanence and the frailty of the human condition. If we truly saw only that, and gained only that much understanding, then I would consider our venture entirely worth our while.

I was taken aback to witness some of the teams holding classes in ladder crossing for their less experienced members, in preparation for the crevasses of the Khumbu Icefall. Some of these climbers were unsure of how to attach their crampons and had difficulty walking in them correctly. One young Taiwanese knew virtually nothing about mountaineering.

It seemed a bit late to be building mountaineering skills, and I took every chance to tell the inexperienced climbers I saw to be careful. In the mountains, however, such a warning can be taken as nothing more than a casual form of greeting. "To climb Everest," as our cameraman Robert Schauer said, "you need experience, and that's not covered by the $50,000 fee." I could understand their eagerness to practice their climbing. It would be my first time through the Icefall, too, and I was nervous. One hears constantly of the hazards there and the people who have died.

The Taiwanese and South African teams were making their nations' first attempts on Everest, and they proudly displayed their national flags. The South Africans appeared to be having even greater difficulties than the Taiwanese, especially after their primary sponsor, the South African *Sunday Times*, withdrew its sponsorship. Their leader, Ian Woodall, was militaristic to the point of outright rudeness, and during the approach to Base Camp three of the group's most experienced climbers resigned due to a "profound lack of trust in [Ian Woodall's] decisions as a leader," and cited his "continued irresponsible and irrational behavior." They added that they felt it would be life-threatening to continue under his directive. The three were seen waiting to catch a plane at the Syangboche airstrip.

But my curiosity about the mountain exceeded my worry, and my confidence slowly grew—until an avalanche once again broke away from the Lho La below Everest's West Ridge. I turned to watch it gather speed and then crash thousands of feet below, at the base of the ridge. Seconds later Base Camp was blasted by a *whoosh* of air that rattled the tents and fogged us in billows of spindrift. It always looked as if these avalanches would roll over Base Camp and sweep us away.

The American guide Scott Fischer knew my mother, and I liked him. He moved with ease around Base Camp, and his upbeat attitude and laid-back style were infectious and thoroughly American. Scott had climbed K2 with Ed Viesturs in 1992, and he had photographed Ed and Paula's wedding a few weeks earlier. He had been on Everest twice before, in 1987 on the Tibet side, and in 1994, when he reached the summit without oxygen. This year his Seattle-based company, Mountain Madness, had taken on several clients, among them the New York socialite Sandy Hill Pittman. For Pittman, Everest was the final peak of her collection of "Seven Summits"—the highest mountain on every continent. Another client was Pete Schoening, admired as a hero after he saved the lives of six team members high on K2 in 1953. If the sixty-eight-year-old Schoening reached the summit, he would be the oldest person to climb Everest.

The New Zealand guide Rob Hall was the inverse of Fischer: meticulous and organized, always planning ahead, anticipating what might go wrong. He was focused and driven. Impressively, Hall had guided twenty-two people to the top of Everest—more than the total number that reached the summit during the twenty-five-year period following my father's 1953 climb. Eight clients had signed up with him this year, and he clearly felt an obligation to do his best to get them to the top.

All of the leaders were apprehensive about the potential for crowding on the upper part of the mountain. Fischer and Hall wanted to confer on the timing of their teams' summit attempts, and they called a meeting to coordinate dates. Initially, Fischer wanted his team to make an attempt on the ninth of May, a day before Hall's team. Even before reaching Base Camp, Hall had envisioned trying for the summit on May 10; in other years he had gone for the top on this date, and he felt it was lucky. Nearly all his clients reached the summit in 1994 on May 10. None of his clients, however, had reached the top in 1995.

The season was progressing. Fischer and Hall looked at the shortage of time and manpower needed to fix the route high on the mountain and agreed it would be best if, above Camp IV on the South Col, their two teams combined their efforts for a May 10 attempt. Then they alerted the other team leaders, urging them to schedule themselves earlier or later. Climbing parties that followed would benefit, they pointed out, from the ropes they intended to fix on the Hillary Step and the summit ridge.

Our IMAX team could climb comfortably without fixed ropes above the South Col, so we chose May 9, one day ahead of the two large groups. For filming, and for safety, David wanted our team to be relatively alone on summit day. From my point of view, May 9 would be auspicious. It was the tenth anniversary of my father's death. His spirit would be with us, as I acutely wanted it to be. I was wishing, vainly perhaps, that he would be there for me after death even more than he was when alive.

WHILE AT SCHOOL in Darjeeling, I had acquiesced to my father's wishes and applied to college, though I often considered it to be little more than an intermission in my unfolding dream.

Saint Paul's—dismissed by some orthodox Hindus as the "beef-eating school"—is one of the finest boarding schools in Asia, but the stifling confinement there only fueled my desire to travel, to seek out adventures. And embarking out into the world could be done wholeheartedly, I assumed at the time, only if I made a clean break from my parents and the strictures of archaic Asian customs and religion. The Christian staff at Saint Paul's did not try to convert the students. They may have figured that a broad liberal arts education would be sufficient diversion from Buddhist thought and the lamas' counsel. Indeed, I began to question Buddhism especially in the last years of boarding school, just when my parents were cultivating their own Buddhism and spending growing sums of money supporting it. They had traveled the world already, themselves, and presumably made up their own minds about what to believe, so why shouldn't I?

In Darjeeling I had seen a number of American war movies and studied the way American soldiers walked and talked. I fell in love with the actors' casual command of difficult situations. They were sensitive and human but maintained firm control over their lives. They engaged life with insouciance, balanced by principled respect for right and wrong. I was curious about what sort of people had built the United States, a country whose name alone commanded wonder and respect.

I was intrigued by my father's honorary degree from Northland College, Wisconsin, which I had seen hanging on the wall of his office. I applied to Northland for admission and was accepted. Consummation of my Everest climbing passion, and of a hopeful relationship with Soyang, would have to wait.

But when I arrived in the United States at the age of eighteen to enroll I was shocked at the college's lack of discipline. There are few social restraints, it seems, on what one can say or do in America. My classmates needed so many personal possessions. They had brought with them televisions, computers, oversized stereos and speakers, even their teddy bears. And then I would hear them on the phone crying to their parents about being stuck so far away, and could Mom and Dad please send beer money? In my first class a student propped his feet up on the seat in front of him, pointing the soles of his shoes at the professor. To a Sherpa that is a chilling display of disrespect, an insult even, for shoes kill insects as they tread, and they sometimes tread in filth. And I was surprised to hear some students call their professors by their first name. The college's administration, too, seemed to reflect the students' relaxed behavior. Or maybe it was the other way around.

On occasion I witnessed this kind of disrespect among foreigners in Nepal and Darjeeling. When my mother died, I was offended to see a small group of tourists taking photographs of her funeral procession and her body, which was secured on top of a carriage, as if they were watching a festival. I felt my privacy was being invaded. In their own country I doubt these people would simply appear at a stranger's funeral and begin shooting pictures.

What student needs more than four shirts? One of my roommates had thirty. I lived in the United States for ten years, and everything I owned fit inside two suitcases. Uncontrolled excess may be excusable, but where was the sense of gratitude? To many of my classmates nothing was ever quite good enough.

One of the strengths of the Sherpas is our ability to adapt to new and changing conditions and to endure discomfort. My father understood hardship, and he wanted to show it to me and my siblings. While on expeditions with the British, in particular, he carefully studied their system of command and execution. He could see what worked and what didn't, and he especially learned discipline as a tool for getting things done.

"Do your homework," he'd say to us at home. "Don't eat with your hands." "Sit there." "Get up and wash the dishes." Offering to wash dishes was a custom he picked up in America, and he made us do it, too. We had live-in help, but he always said,

"There are no servants in this house." On the mountain, when he gave orders, he would always jump in and help the other Sherpas with the work, such as pitching tents and carrying loads. A light-heartedness always accompanied my father's strictness.

In America, where I would wash the dishes after eating with friends (something that many educated Indians and Nepalese feel is beneath them), I was caught between two cultures, as if my head were on a different continent from my body. With both feet I had jumped gleefully into America's wildness and freedom and opportunity, but gradually I started to look back to my parents and what they had taught me. I needed an anchor in America, and their values were all I could find.

In America, divorce is prevalent, and I wondered if this resulted from the expectations that couples place on each other going into the marriage relationship. When I returned to the Himalaya, Soyang and I had a "love marriage," which is universal in the West and is becoming more common in Asia. But I have noticed that our custom of arranged marriages tends to be just as successful in the long term. Sherpas are practical and resigned, which frees us to carry on with raising children and other tasks of a householder. Love grows as a product of that shared, true life experience.

Soyang and I had known each other since we were kids, and from an early age I somehow knew that I would end up marrying her. I'm glad she accepted my proposal, because I suspected there were several other young men prepared to step in and ask her to marry them. Traditional wedding ceremonies were held for us in both Darjeeling and Kathmandu. The food, for instance, was prepared according to recipes in which the numbers of ingredients is prescribed in ancient texts, and the timing for presentation of the more than twenty dishes was strictly adhered to.

I wished that my parents were there. During the Darjeeling ceremony, I told them in whispered tones how grateful I was for their love and guidance and asked that they not worry about me and my brothers and sister. I knew they would be proud to see that we had all grown up and could take care of ourselves.

FROM BASE CAMP, Wongchu had sent a note to an elderly monk from Pangboche, and in the hand-delivered reply the lama specified the date from the Tibetan calendar that would be most favorable for the Base Camp *puja* ceremony of propitiation.

Sherpas won't climb on the mountain until the puja is held, and Western climbers defer to the Sherpas on this bit of expedition protocol. The ritual can be loosely described as a petitioning of the gods for permission to climb, and for good weather and safe passage. Liturgically, however, this is a type of *Ser-kyim* ("Golden Drink Offering") ceremony, and has broader significance. Any new enterprise, such as building a house or climbing a mountain, requires that the deities first be engaged by a lama, who asks for their understanding and tolerance.

The day before the puja, one of the young Sherpas on the team who had taken monastic training directed the building of a crude but attractive stupa-like structure, about eight feet high, which would act as the heart of the *lhap-so*, the worship site.

Early the next morning the lama arrived, followed by a porter carrying a large plastic drum of chang, for this is no somber occasion. Jangbu erected a *tharshing*, a tall prayer flagpole, then secured its base with stones. (Sherpa custom dictates that this be done by a person who has both parents living.) Seven colorful lengths of prayer flags (it must be an odd number) radiated like spokes from the top of the pole, and we anchored their ends nearby. We believe that if the tharshing breaks or is dismantled, bad luck will ensue. On the other hand, if a raven alights on the juniper branch tied to the top of the pole, the expedition will succeed.

By midmorning the entire team had congregated at the lhap-so with offerings of grains and potatoes and fancier items such as power bars, chocolate, and whiskey. Sitting cross-legged on a cushion, the lama read while two Sherpas poured him tea and made him comfortable.

The lama's chants invoked the presence of eight categories of deities, including the guru, the Dharma Protectors, the tutelary deities, the country-gods, the angel-like (but sometimes wrathful) *dakinis,* and Miyolangsangma, the bountiful protector goddess of Everest. The lama had placed three white stones on the chorten's altar, representing Miyolangsangma and two others of the Five Long-Life Sisters. An image of Guru Rimpoche—Padmasambhava, the "lotus-born" saint who brought Buddhism to Tibet—had been fixed to the lhap-so's altar with strips of duct tape.

Despite the traditional Sherpa air of informality at such gatherings, the climbing Sherpas were hardly distracted as they meditated and prayed. We say that the intense disorientation that one encounters at the moment of death—an experience that much of Buddhist practice is meant to prepare us for—is far more distracting than the most disturbing of background noise. In fact, lamas emphasize that for adept practitioners sounds and confusion can act as aids to concentration.

I joined the climbing Sherpas in prayer. Some of the Western climbers did so, too, out of respect for us, but also to be seen as participating. Some foreign climbers have studied Buddhism, while others may simply be superstitious.

Our climbing gear—the tools of our trade—had to be blessed and purified, too, before we could bring them onto the mountain. A Sherpa placed some juniper boughs at the base of the altar and nursed them to flames. The members and Sherpas then passed their ropes, crampons, ice axes, and other equipment through the smoke, bathing each item in protective wafts of incense. Just as the sweet smell of incense cleanses odors, the smoke expels spiritual pollution, clearing the way for favor from the deities.

Wongchu distributed handfuls of tsampa, and as a final consecration we all slowly lifted our right hands while chanting in unison, in a long rising tone, "*SwooooOOO!*" (Go up—may good fortune arise!). We did it again, and the third time we launched the flour skyward. In an exuberant, chaotic moment, we all shouted "*Lha Gyalo!*" (May the Gods be victorious!) and smeared the flour remaining in our hands onto each other's hair and cheeks, to signify hopes that we would live until our hair and beards turn white.

The lama poured chang as a communion. As I had with the holy water from Geshé Rimpoche, I accepted some in my right hand, my left held respectfully beneath it. I drank a sip, then ran the rest through my hair to fully incorporate the blessing. The offerings were passed out for us to eat, and I noted that everyone was careful to not take too much.

We were now released to embark on the climb.

FINALLY, AFTER MONTHS of preparation, I had strapped on my crampons and was standing at the edge of the Khumbu Icefall, headed for Camp I. Geshé Rimpoche had given me a precise time to begin climbing the mountain. Other Sherpas' lamas had prescribed similar dates to enter the Khumbu Icefall, but most of them had set the date two days before our climbing schedule allowed. To accommodate this, two days earlier several of us had thrown on our equipment and formally launched ourselves into the Icefall. We walked up to the first crevasse, then returned to Base Camp. Fulfilling ritual prescriptions this way is perfectly fine, and the lamas know we do it.

The morning of the first day of a climb is critical for Sherpas. We first orient ourselves toward the south, while drawing our mantras into our mouths. Privately, each of us begins to concentrate and invokes the three elements that will guide and protect us: the deities, our lama, and our parents. To do this effectively and genuinely, the lamas say, the mind should be relaxed and the meditation unforced. It is not a matter of actively emptying the mind as much as simply letting go—opening a door so that extraneous and disturbing thoughts can depart, allowing these three elements to take up residence.

The Khumbu Icefall is a labyrinth of house-sized blocks of ice, towering seracs, and gaping crevasses, all seemingly frozen in midcreation, sculpted with an artistic combination of randomness and cosmic order. Their colors range from white to clear to turquoise and change as one walks past them, like the mosaic of refracted light on the bottom of a swimming pool. Mesmerizing as this maze is, the Icefall demands concentration. Chunks of ice weighing hundreds of tons can shift and tumble without warning—Chomolungma's version of Russian roulette. In the passage of a day, crevasses can open up and then close again as the glacier twists and undulates, squeaking and popping in its slow but unrelenting downward progress. Some areas appear more ready to shift and fall than others, but no one can predict exactly when that will happen. The climbers move through the Icefall only in the early morning, when the ice bridges and seracs are still frozen from the night before—or mostly frozen.

"Collapses in the Icefall happen so fast," the Himalayan climbing veteran Pete Athans told me, "that you're just as likely to run into their path as you are to avoid them." The British on the 1953 expedition gave names like "Hell-fire Alley" and "Atom Bomb" to especially dicey areas.

On exposed sections of the Icefall, climbers are protected by fixed ropes, long lengths of stationary line anchored in the snow and ice that span the crevasses alongside the ladders. For safety and as a climbing aid, we use an oval device called an ascender, which is connected by a loop of webbing to our harnesses. We clip the ascender onto the rope and slide it forward as we move upward, and it grips the rope if we lean back or fall.

Before passing beneath one ominous overhanging block of ice, I stopped and pulled from a cotton drawstring pouch some of the blessed grains of barley that Geshé Rimpoche had given me. I cast a small handful onto the route ahead, briefly wondering what the climbers behind me would think of it if they noticed.

The Icefall has claimed more than twenty lives, the majority of them Sherpas. Most Western climbers—the clients at least— waltz through the glacier only three or four times and bypass Camp I to rest comfortably at Camp II—Advance Base Camp. They little appreciate that Sherpas do virtually all of the load-carrying through the Icefall, the most hazardous stretch of the mountain. In 1953, seventeen Sherpas delivered 750 pounds of food and equipment to the South Col, at 26,000 feet, a feat that made my father proud, as I am. Clearly, the British expedition would not have made it above Base Camp—and possibly not even that far—without them.

For me the dangers were momentarily eclipsed by my relief to be climbing, moving forward over snow, feeling vulnerable and human but sublimely energized, tasting the adrenaline that surges during a test of one's faith and hope. While climbing, it is best not to think about death or to be fearful. Fear triggers mistakes. Yet it is fear that also induces respect for the mountain.

Experience is the best antidote for fear. An inexperienced climber doesn't know whether to trust a tiny foothold the size of a penny, but it can feel as safe as a carpeted hallway to an experienced climber.

While waiting for Araceli to negotiate a ladder crossing, I studied the seasonal layers of snowfall on the far side of the crevasse, the annual strata that accumulate like rings on a tree. Counting down forty-three layers, my eyes followed along the layer's serpentine length. That level was deposited the season of my father's successful climb. He walked atop that layer.

It was my turn to cross the crevasse, on four sections of aluminum ladders lashed together with plastic rope. On the longer spans, the ladders develop an unnerving bounce as climbers approach the midpoint above the crevasse. Humbly slowed to a crawl, there is time to stare into the seemingly bottomless blue-black depth—"looking into America," as Sherpas say. We term falling into a crevasse "getting a visa to the United States."

The ladders need almost daily adjustment to correct for the continual movement of the glacier, especially later in the season, when it is warmer. The anchors melt out, screws loosen, crevasses widen, and parts of the glacier collapse, destroying sections of the route. With the British, and the Swiss before them, my father crossed crevasses mainly on logs—entire trees that the Sherpas felled and limbed at lower elevations and carried into the Icefall. In 1953 the British brought a single telescoping aluminum ladder, hoping that it could be transported from crevasse to crevasse as needed. My father's experience with the Swiss had taught him that in order to handle the constant up-and-down traffic, they would need to fully fix a route through the Icefall. He finally convinced the British to have the Sherpas cut numerous pine logs and carry them into the glacier, as the Swiss had done.

One afternoon my father and Hillary, roped to each other, were down-climbing through the Icefall, with Hillary in the lead. While negotiating a steep downward slope, my father suddenly saw Hillary fall, twist around, and raise his ice ax as he shouted, "Tenzing!" Hillary was being devoured by a hidden crevasse, one that he had pointed out to Tenzing only that morning on their way up. My father immediately jammed his ice ax into the snow and wrapped the rope around it to anchor himself and Hillary.

Hillary had fallen about fifteen feet before coming to rest, yet he was in danger of plunging farther into the depths of the crevasse. My father, after positioning himself to gain some leverage, was able to gradually haul Hillary up to the edge of the crevasse, with some help from Hillary's single cramponed foot. He had lost his ice ax and a crampon in the fall.

My father knew that to haul a man over the lip of the crevasse without help would be nearly impossible, but with a final strenuous effort he was able to inch Hillary high enough that Hillary could reach outside the crevasse and help pull himself out.

Both of them were exhausted by the ordeal, and my father's gloves were torn by the rope. The incident bonded the two climbers, and at Base Camp the grateful Hillary told the team members that he would have been lost had it not been for Tenzing. My father was proud that he had been instrumental in saving Hillary's life, but he stressed to me that he had done nothing extraordinary, that he simply acted quickly and decisively, as any international climber would have done.

IN THE ICEFALL, as on the mountain, we hope that we have been imbued with enough *tsin-lap* to handle any situation. Tsin-lap is roughly translated as "blessing," but it really means the mental ability and strength to allow our minds to be changed in the direction of complete awareness. When we pray to the wisdom deities, to the Buddhas, we pray for tsin-lap. It is believed that to some degree it can be triggered and nourished by consuming sacred substances, such as the pills and liquids—also called tsin-lap—that are consecrated by lamas through prayers, mantras, and visualizations. Some of these contain minute pieces of the body parts of the Buddha or high lamas, combined with hundreds of Himalayan medicinal herbs and other blessed objects.

To receive tsin-lap is to make a connection, and any such connection is positive. For instance, we say that even if you view the Buddha as an enemy, simply by taking that view you have made a connection that will speed your enlightenment.

It's not all mental or spiritual, of course. Physically, climbing Everest requires the strength and stamina of a conditioned athlete, and athletes develop their ability partly through repetitive drills. I regarded every day as a form of training, and I forced myself to work hard at a consistent pace, to not overexert or overeat, and to drink plenty of water to avoid becoming dehydrated. It hadn't happened to me, but I'd heard gruesome stories of a dehydration-related affliction among climbers confined at high altitudes called fecal impaction—constipation so bad that digital extraction is necessary. Nicotine has a laxative effect, so I figured that smoking might be a helpful preventive measure. I was trying to quit, but I sneaked a few cigarettes with Bijaya, our Nepalese liaison officer. "Sherpa oxygen," we called it.

For maximum efficiency of movement and to aid acclimatization, we carried loads to successively higher camps and then descended to sleep. When we felt strong enough to sleep at higher altitudes and enough loads had been delivered to the higher camps to form a stockpile, we carried higher still.

As climbers, we have to listen to what our bodies are telling us and fine-tune our rate of ascent: acclimatizing just enough to summit before we become too debilitated by the altitude and shortage of oxygen to do so. To treat altitude sickness, we had an inflatable hyperbaric chamber, basically a reinforced vinyl tube large enough for the patient to climb in and lie down. Helpers continually pump the bag from the outside, increasing the air pressure (and thereby the oxygen available to the lungs and body) so that the patient's effective elevation is lowered several thousand feet. When patients emerge from the hyperbaric bag, they can often descend with minimal help, or even on their own.

Once the four camps are established and fully stocked, the summit push can be made quickly from Base Camp or Advance Base Camp. In 1953 and earlier, climbers established nine camps, which acted as progressive levels of their gradual siege. That system has been replaced by the "climb high, sleep low" strategy: two or three times before the summit attempt, climbers descend all the way to Base Camp for a few days to rest and regain lost weight. It's actually possible to put an Everest climb on hold this way, and climbers delight in releasing themselves, exhausted and depleted, into safe, luxurious sleep at Base Camp. But reducing the number of camps has yielded no shortcuts: it takes as long to establish today's four camps as it did to set up the nine camps of 1953—more than a month and a half.

I felt more experienced than many of those on the mountain, but as I plodded upward, squeezing through awkward clefts in the ice, listening to the groans and squeals of the glacier as it shrugged and shifted, my heavy pack only amplified the weight of my self-doubt.

The tattered hulk of a helicopter lodged in the Icefall below Camp I roused me from my reverie. It had been chartered in 1973 by the first Italians on Everest, who staged what was likely the largest expedition in the history of mountaineering, with 64 climbers, 3,000 porters, and 120 Sherpas. In the attempt to airlift loads to a point above the Icefall, the chopper had twice landed and taken off successfully but after the third landing was unable to take off. Some Sherpas say that the helicopter foundered because it had carried a live sheep to Base Camp, where the team had sacrificed the sheep and eaten it. Killing or roasting meat in the vicinity of the mountain is perhaps the worst defilement imaginable. Nonetheless, the Italians achieved their objective of getting an Italian to the summit at any cost.

That's when I walked past my first dead body—or more like half a body—baking in the intense sunshine near the top of the Icefall. Everest veterans are accustomed to seeing bodies, and the Sherpas refer to them dismissively, probably out of uneasiness, as "raven momos"—a wordplay on the Himalayan delicacy of meat dumplings. A certain amount of gallows humor keeps us from yielding to the ever-present fear of death.

Dead bodies are in fact scattered all over the mountain. Most of them were victims, at least indirectly, of the effects of altitude, bad weather, or bad judgment. They serve as a reminder that, on Everest, the margin of error is extremely small.

Camp I, at the top of the Khumbu Icefall, marks the beginning of the Western Cwm. Camp II, Advance Base Camp, is located at the head of this valley, below the Lhotse Face.

4

FROM
HER HEM
TO HER LAP

4

FROM
HER HEM
TO HER LAP

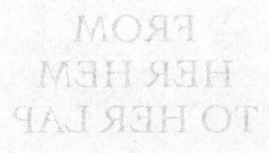

Finally, I had reached Camp I, at 19,100 feet, and was up and out of the shadowy dragon's teeth of the Khumbu Icefall. From the camp's small cluster of tents, I looked up-valley toward the massive Lhotse Face and the astounding spectacle of the Southwest Face of Everest, neither of which were visible from Base Camp.

At its upper end, the Khumbu Glacier has sculpted a cirque, a majestic amphitheater of rock and snow that rises steeply from a narrow but relatively level valley. This valley is known as the Western Cwm, and Camp II—Advance Base Camp (ABC)—sits at its upper end. In the spring of 1952 my father and the Swiss were the first humans to enter the Cwm, and they referred to it as the "Valley of Silence," perhaps because it is virtually surrounded by walls of mountains. My father said that when the wind was still, he could hear only the sound of his breathing, the voices of his teammates, and the crunch of their boots on the snow.

Carrying loads through the Cwm was glorious. I relished the simple physics of climbing, of moving over steep and then flat terrain, of rounding corners to encounter yet another exotic creation out of ice, of feeling the different tones and textures of snow under my feet.

Through the Western Cwm, convoys of Sherpas ferried heavy loads toward ABC, and I jumped in line with them. One Sherpa asked me to leave some of my loads for them to carry, and he was only half joking. The Sherpas work on a bonus system, and my help meant less work and therefore less money for them. Though my father was a sirdar, he always carried loads. It is hard for someone who is walking unburdened to generate in others an enthusiasm for work.

Here in the Cwm I began to feel secure, as if I were cradled in the lap of the mountain itself—despite the avalanches that rumble off of Lhotse and Everest's Southwest Face, raking over the valley. Indeed, most of the Cwm's and the Khumbu Glacier's mass of snow comes from avalanches that tumble into it from the walls on either side.

At midday the sun's rays gather and concentrate here, reflecting off the walls of Nuptse and the western buttress of Everest. Like a giant parabolic solar reflector, the Cwm scorches any climbers passing through its belly with radiant heat, though the ambient temperature may be near freezing. I wore my thickest glacier goggles, used an umbrella for shade, and applied sunscreen, though my skin is naturally dark.

It's a long, meandering trail to ABC, and more than once I caught the features of the landscape moving, seeming to change their position. I figured it was the altitude and hypoxia, though my father and other Sherpas had spoken about seeing rock cairns disappear and reappear, especially while traversing the monotonous rubble and moraine of the Nangpa Glacier on trading trips across the high pass to Tibet.

Our team clicked. We were working with a tuned efficiency that required little discussion. As David directed, I went through the repetitive motions of helping set up the camera and then performing on-camera. The IMAX camera was huge and made a wonderful loud whirring noise—the sound of mountainous grandeur being captured on film. I pictured the images that met our eyes filling a giant screen, superior in breadth and detail to my own peripheral vision. I only wished that it could capture how we felt, too, our transit through emotions of fear and elation, discouragement and achievement.

The bad omens seemed to fall away. My internal chatter slowed down, and a bountiful calmness moved in to replace it. Each pace fell in with my father's footsteps. Yes, this is what he spoke about, this is what drew him back to Everest in 1953 for his seventh attempt: the camaraderie, the exhilaration of strenuous physical effort, and the crystalline, nostril-stinging air. This was what I had wanted to share more of with him while he was alive—the sheer delight, not the celebrity. I dreaded returning to Base Camp and the distracting, human-created landscapes and dramas of lower elevations.

MY FATHER OFTEN spoke about his good friend the Swiss climber Raymond Lambert, and of how much he loved Switzerland and the Swiss. Climbing on Everest with Lambert, as he did in both the spring and fall of 1952, was what climbing should be about, he believed: good friends sharing the thrill and glory of the mountains. Lambert was skilled at steep climbing, which in those days required cutting steps with an ice ax. He had lost his toes to frostbite, and the special climbing boots that had been fashioned to fit his foreshortened feet allowed him to stand like a mountain goat on the tiniest of holds.

Until the early 1950s, Nepal and Tibet were closed to foreigners except selected British, and only Tibet allowed the British to climb. Everest had been a thoroughly British mountain. But in

1950 Nepal opened its doors to international climbers and allowed any nationality to come and attempt the mountain, one expedition at a time. In 1950 and 1951, the handful of Westerners who approached Everest from the south were too unfamiliar with and daunted by the mountain to consider climbing to the top.

The Swiss wanted it badly, and in the spring of 1952 my father and Lambert came tantalizingly close to the summit. Although the weather was excellent and they were feeling strong, they had climbed above the South Col intending only to dump a tent and a few supplies, then return with more Sherpas over the following days. At 27,600 feet on the Southeast Ridge, they picked out a level place where a tent could be pitched, regretting that they had neither sleeping bags nor a stove to melt water or brew tea—only a single candle to melt snow. Then they thought, *Why not?* The two of them spent a sleepless night there, slapping and rubbing each other to stay warm, hoping for a try at the top in the morning.

The next day, the weather was cloudy. Still game, they decided to continue up, and were pleased to find that the Southeast Ridge was broader and less steep than they had anticipated. Their hands were nearly too numb to fasten their crampons, however, and their bottled oxygen was working poorly. Moving excruciatingly slowly through driving wind and snow, they came to a standstill at 28,250 feet, 500 feet below the South Summit, the highest that humans had ever climbed. My father, like Lambert, felt that they could have made the summit, but would not have returned alive. If only they had had bottled oxygen and some tea and water to rehydrate with, they felt they would have been significantly stronger and faster. Before they turned around, my father told me, it was hard for him not to think of the 1924

British climbers George Mallory and Andrew Irvine, heading off upward into the clouds that blanketed Everest's summit, never to return.

WHEN THE EARLY British Everest expeditions passed through the Rongbuk monastery on Everest's north side, in 1921, 1922, and 1924, the abbot and monks were surprised at the foreigners' generosity. Though they had never seen light-skinned people, they were vaguely familiar with Tibet's bloody encounter in 1904 with Sir Francis Younghusband, whose British troops marched in from India to the east of Rongbuk and eventually reached Lhasa.

In 1922, British expedition leader H. W. Tilman told Dzatrul Rimpoche, the first abbot of Rongbuk monastery, that they were not attempting to climb Everest for national prestige, but because they were on something of a spritual pilgrimage to gain merit for the mind and body. Encouragingly, Dzatrul Rimpoche said that the mountain deities would not necessarily be offended by people trying to climb Chomolungma, but he and the monks remained concerned for the safety of the climbers—partly because harm tends to befall those who are not devoted to Buddhism, and partly because of the presence of several yeti. "It is very strange to have to deal with these curious people," Colonel Geoffrey Bruce wrote of the Tibetans following the first British attempt on the mountain in 1922. "They are an extraordinary mixture of superstition and nice feelings."[1]

In the early 1900s it was Dzatrul Rimpoche who had requested that another monastery be built in Nepal to the south

---

[1]C. G. Bruce and other members of the expedition, *The Assault on Mount Everest 1922* (New York: Longmanns & Co., 1923), p. 75.

of Rongbuk, at Tengboche. Tengboche acted as something of a satellite monastery of Rongbuk, and it reduced the need for Sherpa monks to climb over the 19,000-foot Nangpa La to Rongbuk for monastic training.

The blue sheep and Himalayan tahr in Rongbuk's vicinity were completely tame, and they ate out of the monks' hands. But the site's imperturbable peacefulness may have been limited to the animals. My father and then my father's nephew Gombu complained that the senior monks there used to beat them, and both of them stayed less than two years before running home to Khumbu. During the Cultural Revolution, which began in 1966, Rongbuk's exquisite stupa, chapels, and monks' quarters were destroyed by the Chinese. Had my cousin Gombu, who followed my father by nearly two decades, still been studying there, he would have joined the other lamas in their escape over the 19,000-foot Nangpa La into Nepal, bringing with them many of Rongbuk's Buddhist texts and rich traditions.

FOLLOWING MY PARENTS' deaths, I realized that I was drifting away from my family's roots. By learning more about my father's relationship to Chomolungma, I felt I might be able to better understand my own compulsion to climb the mountain. Before my mother died, she told me of a special bond our family had with the mountain, something even more profound than my father's passion to climb it. Without being specific, she said that it was a spiritual connection, and that it somehow involved my late stepmother, Ang Lhamu. My mother urged me to someday find Trulshig Rimpoche, the second and last abbot of the Rongbuk monastery, who is related to us. He now resides in Nepal, and she said that he would be able to tell me the story.

At the age of four, Trulshig Rimpoche had been recognized by Dzatrul Rimpoche, Rongbuk's founder, as an incarnation of his own "heart lama." Before Dzatrul Rimpoche passed away, he appointed Trulshig Rimpoche, at the age of nineteen, to be the abbot of Rongbuk. Trulshig Rimpoche left Tibet in 1959 and took refuge at our house in Darjeeling and at a gompa in Sikkim for some time before moving on to Nepal. He now spends several months each year at a remote hermitage in Solu, meditating and practicing.

After my spring 1995 litter collection trek to Base Camp, I flew back to Lukla that fall. Instead of walking north from Lukla with the crowds of Sherpas and foreign trekkers, however, I followed a much narrower trail south along the Dudh Kosi river, then crossed over the Tragshindu pass and dropped into Solu, the Sherpas' southern heartland. Turning toward the southeast, I hiked through open pine forests and along the margins of terraces planted with millet and corn. In three days I arrived at Trulshig Rimpoche's retreat cave.

The Maratika Cave in Haleshe, almost directly south of Everest, is one of a number of mountain caves where Guru Rimpoche meditated, as did the great yogi-saint Milarepa. Guru Rimpoche predicted that a time would come when Buddhism would see a decline or persecution in Tibet, and that devout people would have to flee their homeland. So he blessed a number of remote enclaves in the Himalaya known as *bé-yül*, or "hidden lands"—sanctuaries where Buddhists would be able to find refuge. The texts say that Guru Rimpoche meditated in a cave above Khumjung village and there vanquished or converted the evil spirits of the time, establishing Khumbu as one of the bé-yül that he identified. Mystical powers are concentrated and spirits abound in these valleys, the Sherpas say, and they should be kept pristine, undefiled by excessive human activity. My father was born in one bé-yül, the sacred upper Peng Chu River valley in Tibet, and moved to another, along the upper Bhote Kosi River in Khumbu.

I wandered through a group of scattered houses at the base of a ragged cliff, then switchbacked upward for several minutes to a cluster of wooden shacks buttressed precariously against the hillside with stilts. As I ducked in through the main doorway, I was greeted by a monk, Trulshig Rimpoche's personal attendant, who gave me a big smile. As had happened at Grandfather Gaga's in Thame, I felt I was coming home.

The monk led me to a colorfully painted antechamber, a waiting room. He told me to wait a few moments, then disappeared behind the door curtain leading to the next room, clearly Trulshig Rimpoche's quarters. I was glad for the wait, to catch my breath and gather my thoughts. My palms were sweating. Even though I am related to Rimpoche, I found myself nervous, excited even, as I was when visiting with my father in the sunroom where he would sit to get warm on winter mornings.

The attendant ushered me through the door curtain and into a room that was less than ten feet square. To one side Trulshig Rimpoche, rotund and somehow ageless, looked up from his sitting platform. He smiled congenially, as if he had something to tell me and had been waiting for me, his lost relative, to arrive. Out of respect for Rimpoche's stature, I didn't smile myself but first did three prostrations, thinking that even the mothers of the Dalai Lamas used to prostrate before their sons. I stepped forward, crouching, to present him with a kata and some offerings. He motioned me to sit down.

He called for tea, then took out an ancient-looking text, one of many that he and the Rongbuk monks had transported over the Nangpa La. He set the book—long, loose rice-paper folios sandwiched between carved wooden blocks and wrapped in a saffron-colored scarf—on the low prayer table in front of him. One by one, he flipped over the folios, mouthing words as he read. Then he stopped, threw the trailing edge of his robe over his shoulder, shifted forward on his cushion, and looked up at me.

"When I arrived in Khumbu and Solu in exile from Tibet," he began slowly, "I became acquainted with a respected Buddhist known as the 'Ladakh Lama.' At the time, he was living at Swayambhunath, near Kathmandu, but he later moved to Darjeeling.

"The Ladakh Lama was widely known for his skills at seeing the future, which he did by looking into his brass *melong*, a ritual mirror. In one of his prophecies, done in the 1930s, he told me that he clearly saw that a Himalayan Buddhist would be the first person to climb Chomolungma." He reached for his cup and took a sip of tea. "I thought you might be interested to hear that."

I was stunned by this pronouncement. For the devout people who believed that my father was the first to step on the summit, the Ladakh Lama's prophecy was further evidence that he may have been first—although my father discounted the issue of who was first as immaterial.

More important, the prophecy explained why my father had abandoned monastery life. Unconsciously, he may have been advancing his journey down a predestined spiritual path, as the vehicle for this prophecy. It explained why he ran off to Darjeeling, why he climbed mountains, and why he worshiped Miyolangsangma.

I recalled a story I had heard from Thame villagers some years earlier. A fellow yak herder once saw young Tenzing napping in a meadow above the hamlet. His yaks had wandered off, and a cobra, which is not exactly native to Khumbu, had slithered up in the grass behind him. Then the cobra opened its hood and arched itself directly over my father's sleeping head. The snake appeared identical, the yak herder said, to the snakes of the seven *naga* serpent spirits depicted in Buddhist and Hindu iconography, forming the halo of cobra heads that accent and shield the deity beneath them. Then the naga disappeared.

According to folklore, such an event is an auspicious blessing. The Thame people who were aware of this story said later that they weren't surprised by the news that Tenzing had climbed Everest.

Rimpoche continued to shift on his cushion, as if he were building up to say even more. He flipped over several folios, then stopped. He rocked back and forth as he scanned a passage, the one that may have unsettled me the most. He read loudly.

"Much attention will come to be focused on the mountain where Miyolangsangma resides, and people will suffer hardship as a result of defilement and negative deeds generated in her vicinity." He looked up at me, then continued in his own words. "Yes, the histories say that, centuries ago, many people in the Chomolungma region became ill, and some died. Seeing that, Milarepa asked Miyolangsangma, 'Why are you harming these people?'

"Her reply was, in effect: 'This is my home. These people have polluted my living space, causing me sickness, and when I become sick, they become infected, too, and some may die.' In those days people were taking the mountain for granted, as they are now, with the same consequences people now are facing—all these accidents and deaths that I have heard about."

Rimpoche took a sip of his tea, exhaled loudly, then launched into another story. I wasn't sure how much more revelation I could handle.

"Did you know there are indications that your stepmother, Ang Lhamu, the heavyset one, was actually—herself—a manifestation, a human embodiment, of Miyolangsangma?"

I was struck by disbelief. It must have been a joke.

"But she was such a homebody, such a nurturer, such a—"

"Precisely," Rimpoche interjected, as if he'd anticipated my response. "She was a protectress, a grantor of good fortune. She was the one who guided your father up the mountain. She provided him with the home life, the stability, the *sense* that he needed in order to climb it safely—through her blessings. She was the platform for his mission, the mission that the Ladakh Lama saw in the melong. Ang Lhamu came to him to fulfill that prophecy, and she guided him because she knew the way." When British expedition member George Band had described her as "formidable," I thought, he too may have been referring to something more than her size.

"Did my father know this?" I asked, incredulous.

"Your father never knew about the prophecy, and no, I never spoke to him about Ang Lhamu. On some level, however, I think he might have known the two of them had more than a simple worldly connection."

Their connection never seemed all that worldly either. She never bore him a child, for one thing. Knowing that my father wanted a son, she had introduced Tenzing to her cousin, my mother, Daku, and then by some accounts invited Daku to come live with them so that he would have a wife who could bear children.

Taking two wives was fairly common as recently as a couple of decades ago, if the husband could afford to support them. Polygamy often took the form of two sisters marrying a single man, generally in the same ceremony. Polyandry, in the form of two brothers sharing a single wife, was also not uncommon because many Tibetan and Sherpa husbands were away for extended periods on trading trips.

Ang Lhamu had passed away shortly before I was born, but I remember hearing relatives say that she and my father were well matched karmically, but they couldn't quite understand why he had married her. She didn't like to mix much, socially. But she had provided him with closeness and strength, especially after the death of his first wife, Dawa Phuti.

Dawa Phuti had given birth to a boy named Nima Dorje. My father adored him, but he died in 1939, at the age of four. Around that time Dawa Phuti gave birth to two girls—my elder half sisters, Ang Nima and Pem Pem. Dawa Phuti died while the girls were still young, and Ang Lhamu raised my half sisters as if she were their real mother.

Ang Lhamu's quiet determination and self-confidence touched everything she did. It wasn't so much that she loved my father. Trulshig Rimpoche was suggesting that she had a divine mission to protect him and see him to Chomolungma's summit. Her intuition about people and events was of great help to my father, and he must have sensed that she was a soul mate, beginning in the 1930s when she brought milk to him as a young laborer on the church at Saint Paul's School and they argued good-naturedly over the price.

She was a traditional, hardworking Sherpa woman, and she concealed her depth of knowledge about the Western world. In 1938 a British family for whom she was working returned to England and took her with them as an *ayah*, perhaps the first Sherpa woman to go to England. For two years she lived at a hotel near Hyde Park, in the center of London, where she carefully studied the ways of wealthy foreigners. That experience prepared her nicely for the international celebrity that followed my father's Everest climb.

"Ang Lhamu's father, Lama Sangye, was a devoted follower of Dzatrul Rimpoche, the first lama of Rongbuk," Trulshig Rimpoche went on, "and he settled in Darjeeling and eventually became a highly respected lama there. He and his wife used to come to Rongbuk, and they stayed for extended periods. There is a remarkable story that, before Ang Lhamu was born, her mother took her yaks into the hills to graze. As she napped on the hillside, a dream came to her in which she had an affair with a man with white hair and a white beard, dressed all in white. Ang Lhamu was conceived right after that. Although Lama Sangye is clearly the father, this was a sign that Ang Lhamu was not an ordinary child. She was clearly blessed."

I looked up at Rimpoche and nodded, but could find little to say. Our family's connection to Chomolungma was far more profound than I had ever imagined.

"And someday she will guide you, too, if you are faithful to her," he said, referring to Ang Lhamu, but also meaning Miyolangsangma, I deduced. He then reached into a carved wooden cabinet next to his sitting cushion and pulled out a small item and handed it to me. It was a gold ring. "This is for good luck in reaching the summit," he said.

I hadn't told him that I was intending to climb the mountain. I must have looked dumbfounded as I thanked him and backed respectfully out of his quarters.

A monk directed me to the Maratika Cave, immediately below the monks' houses. I descended into the granite depression as far as I could go and peered in. The cave's holy water sits in a dark pool at the bottom, but pilgrims and monks place glass jars on small rock platforms along its walls to collect the water that drips into it. I placed my hand against the wall and collected some in my palm, then drank it slowly.

The lamas describe peering into bodies of water, or into their brass melong mirrors in which they see the future, as similar to watching a movie. Some laypeople are born with an ability to see the future, too.

I turned and again looked into the depths of the pool. A progression of still images, events, and scenes of my life, past and future, slowly gathered and unfolded before me. I saw myself in the midst of suffering and hardship, but also on the summit of Everest. The images seemed to grab me by the chest, their sheer visceral intensity overpowering my sense of wonder and disbelief.

PARTWAY UP THE Western Cwm, I could make out several tents scattered across a pile of rocks. This was ABC, or Camp II, at 21,400 feet. Still clutching my umbrella, aiming it like a shield toward the fiery sun, I continued plodding, and within an hour I reached ABC.

ABC is a smaller version of Base Camp, with a cooking tent and cook, dining tent, and individual tents. Once acclimatized, climbers can leave Base Camp, bypass Camp I, and reach ABC in a long morning. Most of our rest time above Base Camp would be spent here.

In a sense, this is where the Everest massif begins. From ABC, the summit lies only one and a third miles away horizontally, plus one and a third miles vertically. The grandness of the landscape deceives one's sense of scale, leading one to perceive the mountain as fairly modest and its summit as no more than a day's climb—until one sees minuscule climbers on the route high above, if they can be seen at all.

In the late afternoons the winds on the upper mountain had been building to a crescendo as dramatic and frightening as those my father had described, roaring away like packs of terrible wild animals unleashed by the demons. His description pre-dated the age of commercial jets, which the Everest winds are more commonly compared to nowadays. Robert Schauer called the gales "the Kathmandu-Lhasa Express." Whenever it was howling, we would say, "Well, the train's running again today."

Our goal was to climb through the heart of that wind. As we stood at ABC looking up, I tried to take solace in David's words: "The wind you hear is always worse than the wind you're actually in." Most of the time. Perhaps.

Combined with the cold, the winds are unbearable. In the late fall of 1952 on my father's second try with the Swiss, he rested and camped for many frigid days on the rocks here at ABC. The fall days are shorter than in the spring, and the sun disappears behind the summit ridge of Nuptse by two each afternoon. The Swiss expedition members and Sherpas were bitterly cold until sunrise, which didn't come until late in the morning. The cold was affecting the Sherpas psychologically as much as physically, and they wished to be off the mountain entirely. Arguments grew in intensity.

Progress was slow. My father and Lambert reached the South Col near dark, and for two hours they staggered about trying to set up their tents near the still-visible remains of their spring campsite. Lambert's thermometer registered thirty below zero.

They left the South Col early the next morning, but the wind and cold continued to batter them. My father was wearing three pairs of gloves, but his fingers had gone numb, and their noses, lips, and cheeks began turning shades of white and blue. The Sherpas and the Swiss behind them had virtually ceased to move forward. Retreating was their only choice; they turned around well below the point they had reached in the spring.

My father and Lambert always wanted to reach the summit together, and they knew this was their last try, at least for some time. As they turned and headed down, they didn't even look at each other, but each knew what the other was thinking in the way that climbers can communicate beyond language when they have spent months together, entrusting their lives to each other. I think they also shared a certain resolute pride, knowing that in those conditions no humans could have possibly succeeded.

On the walk out, my father was exhausted. He sprained his ankle and then became feverish. It had been his second Everest attempt in only six months, and he told the other Sherpas with him that he was tired of the mountain and was close to admitting defeat. In Kathmandu, however, the king himself presented my father with the Nepal Pratap Bardhak ("Rising Glory") medal, a high honor.

His sickness turned out to be malaria, what was termed "marsh fever" at the time. The Swiss flew him out to Patna, in northern India, where he stayed at a missionary hospital for ten days.

He was still in the hospital in December 1952 when he received a letter from Major Charles Wylie, inviting him to return to Everest in the spring of 1953 with a British expedition. Major Wylie, who would be the transport officer, spoke Nepali, and his father had been a recruiter for the Gurkha Regiments in Darjeeling in the 1930s and his grandfather was British Resident in Nepal in the 1890s. Wylie was aware of the respect that my father commanded among porters and the other Sherpas, and desperately wanted him to join them. Even though my father was still weak and nearly twenty pounds underweight, he relented. It would be his lucky seventh attempt.

My father had many close British friends, as I do. The English are more reserved and formal than other foreigners. They are brave, just, and fair, and even good-humored, but in my father's day they didn't fully treat outsiders as equals. I've detected this disposition myself in some older Brits. With the Swiss in the fall of 1952, my father had been invited along as a full climbing member of the team; the Swiss and French treated my father as a friend and partner in a way that the British didn't, and perhaps couldn't. Even today, some expedition accounts—not necessarily British—don't list by name the Sherpas who made the summit or who were on the expedition, but lump them into the generic category of "Sherpas."

My father would have preferred to return to Everest with the Swiss, but he didn't mind the British and knew they would make a grand effort, having always considered Everest to be their mountain. It would be their last shot at the peak before the more dangerous fall season, for which they had a contingency plan. Then the French would have a chance. They had been granted permission for 1954. There were rumors, too, of an even greater threat: a Russian expedition might set forth in the spring from the north side, the same season the British would approach the summit from the south. The world of mountaineers and politics were quickly converging on the roof of the world.

FORTUNATELY, OMINOUS BEGINNINGS don't always lead to unfavorable outcomes.

The 1953 expedition certainly had its share of unsettling early difficulties. My father had rounded up about thirty Sherpas from Darjeeling and Khumbu and summoned them to Kathmandu early that spring. They gathered outside the British embassy, near the heart of the city. Sherpa women came as well, wearing boots made by hand from buffalo hide, with felt uppers. The men wore battered sneakers and well-broken-in climbing boots, relics from previous expeditions.

Nowadays many Sherpas own houses and apartments in Kathmandu, and growing numbers of them drive cars and motorcycles. But in 1953 Kathmandu didn't even have hotels, and none of the Sherpas had relatives living in the city. A British official assigned them sleeping quarters in a garage, recently converted from a stable, on the grounds of the British embassy. The British and New Zealand "Kiwi" climbers were housed within the embassy itself.

Understandably, the Sherpas were indignant. They had endured hardship and slept with equanimity in places far less inviting, but this was a poor beginning symbolically. At a late hour my father presented the Sherpas' complaints to Colonel John Hunt, the leader. For a moment my father considered leaving to find a monastery to sleep in, as a form of protest, but he stuck with the other Sherpas. Grumbling, they agreed to make the best of it for that one night.

In the morning insult was added to injury when they were scolded by the embassy staff for having used the road in front of the garage as a latrine. The British hadn't even given them a place to go to the bathroom. The dressing-down made them only more annoyed—to whatever degree they bothered to listen.

The British team members had signed an exclusive agreement with the *London Times* for their accounts of the expedition, and they were sworn to secrecy. The Sherpas had signed no such agreement, so my father was surrounded by competing journalists setting him up as the spokesman for the Sherpas and as a possible leak for inside information. He didn't know how to read, but he learned quickly that what one says and what appears in the newspaper can be widely divergent. It is to my father's credit that he didn't report the garage incident to the handful of reporters who would have gladly blown the issue out of proportion, getting the expedition off to an even rockier start.

Then, in a break from expedition custom (however rudimentary and variable such traditions were at the time), the Sherpas were told that the sleeping bags, boots, and clothing to be issued to them would be distributed only in Namche Bazaar or at Base Camp, rather than at the start of the expedition. At first, the Sherpas considered this to be a cheap slight, but they decided to go along when one Sherpa pointed out that the porters would then be responsible for getting the gear to Base Camp.

The Sherpas were also given a physical fitness test before leaving Kathmandu. A man named Gyaltsen, who was as strong as any other Sherpa, was disqualified because of an apparent heart irregularity. Distrustful of Western medicine, the Sherpas felt that he had been unfairly culled from the expedition, and his departure led to more grumbling in the ranks.

Major Wylie and my father were accustomed to handling complicated porter problems. He and my father were usually the ones thrown together into the middle of these disagreements, and their diplomacy skills were fully taxed. Wylie offered an apology to the Sherpas on behalf of the British—whether he was authorized to do so or not. He later became the military attaché in Nepal, from 1961 to 1964, and remains a good friend of our family.

Another disagreement occurred at Tengboche when the British announced that the equipment to be issued to the Sherpas would have to be returned after the climb. No previous expeditions, including British, had made such a demand, and it nearly caused a mutiny. Colonel Hunt retracted the directive, saying that they had wanted the equipment returned only in order to present it formally as a bonus in Kathmandu, following the expedition. One consequence was that the Sherpas, who generally regarded the sah'bs with great respect, began to realize that they could be unpredictable and impulsive—human, in other words.

Then my father learned that Pasang Phutar, a politically oriented Sherpa, might have been recruited by the Communists, who were gaining favor in Nepal at the time, to stir up trouble on the expedition. A "trial" was held near Tengboche, and Pasang appeared before Wylie, Hunt, and my father. Hunt and Wylie determined that Pasang would have to go, a decision that my father supported, though it was difficult for him because Pasang was a competent sirdar, a strong climber, and a good friend. It turned out that the expedition dynamics improved with his departure.

AT ADVANCE BASE CAMP, I kept visualizing the 1953 film clip in which my father and Hillary are walking slowly into ABC on their descent from the summit. I wanted to see the precise location of that shot, relative to where we placed our tents, and I found it on a flat space at the bottom of the Lhotse Face, about ten minutes' walk away. The sight of it transported me to the excitement that occurred there forty-three years earlier.

The British expedition members waiting at ABC had heard no news and had spotted no sleeping bags laid out on the snow near the next higher camp on the Lhotse Face, an agreed-upon signal for victory. They stood silently, watching Hillary and my father approach along with George Lowe, who had accompanied them from the South Col. The languid quality of their walk seemed to telegraph defeat—a recurring theme for the British on Everest over the previous three decades. It was the eve of the queen's coronation, and once again there would be little to show her from this part of the world.

Hillary and my father were simply too exhausted to raise their arms. Then George Lowe suddenly lifted his ice ax jubilantly and pointed toward the summit. It began to dawn on the team members at ABC that they had triumphed. They started walking toward the climbers, then broke into a run as Hillary weakly lifted his ice ax in a positive gesture. My father gave a thumbs-up. Then a certain fullness and depth came to the smiles on both their faces, unambiguously saying, "We made it."

Hugs and good cheer were exchanged all around, and tears came to Colonel Hunt's eyes. "Is it really true?" Hunt kept asking Hillary and my father, hugging them both. The other sah'bs were jumping about as if possessed, and the Sherpas were nearly as excited. At least for that moment, sah'bs and Sherpas became one. My father's broad smile, brimming with white teeth, filled the scene.

He immediately became a living legend to the expedition Sherpas; some of them bent at the waist toward him and placed their palms together, prayer fashion. One of them guided my father's hand to his forehead, to take blessing. Then they huddled around him and reverently served him tea as he recounted the climb in full Sherpa storytelling fashion, dramatically mimicking sounds, pausing at moments of tension, and letting them in on his reasoning, his apprehensions, and his joy. Through great struggle, Tenzing and Hillary had found their way to the highest point on the surface of the earth.

For my father, and for the many Sherpas who had dedicated parts of their lives to getting themselves and others up Everest, the success had been a long time coming.

OUR CHANCE FOR the summit might be a while in coming, too, I conjectured. By the first week of May 1996, a Frenchman, two Spanish brothers, and Göran Kropp, a lone Swede, had made unsuccessful summit attempts via the South Col route. Three of them had reached the South Summit, at 28,700 feet, or just below it, but were forced back by deep snow and high winds.

One wealthy Norwegian climber arrived at ABC, intending to climb the near-vertical, avalanche-prone Southwest Face. He described his attempt as solo, though he had hired ten Sherpas. He was another one with limited climbing experience, and a Sherpa carrying loads for him said that the man had never seen crampons before entering the Khumbu Icefall. From ABC the Norwegian reached a short way up the face, climbing in an area dangerously exposed to avalanches. There he abruptly decided to abandon his attempt altogether, saying that he had received news of a sickness in the family. We were all relieved.

I was amazed by Göran Kropp, who had bicycled and walked all the way from his hometown in Sweden to Nepal, and on to Everest Base Camp, without any external assistance. After hauling his supplies through the Icefall on a route that he found and fixed himself, he planned to climb the mountain—solo and unassisted—and then walk and bicycle back to Sweden. Unlike many other eccentrics, he was strong, experienced, and smart, though when I got to know him I suspected that his infectious sense of humor alone could spirit him a good ways up the mountain.

Kropp's dedication to making his attempt a true purist's effort far exceeded anyone's curiosity as to whether he might be cheating. He was adamant about not accepting even a cup of tea from outsiders, not even from his girlfriend, who traveled alongside him. At Base Camp he was still agonizing over some modest help he had accepted when his bicycle broke down on a remote road in the Middle East.

Göran reminded me of my father—they shared a relentless good cheer, a passion for strenuous work, and an appreciation for the value of hardship and honesty. They never lost faith.

For Miyolangsangma to guide me, I was beginning to sense that my faith would have to be similarly genuine and unwavering. It would have to come from deep within. As I stood below the daunting Lhotse Face, where a Sherpa had been killed while climbing near my father in 1952, the fearful and family-oriented side of me was mustering what faith it could. If my daughter were to be left fatherless and my wife without a husband, this all would be a horrible mistake. As it was, I had made the decision to be away from my family for an extended period to chase dreams—or chase down demons. This was what my father had done, leaving his family alone for months on end. His absence was what I had resented when I was a boy—a boy who wanted to join him and be with him, and to grow up to be like him.

THE LHOTSE FACE is a 4,000-foot-high, 50-degree wall of blue ice, parts of it as hard as polished rock. Establishing the fixed ropes up the Lhotse Face to Camp III, at 24,500 feet, was the joint responsibility of three teams, and we contributed some of our Sherpas to the effort.

To fix Camp III itself, we almost literally had to fight with other teams for space. After we roped off an area for our tents, the Yugoslav team's Sherpas removed them and began setting up their own tents. The Yugoslav sirdar was hostile and abrasive, and over the radio he threatened to cut our throats if we stepped into Camp III and tried to reclaim our site. David managed to contact the Yugoslav team leader on the radio, and they smoothed out the situation. The Yugoslavs ended up pitching their camp on a terrace below us.

To create a platform for our tents, we had to painstakingly carve terraces out of the steep slope. We needed only two tents because the Sherpas do not generally stay here but go directly from ABC to the South Col.

Once Camp III was in place, we worked on stocking Camp IV with food, oxygen, and other supplies. Camp IV is located on the South Col, the broad, nearly flat saddle between Lhotse and Everest. At 26,000 feet, higher than all but about twenty of the world's highest peaks, the South Col is in the "death zone"—the enigmatic altitude above which a climber's condition only deteriorates, and where he must limit his time. Six of our tents were pitched here, but until the night before the summit push, Camp IV is little more than a place to store oxygen and equipment. For more than a week the Sherpas left ABC in the early morning, climbed empty to Camp III, picked up fifty-pound loads, carried them to Camp IV, and then returned to ABC before evening. By early May we had all of our camps stocked.

To REST AND refuel before the summit attempt, the entire team descended from ABC and Camp III to Base Camp. Mentally, this was difficult to do when the summit was much closer to us than Base Camp.

Coming from the austerity of the Icefall, the sprawling tent city of Base Camp seemed luxurious compared to the stark, cold remoteness I registered when I first saw it three weeks earlier, arriving from the other direction.

At mealtimes the IMAX team relaxed, and we listened to Roger Bilham's impromptu evening geology lessons. Overall, however, tension was building. Climbing requires concentration and patience, and the crowding and changing weather conditions had increased the general stress level. Possibly as an outlet for the tension, in the late afternoon of one of the rest days Rob Hall's group held a boisterous party in their dining tent. (One American climber quipped to me that he prepared for the low oxygen levels of altitude by drinking himself into a state of hypoxia.) Hall had taken on two more clients than he had the year before, when none of his clients reached the summit. The stakes had been jacked up, it seemed. I could understand the need for a party to relieve tension, but it seemed strange to have one before their summit attempt.

Wongchu and I worked together on coordinating the movements of the loads, and he took on the task of cracking the whip over the Base Camp Sherpas. Soon after we arrived at Base

Camp, he lined up a group of young and rebellious support Sherpas and lectured them on getting their chores done on time and on cooperating with Changba, the cook. He emphasized that he didn't want to hear stories about extramarital sex at Base Camp, which would very possibly attract misfortune. And he forbade the roasting or frying of meat, the smell of which offends and defiles Miyolangsangma—resulting in high winds on the upper slopes, the Sherpas believe. Any activity that generates emotions such as anger, jealousy, lust, and pride should be avoided on the mountain, we say, because these will affect one's mindfulness when climbing.

Wongchu humored and cajoled the Sherpas as much as he threatened them, but he still kept a stick in the kitchen and would whack miscreant Sherpas hard on the butt when they acted up. "You came here to do work," he would say loudly. This reminded me of my father: single-minded and tough. There wasn't a Sherpa who wasn't afraid of Wongchu—and of Tenzing.

There are pitfalls of single-mindedness, too, as the Tengboche Lama had once cautioned me with a reflective chuckle. "Often, when you tell people not to do something, they want to do it that much more. Like our respected elder, Konjo Chhumbi from Khumjung, the former village leader. On special occasions the villagers gather in the monastery compound and run around, shouting and making a fuss over the festivities. He would stride back and forth holding his hands up importantly, but the more he told them to sit down and be quiet, the more commotion they made."

In America I had become used to seeing men and women kissing in public—Sherpas are extremely shy about public displays of affection—but it caught me off guard to see this happen at

Base Camp. Sexual abstinence, general modesty, and care with cooking meat were important elements of our team's professionalism and respect. Ultimately, most Sherpas are more afraid of the law of dharma than the law of man.

At Base Camp the Sherpas and team members ate separately, mainly because of our dissimilar diets. I developed my own routine. Each evening I wandered over to the dining tent to see what the climbers were eating, then I'd stroll across to the kitchen tent to see what the Sherpas had cooked for themselves. The Western food didn't sit well with me, so I usually ate with the Sherpas. And it was hard to beat *shyakpa*, Sherpa stew cooked in heavy yak meat broth, unless the team members were serving wine. Miyolangsangma wouldn't mind wine, if consumed in moderation.

Even our expensive high-energy bars, loaded with nutrients, didn't satisfy me, and I was glad to have brought my own version: tsampa mixed with sugar and nuts and raisins. I used a small leather sack to knead it into dough balls called *pak*. I even added tsampa to my morning tea—the Sherpa breakfast. Tsampa digests slowly and provides lasting fuel; some Sherpas even eat the dry flour, which is hard for the uninitiated to get down.

The evening when I returned to Base Camp, our historian, Audrey Salkeld, phoned Charles Warren, the oldest surviving Everest climber, to wish him a happy ninetieth birthday. My father made his first attempt on the mountain in 1935, when he joined Warren, Eric Shipton, and other Brits on the north side. They encountered the customary bad weather and retreated before reaching much of an altitude, but they did find the body of Maurice Wilson, the eccentric pilot who, a year earlier, had hoped to reach the summit, solo, through prayer and fasting.

The Tibetan authorities knew of Wilson from a previous secretive attempt, and he had signed a paper saying that he wouldn't attempt to enter Tibet again. To reach the mountain, he and his three Tibetan companions evaded the border patrols and checkposts by traveling at night and taking lengthy detours. When they reached their highest camp on the Rongbuk Glacier, directly below the North Col, the three Tibetans refused to go farther. Wilson was determined to forge on toward the North Col and the summit, alone, and he asked them to wait at Base Camp for him for three days. At least that's what the Tibetans told my father.

Wilson's skeleton was still covered in a veil of dry, frozen skin, and his frame was contorted, as if he had been trying to remove his boots. One boot was off, and the lace of the other boot rested in his bony hand. My father told me that he and Warren buried the remains of the "Mad Yorkshireman," as the press had called him, under the rocks of the glacial moraine.

Back in Darjeeling, the three Tibetans were displaying visible signs of wealth that could only have come from Wilson. My father wasn't so sure they had waited three days for him, and he scolded them for not having dragged him off the mountain before his suicidal death. Wilson must have returned to his tent in a depleted state, found no one there to take care of him, and then died from cold or exhaustion.

By 1935 Chomolungma had fully engaged my father's fascination and fear, and he began to wonder whether the mountain, or maybe just the route on the north side, was impossibly difficult— or even hexed. He was seven years old when the British made their first attempt in 1921. The following year, seven Sherpas were lost in a massive avalanche, a tragedy that sent a shudder through the Sherpa community. After the third British attempt, in 1924, it was a month or two before news of that expedition arrived in the village of Thame, along with the story that George Mallory and Sandy Irvine had last been seen heading into the clouds, just below the summit. My father was ten years old and had never seen a Westerner before, but the foreign-sounding names of Mallory and Irvine stuck firmly in his memory.

In defiance of the odds—or messages from the gods—the sah'bs and Sherpas kept returning to the mountain, or trying to, in increasing numbers. Except during World War II. There were no expeditions between 1938 and 1947, the year when another eccentric Brit, named Earl Denman, arrived in Darjeeling hoping to sneak into Tibet and solo the mountain. My father jumped at the opportunity, despite cautions from all who knew Denman that he had little chance of succeeding. As predicted, they didn't make it, but my father grew fond of Denman, as he did of all the other foreign eccentrics. He shared their spirit of adventure, certainly, but there was more to it than that. Like my father, these outsiders believed in possibilities. Their plans always overflowed with hope, and they remained committed to their dreams.

THE NIGHT AFTER our descent to Base Camp, some of our team's crampons and harnesses were stolen from the spot where climbers customarily left them, at the edge of the glacier. The veteran climbers especially were saddened that such a thing would happen within the mountaineering community. In a couple of instances in the past, some oxygen and equipment had been stolen at the South Col, resulting in the unfortunate practice of locking the tents at Camp IV. I recalled Nepal's fuel embargo of 1990, when I was trekking to Base Camp from the town of Jiri with fifty plastic jugs of kerosene. We had to carefully glue the tops shut to keep people from stealing it—including the porters but mainly the police, who would want to inspect it and then confiscate some for their own use.

The loss of important equipment, which was difficult to replace in this remote valley, could ruin an expedition. David called a meeting of the team leaders in the IMAX dining tent. Knowing that it would be difficult and nonproductive to stage a search or to cast blame, everyone at the meeting discussed the theft's meaning in the context of the normally selfless and considerate spirit of mountaineering.

The meeting also provided an opportunity for the leaders of the commercial groups to flex their agendas and reinforce their personal and team pecking orders. It was sometimes hard to distinguish between displays of national chauvinism and personal ego, but the team leaders who had been on Everest the most were conspicuously proprietary about what should be done on the mountain and at Base Camp.

I was a bit surprised to find that all the team leaders—David Breashears, Scott Fischer, Rob Hall, Todd Burleson, Henry Todd—knew each other. Even still, I sensed an undercurrent of competition between them, and between the groups. The guides who had bagged more peaks had a professional advantage, and Everest was their gridiron. Rivalry could be expected.

A buzz was circulating among the veteran climbing Sherpas at Base Camp. They had never seen so many ravens—we call them *gorak*, for their throaty call—or heard them calling so noisily. The gorak were making the Base Camp cooks and others stationed there anxious and uneasy. They are believed to be psychic, with the ability to see and understand on the level of humans. Also, they are regarded as messengers, and a whole study of raven and crow "auspicy" has developed in Tibet, which catalogs the meaning and auspiciousness of these birds' calls and behavior. Most Sherpas do not know how to decipher the goraks' calls, but when goraks gather at Base Camp, cawing away, we tend to suspect that something will go wrong on the mountain. They have been seen squawking about and cadging food as high as the South Col.

Not surprisingly, the first injury of the season occurred in the Icefall. Rob Hall had wanted to get his team to ABC first, to secure the tent sites he had used in previous years. He had sent five of his Sherpas up to claim these sites before the fixed ropes had been established, and before Hall himself had arrived at Base Camp. And before their puja had been performed.

Approaching a landmark called the Nuptse Corner in the Western Cwm, Ngawang Tenzing, one of Hall's Sherpas, broke through the surface of a smooth stretch of snow and fell— unroped—into a hidden crevasse. Miraculously, he landed on a narrow ledge of snow, surrounded by depth and darkness. If he had rolled off the ledge, he would have died. After being pulled out by his teammates, Ngawang was stranded at Camp I for two days with a suspected broken femur.

Hall asked if we could dedicate some of our Sherpas to Ngawang's evacuation. Wongchu said that using our Sherpas would be fine, but he wanted them to be reimbursed at the rate of about $6 per day.

Hall grumbled at this, though it wasn't much to ask considering the Sherpas sorely needed a rest day, and they regarded it as a non-emergency rescue—even though it was another Sherpa who was injured. David and some of the other team leaders don't like to simply order expedition Sherpas around, or to contradict their instincts. The difficulty Hall faced in gathering other teams' Sherpas for this task illustrated the mild rivalry that smoldered along not only between the various teams. The Sherpas are as loyal to their expeditions as the members are.

Eventually, thirty-five climbers and Sherpas, including six from our team, convened for the complicated evacuation. From Base Camp Ngawang was airlifted to Kathmandu.

Not long afterward, Ngawang Topgay, a Sherpa on Scott Fischer's team, was found in the Icefall in great distress. Fluid had gathered in his lungs, a symptom of severe pulmonary edema. His team members helped him to Base Camp and then to the Pheriche health post, at fourteen thousand feet, but he remained in critical condition. A lama was called up from Pangboche to do a long-life puja for him, and when the weather cleared three days later, he was helicoptered out.

In the latter half of April, a member of Mal Duff's party suffered what may have been a heart attack and was evacuated. Some days after that another climber on Duff's team fell and broke some ribs while descending from Camp II. Robert Schauer and Thillen, one of our team's high-altitude Sherpas, found him in the Icefall, walking slowly and with great difficulty as if he were lost. They helped him downward until he was met by some of his teammates near the bottom of the Icefall. He, too, was choppered out to Kathmandu.

The busy, somewhat stressful atmosphere at Base Camp wore on me. More time for rest here might have helped, but I preferred being on the mountain—carrying a load if nothing else. Before sunrise one morning I lit some incense and recited some prayers at the lhap-so, circled it three times, then shouldered a load and stepped into the Icefall, headed for ABC. Bursts of moonlight sparkled on the fresh snow crystals left by the localized snowfall of the afternoon before. I inhaled several deep drafts of the cold air, like a mountain bush pilot taking some hits of compressed oxygen before takeoff, and released myself again into the arms of Miyolangsangma.

Over the radio from Camp II, Wongchu, our team's sirdar, urges the Sherpas on the South Col to rouse themselves—however exhausted they are from reaching the summit the day before—and look for survivors stranded higher on the mountain.

5

THE WRATH
OF THE
GODDESS

5

THE WRATH
OF THE
GODDESS

After seven passages through the Icefall, I had begun to develop a close but uneasy relationship with it. My face was already sunburned and swollen, and when I again reached the Western Cwm, the sun struck me full force.

At ABC, David was cautiously optimistic. We were on schedule, and if the decent weather and our health remained stable and the IMAX camera continued to function smoothly, we might make it to the top and be able to film there. Araceli, Sumiyo, and I, the three members of our team who had never been above the South Col, remained apprehensive. We spoke little about the mountain.

The night before our climb to Camp III, Sumiyo cracked a second rib from violent coughing. She was still nursing the rib she had cracked three weeks earlier. Unfortunately, little can be done for cracked ribs and healing is slow at this altitude. She downplayed her handicap and maintained that it wouldn't affect her performance, but I could see that she was in genuine pain. David and I sensed that she was covering up. It was then that she mentioned to us that she hadn't notified her father that she was climbing Everest, out of fear that he would worry.

Ultimately, I feared that weakness of other teams on the mountain would affect us more than our own shortcomings. Normally, it takes no more than three hours to climb from Base

Camp to Camp I through the treacherous Icefall, but the guided clients and some of the Taiwanese and South Africans had been taking five or six hours—nearly double the usual time. Their slow progress not only raised questions about their fitness for climbing higher on the mountain but made us wonder whether they might cause potentially dangerous delays.

On May 7, we climbed from ABC to Camp III, still carrying loads. I shared a tent at III with Robert and Sumiyo; David, Ed, and Araceli were in the other. That afternoon the weather began acting strange—not bad exactly, but the high haze and wispy cirrus clouds were telling us that conditions might change for the worse.

From Camp III, we watched the upper part of the mountain. The "train" was still running; the wind continued to rip past the Southeast Ridge and siphon over the South Col, as if it were about to drop into the Western Cwm. Now that we were finally poised for the summit, perhaps the mountain was preparing to reject us. The jet stream was still sitting on the summit, and eight other teams were climbing only a day behind us.

Late that afternoon we peered steeply down into the Cwm and watched a near-endless procession of climbers heading up from Camp I toward ABC. Most of them were Scott Fischer's and Rob Hall's clients, plus the Taiwanese and South African teams, and several dozen Sherpas in support. All of them would be heading up to Camp III the next morning.

"We're being squeezed; that's how I feel," David said, his gaze shifting from the climbers below to the high clouds above. Ed and David sensed that the real window of good weather this particular year would come later in the month. Putting all the factors together, it seemed prudent to let the others "climb through," so we decided to retreat to ABC and wait.

As we descended, we passed the leaders of the commercial guided teams, spiritedly goading their clients up the Lhotse Face. Their eyes met ours with uneasy curiosity. David was taken aback when one of the guides who passed him said that he expected to get every one of the clients to the summit. David didn't say anything, but later he mentioned to us what he was thinking: *Well, sure, they're moving along now, and if the weather and their strength and several other conditions continue to work in their favor, yes, they might make it.*

I shook hands with some of the ascending climbers and wished them luck. Robert passed Rob Hall, who expressed concern about falling ice or rocks that our team might dislodge onto his group, though we were being extremely careful. Robert felt that Hall might benefit by focusing his concern on his clients.

Shortly afterward a rock that must have been dislodged by someone above us whizzed by within a foot or two of Robert's head.

Something didn't feel right. Although these climbers might have adversely affected our own summit attempt—and our safety—I was more concerned about them, about how they would do, and about what might go wrong within their parties. I hadn't yet been high on Everest, but I was well aware that hypoxia and exhaustion in the death zone, above 26,000 feet, would be a dangerous mix for novice Himalayan climbers. Even the route from ABC to Camp IV was risky, though much of it was along fixed ropes. Each time we passed someone, we had to unclip our safety lines from the fixed rope and reclip them to the rope beyond them, then do the same with the ascenders, so that we always had one line clipped onto the fixed rope. And might the clients step on the rope and cut it with their crampons? If a climber fell, he would pull another along with him, then another, until the anchors popped out like a burst seam.

On the Lhotse Face especially, many of the climbers used the fixed ropes to haul themselves up, leaning back heavily on their ascenders each time they slid them up the rope—using the rope not as a safety device but as a climbing aid. I never had great confidence in the anchors and avoided placing my weight on them even when there were few others climbing on the route.

At the rate these climbers were moving, it was easy to envision crowding and bottlenecks on summit day that could dangerously delay the faster climbers. And if one or two climbers collapsed or sustained an injury, those around would be obligated to help them, severely stressing their own reserves of energy.

We would never hesitate to help a marooned climber, but we knew that doing so could jeopardize our entire expedition. By David's calculation, in order to get the IMAX camera to the summit and film there we would have to place a minimum of ten team members and Sherpas on the summit: David and Robert filming; Ed, Araceli, and me on camera; two Sherpas to carry the camera; one to carry the monopod, camera head, and film magazines; and two to carry oxygen bottles. Every one of these people would be essential for the climb, and for the film.

When I arrived at the *bergschrund*, a cliff of vertical ice at the bottom of the Lhotse Face, Yasuko Namba of Japan was in the midst of climbing it. She asked me for assistance, and I extended my hand and helped her up and over the lip. She would have made it on her own, but with difficulty. It made me wonder that a climber with moderate experience had made it this far.

During our descent I felt angry and envious, as if we were abandoning our fellow mountaineers and friends. Were we throwing away a good shot at the peak? The decision seemed right in my head, but my guts were telling me to turn around and continue upward. Why was I descending in good weather? This might be our only chance, and even if a clear climbing window were to open again, it is misery to rebuild the energy to climb to a point that we had reached and then retreated from. We were already tired. Would we have the strength and motivation to try again? And May 9 was the auspicious anniversary of my father's death.

Perhaps crowding would not be a problem. In 1993, twenty-nine climbers reached the summit on the same day. But 1993 also saw deaths on the mountain, including the loss of my cousin Lobsang Tsering. I thought of my father's six retreats before his successful seventh attempt, and understood the message he had been trying to teach me as I grew up, seeing my eagerness to get out and climb: *patience*. All boons and benefits will come to those who are accepting and diligent. The mountain isn't going anywhere; there will always be another chance to climb. On Everest, impatience can be fatal.

In the mid-1980s no one reached the summit for three consecutive seasons, yet few of this year's guides were on Everest in those seasons. Over the long term even the best climbers don't beat fifty-fifty odds in their attempts on the mountain. The veteran climber Pete Athans reached the top only on his fifth try. Until 1996, "Steady" Ed Viesturs, arguably America's strongest climber, had made the summit on only three out of seven attempts.

The guided clients, on the other hand, might look at the odds differently, especially those who have been turned back from the summit once or twice before and would again face investing significant time, effort, and funds to make another try. It may be Everest's intimidating size that causes some climbers to lose a sense of priorities. In the midst of their climb, far from their home countries and familiar surroundings, the mountain becomes an all-consuming passion. It seduces some climbers into a sense of importance, of having a mission, and this perspective leads to the suspension of cautious thought and behavior. If a last-chance desperation kicks in, too, these climbers may push their luck and take risks—without the experience needed to carefully gauge those risks.

The Sherpas grudgingly admitted that we might have done the right thing by descending, though they would forfeit their high-altitude bonus if we didn't try again. I wasn't sure they would want to wait very long for another chance.

That night at ABC, a premonitory dream, a message dream, gripped me by the stomach: an accident would occur on the Lhotse Face. I sensed that the dream was delivered to me by my father. In the morning I rationalized that it may have been no more than auto-suggestion generated by the image of the commercial groups heading up the Lhotse Face like a line of ants up a tree. Or it might have been my father's disturbing stories of climbing the Lhotse Face four decades earlier.

IN 1952, no one was confident that the mountain could be climbed in the fall. The Swiss didn't have the leisure to wait, however, because the British had been granted the lone permit for the spring of 1953.

Until the fall of 1952 climbers took a relatively direct route from ABC to the South Col, passing beneath the Geneva Spur. That line is exposed to avalanches and rockfall, they learned, especially a thirty-foot section that acts as an avalanche chute. An accident occurred there when my father was at ABC, and in horror he watched it unfold through a telescope. About ten Sherpas had joined a Dr. Chevalley and a Mr. Spöhel, and they were roped together below ABC in four teams, three men on each rope. After going only a short distance above ABC, they heard a rumbling sound above them, but it was insufficient warning for them to avoid the sheets and blocks of ice that came pouring down. The climbers flattened themselves, finding what haven they could behind protrusions on the slope. Several of them were struck by small pieces of ice, but none were seriously hurt—except for Mingma Dorje, who was on a rope with my cousin Topgay. He may have been looking up at the time, because he was hit squarely in the face by falling ice. He went limp on the rope, and Topgay and another Sherpa hurried to help him.

As they were escorting Mingma Dorje toward ABC, a second incident occurred. Three Sherpas, perhaps spooked by the first accident, were climbing closely together when one of them missed his footing and slipped. He pulled the other two off balance, sending all of them tumbling down the slope. They came to rest where the slope leveled out a few hundred yards below. The three were injured, one with a broken collarbone, and they returned to Base Camp, leaving the expedition deprived of three of its strongest Sherpas.

Mingma Dorje, it turned out, was in serious condition. In addition to the injuries to his face, Dr. Chevalley found that either a shard of ice or a broken rib had pierced his lung. Chevalley and others struggled to keep him alive on oxygen throughout the night, but he died before morning.

Understandably, the Sherpas were upset and frightened. Mingma Dorje was the first person to die on Everest in nearly eighteen years, and the first casualty on the south side of the mountain. The Swiss, who were always accommodating of the Sherpas and their needs, conferred with my father. They said that if most of the Sherpas wished to abandon the attempt at that point, they would agree to retreat. The spring season of 1952 on Everest with the Swiss hadn't been much easier, and my father had had great difficulty finding thirty-five Sherpas willing to sign up for the mountain that fall season. After some reflection and discussion, however, the Sherpas agreed to carry on.

Following those accidents, the Swiss and the Sherpas spent many days forging the safer route that is used today, leading far to the right, up the Lhotse Face, then across the middle of the Geneva Spur and down one hundred feet to the South Col.

MY DREAM, THE lamas' divinations, and the prophecy about the suffering of people in the mountain's vicinity would be proven accurate sooner than I expected. On the morning of May 9, I was sitting at the entry to the ABC kitchen tent, sipping tea and listening to conversations on the walkie-talkie. I watched a Sherpa putter around camp, moving stones and checking on tent guy lines. The Sherpa was sixty-year-old Au Passang, who had been on an incredible thirty-five Everest expeditions. Over the years Au Passang had made countless trips to the South Col but he never cared to go on to the summit. He was always praying, chanting a mantra, and either working or looking for something to make himself busy with. His gentle wrinkled features expressed compassion and understanding, and I somehow felt safe whenever he was in the vicinity, as I did in Grandfather Gaga's presence.

That morning Jangbu Sherpa had climbed from ABC toward the South Col, carrying a large load. As he approached Camp III, he was taken by surprise by a small but frightening avalanche cascading toward him from the Lhotse Face. He dove into a recessed area in the snow as lethal chunks of ice shot past him like fragments from an exploding car. He remained there for ten minutes, breathing heavily, shaken up.

He continued climbing—quickly, in case more snow and ice should slide. As he approached Camp III, he watched in shock as someone standing near the Camp III tents slipped, then slid downhill some twenty-five feet below camp and into a crevasse. He hurried toward camp as fast as he could, but when he got there he found no one about. He began looking into tents, asking those awake whether they knew who might have fallen into the crevasse. Remarkably, no one seemed to know, and no one was missing a teammate. Jangbu grabbed a rope and carefully down-climbed to the edge of the fissure.

On a ledge about fifteen feet below the rim, the Taiwanese climber Chen Yu-Nan, a thirty-six-year-old steelworker from Taipei, was groggily rousing himself. Jangbu descended and tied a rope to him, then with great effort pulled him out. Apparently, Chen had stepped out of his tent to relieve himself while wearing only his smooth-soled inner boots, not crampons.

Jangbu helped Chen back to camp, where most climbers were still asleep, and returned him to his tent. Then he radioed down to ABC to tell us what had happened. Slowly, Chen seemed to improve, however slightly, and we all assumed he would recover. Chen urged the Taiwanese team leader, Makalu Gau, to carry on without him.

Gau left for Camp IV alongside Hall's and Fischer's teams, and Jangbu picked up his own load and also climbed toward the

South Col. Along the way Jangbu passed Scott Fischer, Sandy Pittman, and his friend Lobsang Jangbu, Fischer's sirdar. After the morning's experience with the avalanche and with Chen Yu-Nan, Jangbu felt compelled to urge them all to be careful. He dropped his load at Camp IV on the South Col and returned to Camp III.

At III, Jangbu was surprised to find that Chen's condition had deteriorated; he seemed to be in pain, probably from internal injuries. Passang Tamang, a high-altitude "Sherpa" on the Taiwanese team, did not feel confident in helping him down the mountain alone.

Chen could walk haltingly. Jangbu gathered some coils of rope, and he and Passang began to assist him down the Lhotse Face. Evening was fast approaching, and neither of them was sure they could reach ABC before dark.

At 3:00 P.M. Jangbu radioed us at ABC to say that Chen's condition had deteriorated even further. Less than twenty minutes later, two-thirds of the way down the Lhotse Face, Chen collapsed. Several minutes later, while holding Jangbu's hand, he died.

To us at ABC, it seemed very sudden, and we wanted Jangbu to be sure that Chen wasn't simply unconscious. On the radio, we asked him to hold his glacier goggles to Chen's nose and mouth, to see whether any breath condensed on them. Nothing. Passang and Jangbu left Chen's body, still attached to the fixed rope, and descended to ABC.

Monks remind lay Sherpas that seeing a corpse can be propitious, especially in dreams or when traveling. Still, Sherpas are often reluctant to touch a dead body, especially if their astrological sign, based on the twelve-year cycle of animal symbols, has been identified by a lama as vulnerable to spiritual pollution from death. Touching a corpse in these cases can bring them misfortune, and as long as Chen was attached to the fixed rope, the Sherpas did not want to use it.

The light was fading and the weather had turned bad, but someone would have to evacuate his body. Wongchu, Lhakpa, David, Robert, and Ed packed quickly and departed. When they reached the Taiwanese climber, they could barely see through the blowing snow. Chen was clearly dead, and he had died with none of his countrymen present.

David closed Chen's eyes and covered his face. Then he and Ed slowly lowered him over the bergschrund, where two Taiwanese team Sherpas had arrived from ABC with a sleeping bag. They packed him in the bag, dragged him down to ABC, and left him in a cleft of snow not far from camp. Chen's teammates could carry his body to Base Camp.

By continuing upward to the South Col, Makalu Gau had left Chen in our hands, and we had to sacrifice our energy and resources to fill in for Chen's missing teammates. His death, clearly the result of lack of experience, was avoidable. It occurred on the tenth anniversary of my father's death. And, one year earlier to the day, a Sherpa had fallen on the Lhotse Face during a brief moment when his rope was unclipped, and died.

Chen Yu-Nan's death scared me to the point of sickness. At ABC, I fashioned a small lhap-so and burned incense and prayed. After having nearly forgotten my rudimentary Buddhist teachings and meager faith while in the United States, my supplications suddenly felt urgent and sincere. I imagined the fragrance of the incense perfusing the universe, purifying sickness and obscurations. I made offerings and chanted the Guru Rimpoche mantra, *Om Ah Hum Vajra Guru Padme Siddhi Hum*, and the

Avalokitesvara mantra, *Om Mane Padme Hum.* Those at Base Camp did the same at the lhap-so. The more I thought about it, the more it seemed to me that May 9 had not been a good date to make a summit attempt, though I originally envisioned that my father's spirit would be out then, protecting us all.

Chen Yu-Nan was eventually taken by helicopter to Kathmandu, where he was cremated near the hilltop stupa of Swayambhunath. I heard that his parents were able to attend the ceremony.

I could picture my own body being carried out to Everest's dedicated cremation site, a half-day's walk below Base Camp. If a Sherpa is killed on Everest or on nearby peaks and the body is recovered, it is transported to a level area at sixteen thousand feet called Chukpö Laré ("Rich Man's Yak Corral"). Here, about thirty small *chö-lung* shrines, in some cases no more than large stone cairns, have been built by the Sherpas. The larger of the chö-lung are carefully made by lamas, according to sacred dimensions.

After the cremation, the deceased's ashes are molded into clay votive tablets called *tsa-tsa,* which are placed inside the chö-lung, along with sacred objects such as mandalas, purified offerings, chiseled stone prayer tablets, religious texts, and incense. A piece of juniper wood carved with Buddhist inscriptions, representing the Life Force Tree, is also placed inside, and this must be oriented in the precise alignment it had as part of the standing tree. All of these items are arranged in discrete layers and in prescribed numbers.

The chö-lung represent aspirations for nirvana, for a permanent state of peace, and the prayers we recite there are offered for all sentient beings, not just the deceased. The chö-lung are not monuments as much as ritual vehicles, because humans lose their individuality after death. For this reason, the lamas discourage keeping souvenirs or remembrances of the dead, and names are generally not carved on the chö-lung. Such remembrances would invoke the deceased's personal identity, causing him to believe he is still alive in human form and thereby hindering his transit into the next life.

Those cremated at Chukpö Laré all died untimely, accidental deaths. Reincarnation becomes complicated when one's normal life span has been abruptly foreshortened. Dead bodies do not immediately become empty vessels, and Sherpas believe that a vestige of the living person lingers within and around the corpse for some time. If a body is left on the mountain without proper death rituals, its consciousness can wander and possibly cause harm.

Especially in accidental deaths, lamas and monks are needed to properly dispatch the deceased into the next life. When the lama arrives, he asks for the time of death, then reads from the Tibetan Book of the Dead. The deceased's last thought is critical, and lamas say they can sometimes determine what the person was thinking at the instant of death, then interpret how it will affect his reincarnation.

At the cremation, the lamas do preparatory chanting and rituals, treating the fleshly body as a sacred offering to the deities. It is then ritually purified and given by fire. In a similar ceremony on the north side of Everest, dead Tibetans are flayed and left for consumption by vultures in what is known as "sky burial." Not only are the vultures nourished, but insects are spared the lethal smoke of the crematory fire, Tibetans say.

If the deceased Sherpa was wealthy, relatives in his home village light 100,000 butter lamps in their private chapels and local monastery in an appeal for a favorable rebirth. Monks are called to chant and to read from texts, and the consciousness is prepared for travel through the intermediate, after-death state of *bardo*, a journey said to last forty-nine days. On the forty-ninth day after death, the person is reincarnated.

If the body wasn't recovered, an effigy of the deceased climber is made, and relatives take it to a nearby ridge, generally, where it is buried along with the dead person's clothes. In cases in which the Sherpa was poor, a lesser ritual is done, and the lamas can ritually cleanse the clothes so that other people can wear them.

Chukpö Laré was identified and sanctified by the Tengboche Lama in 1970, after six Sherpas were killed by an avalanche during the monumental Japanese "Man Who Skied Down Everest" expedition. The movie made of this bizarre stunt conveyed the impression that the Sherpas had sacrificed their lives for the glory of Japan. And the skier, Miura, appeared to have fallen and slid down the mountain much farther than he successfully skied it.

I should feel lucky, some say, that ten relatives of mine have reached the summit of Everest and only one of them has died on the mountain. Most veteran expedition Sherpas have relatives who were cremated at Chukpö Laré, and it is where they brought my cousin Lobsang Tsering. While descending from the summit in 1993, Lobsang fell to his death below the Balcony, at about 27,000 feet. No one was able to tell me exactly what happened, but it is thought that he became delirious when he ran out of oxygen.

Lobsang Tsering's father, my uncle, died not long afterward of what people described as heartbreak. After that, Lobsang's mother, Ani Chö-e, became "lost"—despondent, hearing voices, sleeping poorly. The thought of my wife, Soyang, in such a state haunted me. Ani Chö-e was my father's elder sister and my only remaining aunt, until she too passed away in the fall of 2000. She had been ready to go for some time.

For climbing Sherpas, Chukpö Laré is an arresting reminder of our mortality, and of the insignificance of man in the shadow of a giant mountain. We always stop there to recite a prayer. Standing before my crude lhap-so at ABC, I placed Chatral, Trulshig, Geshé, and Tengboche Rimpoches in the front of my mind and, with as much inner peace as I could muster, said a prayer for Chen Yu-nan.

The Sherpas agreed that Chen's death was a harbinger of other bad news. Jangbu felt that this death was telling us to leave the mountain, and that it might even precipitate more deaths. This didn't sound logical, but something about it felt plausible. In Kathmandu, Soyang had heard the news and was distressed; I was at Camp II when she called Base Camp, so I did not speak to her directly. I would have liked to reassure her, but I knew my words would have fallen on deaf, worried ears.

OTHER ACCIDENTS THAT my father and the Sherpas of his generation had witnessed tumbled through my head. My father had viewed one bad fall at close range while climbing a small peak near Kangchenjunga with a lone sah'b, a Swiss climber named George Frey. Frey and a Sherpa named Ang Dawa were climbing ahead of him, in good conditions over steep but fairly easy terrain, at the low elevation of seventeen thousand feet. Frey, who was unroped but an excellent climber, slipped and began falling. It looked as though he might fall on my father, but he passed by to one side, far too fast for my father to stop him. Frey came to rest about one thousand feet below them.

My father said that the experience was similar to what others have described—a few moments of shock and numbness, with little thought beyond the inevitability that he would be falling in a moment, too. Once he realized he was safe, he stood in disbelief. He said he expected to look up and see Frey still standing there above him on the mountain. But Frey was gone. My father decided to name the unnamed peak after him, and he built a memorial for him at its base.

That was only one man, one death. Before the early 1950s, when it was first climbed, India's Nanga Parbat, the "Naked Mountain," had earned a reputation as the world's most brutal and dangerous peak. The Sherpas knew it and feared it, and my father avoided it—until 1950.

On the German expedition of 1934, my father's friends Ang Tsering and Dawa Thondup were lower on the mountain, and they survived to tell him what happened. One member died of altitude sickness, and then four members and five Sherpas died in a blizzard that lasted more than a week. Gyali, another of my father's friends, was high on the peak with the expedition leader, Willy Merkl, when the storm set in. Merkl was in bad shape, and as Gyali struggled to help him descend, Merkl grew weaker and more listless, until he couldn't go on. Gyali probably could have descended to safety on his own, but he decided to stay with Merkl.

Their frozen, preserved bodies were found in 1938, and it appeared that Gyali had lived longer than Merkl but decided to remain with him. When my father spoke of his pride at being a Sherpa, he used to recount this story.

Again on Nanga Parbat, in the late spring of 1937, seven sah'bs and nine Sherpas of a German expedition were buried by an avalanche, at 21,450 feet. As in 1934, Dawa Thondup was one of the few Sherpas to survive. The team had barely pitched Camp IV, and while they slept, an avalanche came off the East Ridge and entombed them, leaving not a single person in the camp alive. A party was sent to bury them that summer, and their bodies were found lying peacefully in their tents, as if still sleeping.

The Germans returned to the mountain the following year, and the year after that, but could get no Sherpas to join them. By 1950 climbers and Sherpas may have felt that enough time had passed, and late that fall my father signed up for Nanga Parbat with a small British expedition led by Captains J. W. Thornley and W. H. Crace. As if sensing that a pall of death from the earlier expeditions threatened to claim them, as well, the sah'bs didn't actually say they were climbing the mountain—a truly Asian way of diverting the attention of wrathful demons. The Brits said that they had come only to do research on snow and cold. But each day they climbed higher and higher.

When the local porters refused to go farther, the four Sherpas and three sah'bs strapped on tumplines and carried equally heavy loads up the mountain. The weather deteriorated and became excruciatingly cold, and the Sherpas reached a point where they, too, refused to go higher. My father, caught between the Sherpas, his professionalism, and his faithfulness to his employers, decided that his friends were right, that it was too dangerous to climb higher.

Undaunted, the sah'bs continued on by themselves, while the Sherpas waited at Base Camp. Within two days the third British member, Richard Marsh, returned to camp with frostbitten feet. Together they waited, following the progress of the other two Brits through a telescope. One bitterly cold late November evening, they saw that Thornley and Crace—fortified with strength and enthusiasm but little experience—had pitched a tent high on the mountain in deplorable, frigid conditions. In the morning, however, their tent was gone.

My father, the Sherpas, and Marsh decided to head up the mountain to attempt a rescue, but at their first camp the temperature dropped to well below zero. Marsh's feet were doing poorly, and the Sherpas were also courting frostbite, so they descended to Base Camp. They climbed once more to high altitudes to search for them, in even worse weather, before they finally gave up.

By the end of that season, a total of thirty-one people had died on Nanga Parbat, and the mountain had yet to be climbed. A stone monument stands at the base of the mountain, inscribed with the names of the twenty-nine Germans and Sherpas who died in 1934 and 1937. My father felt that a pall of death indeed hung over the mountain, and it chilled him deeply.

THE HIMALAYA HAVE taken a toll, especially on Sherpas, and Everest has taken the most. During the first seventy years of Everest climbing, fifty-three Nepalese and Indian Sherpas were killed—more than one-third of the climbing deaths in that period. In addition to the six Sherpas lost on the Japanese skier's expedition, the two worst accidents on Everest occurred in 1922, when seven Sherpas were buried under an avalanche on the North Col, and in the fall of 1974 when one Frenchman and five Sherpas were killed in an avalanche.

When Sherpas are killed climbing, little notice is taken by people outside our community. I can't help but think of their families and am greatly saddened. For many Sherpas, climbing is like mercenary military service. Had these fathers, sons, brothers, and cousins lived, entire family lineages and community histories would have developed very differently.

Compared to foreign climbers, Sherpas may have given their lives disproportionately to this mountain. Nearly half of all Himalayan climbers killed have been Sherpas. One reason is that the Sherpas face greater risks: the foreign teams pay them to make numerous trips ferrying supplies through treacherous stretches such as the Khumbu Icefall, exposing them to danger for longer periods than the team members are. When behind schedule, some expeditions will pay a premium to the Sherpas for carrying loads in the afternoon through areas that are prone to melting and collapse at that time.

In the early 1950s the loss of a Sherpa was compensated with a payment of $20 to $50, with the higher amount going to a married Sherpa with children. The insurance for loss of a hand was $15, with proportionately smaller amounts for lost digits. Now, the trekking agency that the climbing sirdar is attached to must carry a $3,500 life insurance policy for every Sherpa on his team who sets foot on Everest. This is still a paltry amount, though poorer Sherpas, especially, continue to seek the work. One of them told me that climbing beats service in the Nepalese or Indian Army, in terms of both pay and compensation for loss of life.

WHILE STUDYING IN the United States, I tended to think that the Sherpas' attention to the mystical and religious aspects of the mountain was little more than superstition and imaginings. But once I arrived in the lap of the mountain, surrounded by Sherpas who believed, and confronted by a rich history of death—and death itself—I could no longer remain cynical.

Early in the morning of May 10, nearly thirty climbers struck out from the South Col for the summit. At ABC, as soon as it became light enough to see, Robert hauled out the telescope and we scanned the Southeast Ridge far above us; from ABC it is possible to see climbers as they traverse the knife-edge ridge between the South Summit and the Hillary Step. In the early afternoon we finally spotted them—little more than minuscule dots. We knew the colors of some of the climbers' jackets and tried to identify them.

At this late hour, surely they would have reached the top and would now be descending. Unbelievably, they were still heading up! At this slow rate, if they were still going for the summit, they would be coming down in the dark and would encounter the rough weather and high winds that had been raking over the mountain nearly every afternoon since we had arrived at Base Camp.

The Sherpas at ABC were convinced that those still plodding for the summit were headed for trouble. "These mikaru—white eyes—which ones will return, and which ones will remain on the mountain forever?" one of them voiced as we sat in the kitchen tent, drinking tea. All of us sensed that they were stressing their lungta. They were pushing their luck.

The guides of the commercial groups, aware that some of their clients might be slow, had set a strict rule about turnaround time: on summit day, any clients who had not reached the summit by 12:00 noon, or 1:00 P.M. at the latest, would have to turn back for the South Col. To have to collect clients in the dark above the South Col would be a guide's worst nightmare.

It wasn't until after 3:00 P.M. that we heard on the radio that most of Scott Fischer's team had reached the summit, although

Fischer himself still lagged behind. Over the walkie-talkie, Fischer told his climbing sirdar, Lobsang Jangbu, to inform Rob Hall that three of Hall's clients had abandoned their attempt short of the summit, below the Hillary Step, and were returning to the South Col. Why hadn't the others turned around, as well?

Fischer's guides, Anatoli Boukreev and Neal Beidleman, reached the summit about 1:00 P.M. Rob Hall's guide, Andy Harris, also reached the top, along with his clients Yasuko Namba and Jon Krakauer, who was on assignment for *Outside* magazine, and Sherpas Ngawang Dorje, Kami Rita, Lhakpa Tshering, Gombu, and Dorje.

Rob Hall and his client Doug Hansen arrived later, followed by the Taiwanese leader Makalu Gau. Climbing not far behind Gau, Fischer passed his team members on their descent from the top. He chose to slowly continue upward rather than help guide his group down. Sometime after 3:30 P.M., Makalu Gau and then Fischer and his sirdar Lobsang Jangbu arrived at the summit. On the radio, Fischer told those at Base Camp that he was very tired.

Rob Hall arrived on the summit shortly after Fischer and Lobsang, and they overlapped there for some minutes. Then Fischer and Lobsang descended, but Hall decided to wait on top for Doug Hansen, though he was certainly aware that daylight was running out. Hansen arrived on the summit at 4:00 P.M., three hours after the later of the "turnaround" times that Hall had specified.

Altogether, twenty-three people had reached the summit of Mount Everest from the Nepal side that day, May 10, 1996.

DAVID, ED, ROBERT, and I looked down the Western Cwm in the direction of Base Camp. A thick bank of clouds was gaining mass and momentum and was moving uphill toward us. This gray-black mass appeared more ominous than the locally generated clouds that filled the valley each afternoon, and by around 4:30 P.M. Base Camp was blanketed in fog. An hour later the cloudbank rolled over ABC. When I spoke later with Changba, the cook, and the other Sherpas at Base Camp, they said they felt that the weather was unusually sinister. An eerie quietness befell Base Camp.

Meanwhile, a higher level of clouds enveloped the mountain above us.

Then, just before dark, we heard a startling radio call.

"Doug Hansen has collapsed—I need oxygen!"

Sitting in the dining tent at ABC, we were informed of a shocking radio interchange between Rob Hall and Andy Harris. Hall and his client Doug Hansen had reached the summit in the late afternoon, and both were now stranded at 28,200 feet, above the windswept South Summit. Darkness was fast approaching.

They would have to move, or they would most certainly lose their lives. As far as we could tell, Hall had decided to stay with Hansen, though Hansen's condition and location were unknown. Hall certainly knew that he couldn't get Hansen down on his own, and once their oxygen ran out—and once they had used up the oxygen in whatever bottles were left at the South Summit— they would undoubtedly become hypoxic, a condition that would lead to the freezing of their extremities. For Hall to struggle down alone through pitch darkness in a furious, chilling wind would be impossible. And could he really abandon Hansen there, to die alone? Those who spoke with Hall on the radio pleaded with him to come down, stressing that a rescue party could be sent for Hansen.

At Base Camp, it had begun to snow. Other than queries about where the climbers were, there were few radio calls. Then at eight o'clock that evening, Paula Viesturs called us with distressing news: seventeen of the climbers descending the Southeast Ridge had not returned to the South Col. Frustratingly, the radios on the mountain were not operating properly, and we could only assume that these climbers were either battling their way through severe storm conditions or were hunkered in at a place they'd rather not be. Or worse.

The Base Camp support staff stayed up all night, scanning the radio frequencies for news. During their frantic pleas into the radio, we could hear sporadic crying in the background. And praying. They made a list of names, slowly checking them off as climbers were reported safe. They didn't get very far down the list.

I WAS DISMAYED by the situation, but not entirely surprised. The divinations had been right. Both Chatral Rimpoche and Geshé Rimpoche, the Buddhist lamas for my family and my wife's, Soyang's, family, had identified the season as problematic, plagued with obstacles.

Wongchu told me that when he was on Everest the year before, he had a dream of a beautiful goddess who, smiling and laughing, approached him and caressed him. The dream had recurred this year, and the goddess again smiled seductively as she advanced toward him. But this time she turned wrathful and angry. Wongchu said that he hadn't mentioned the dream to the other expedition Sherpas.

Jangbu had a similar, startlingly realistic dream at ABC. A beautiful young woman appearing much like Miyolangsangma approached him, and she was complaining, saying that people had been stepping on her head, defiling her and degrading her. In the dream, Jangbu felt afraid at first and then felt bad for this woman. He prostrated to her and asked for forgiveness for anything he might have done to offend her, for any contribution he may have made to her defilement. She smiled and thanked him, then walked off up the mountain.

Jangbu awoke, unsure whether what he saw was a dream or reality. Unable to sleep for the rest of the night, he sat up in his sleeping bag, lit some incense, and prayed.

"Ten Times" Ang Rita, who was climbing with the lone Swede Göran Kropp, told Wongchu that he had been experiencing remarkably similar dreams, and in each case the girl wandered off up the mountain, as she had for Wongchu and Jangbu. They agreed that if the girl had headed down instead, it would have been an extremely bad omen. At the least, Miyolangsangma's appearance in their dreams indicated to them that she was unhappy with the pollution and disrespect surrounding her.

It didn't take a belief in dreams or divinations, however, to see that the ingredients for disaster were all present: crowding, inexperience, excessive desire, and sheer numbers, all stirred into a change in the weather.

I retired to my tent at 11:00 P.M., knowing there was nothing we could do but wait. I lay on my back and wondered, fruitlessly, how we had all gotten into this situation. Why had these people come halfway around the world to voluntarily place themselves in harm's way? Returning to Everest after eighteen years, Robert especially was bewildered by the shift in attitude toward Everest. The motivation behind mountaineering seemed to have taken a turn away from awe and respect for the mountain and drifted in the direction of ego gratification, business, and trophy hunting.

Only one day before, Araceli, Sumiyo, the other Sherpas, and I had shared some regret that we had decided to retreat. Now we felt confident that we had made the right decision. On the other hand, if we had been climbing with these teams, we might have been better positioned to provide help.

ANATOLI BOUKREEV, the Russian climber who was guiding for Scott Fischer, had descended from the summit quickly and arrived at his tent on the South Col at about the same time as some of the clients who had turned back before the top. Upon arrival at Camp IV from the summit, climbers naturally feel an urge to simply crawl into their tents and pass out in a haze of exhaustion and hypoxia, hoping the climbers behind them make it back all right. It's as if humans can carefully gauge and ration their physical energy, leaving only enough to reach their destination. It is not unknown for climbers to collapse within yards of the South Col tents, and I doubt that many have felt they could have walked much farther.

The later returning climbers were not so fortunate. Not far above the Col, fierce winds and blowing snow had slowed the descent of those who reached the top late in the day. At the bottom of the fixed ropes above the "ice bulge," a tricky patch of rock-hard ice just above the Col, one group of eleven climbers veered slightly to the east in an attempt to avoid an encounter with the treacherous Lhotse Face in the dark. That morning they had climbed over the ice bulge in darkness, and now it was debilitatingly dark again.

To follow the Southeast Ridge and the slopes below it is fairly straightforward, but when climbers issue out onto the broad and flat South Col, it is easy to become disoriented in whiteout and darkness. People don't normally think of carrying a compass or a GPS device on Everest, but those conditions on the Col might have been one time and place that such an instrument would have come in handy.

Visibility had dropped to only a few feet, and as the light faded they removed their dark-lensed ski goggles, forcing them to squint into wind-driven snow particles coming at them at fifty miles an hour. Some of the clients were having trouble walking and at times sat down. Beck Weathers, a fifty-year-old Dallas pathologist who had been unable to see all day long, was tethered to Hall's guide Mike Groom, who was pulling him along as best he could.

Unable to tell where to go next, the group formed a huddle in an attempt to keep warm. Their hunger, hypoxia, exhaustion, and dehydration would have reduced the circulation in their feet and hands and affected their ability to think. Some of them were certain they would die there.

At about 2:00 A.M., the clouds overhead parted, and Klev Schoening—Pete's nephew and a strong climber—was able to get his bearings from the stars and surrounding ridges. He recognized the mass of Everest above them and also identified Polaris and the Big Dipper. He and the guides Neal Beidleman and Mike Groom and Sherpas Ngawang Dorje and Tashi Tsering goaded and pulled at the others. They got the huddle moving haltingly in the direction in which Schoening was positive they needed to head.

Clients Yasuko Namba, Beck Weathers, Sandy Pittman, and Charlotte Fox were barely able to walk. Those who were able to stumble forward gradually broke away from them. Tim Madsen could have joined the first group but selflessly decided to remain with Charlotte Fox, who was in poor condition. Having barely progressed, they formed a second, smaller, huddle.

The first group found its way to Camp IV. Beidleman attempted to describe to Anatoli Boukreev where the others were bunched, somewhere near the Kangshung Face on the South Col's far eastern side, but he was too exhausted to speak clearly.

With a bottle of oxygen, Boukreev set out to find the stranded climbers, despite his own exhaustion from climbing to the summit without oxygen. Unable to find them, he retraced his steps to get better instructions from Beidleman and then Lene Gammelgaard, who was more coherent. On the next trip out he found the climbers just beyond the point he had reached earlier. Boukreev left some oxygen and escorted Sandy Pittman back to Camp IV; then he returned with some tea and more oxygen. He helped Charlotte Fox and Tim Madsen back, leaving behind Beck Weathers and Yasuko Namba, clients of Rob Hall's, who were immobile.

The next day Lhakpa Tshering Sherpa and Stuart Hutchison, a doctor from Hall's expedition who had also reached the summit, hiked out to look for Weathers and Namba. The accounts of what they saw varied. One was that Namba was still breathing, quite shallowly, but her pupils were dilated. Another version said she was completely inert. They found Beck Weathers either already dead or so close to death as to be impossible to revive. The two climbers were only four hundred meters away from camp.

Helen Wilton, Rob Hall's Base Camp manager, phoned Weathers's wife, Peach, in Dallas to deliver the news before the media learned of it. Wilton told her that her husband's body had been identified.

◆————◆

MEANWHILE, AT ABC and Base Camp, nothing was known of the whereabouts and condition of Scott Fischer and Makalu Gau. The fact that Fischer was feeling poorly when he reached the summit the day before was not a good sign. Veterans and novices alike are generally unable to sleep on the South Col and are already tired when they arrive there from Camp III. As a matter of course, many suffer from bronchitis, cracked ribs, exhaustion, or symptoms of high-altitude sickness. Moreover, any preexisting condition tends to be aggravated in the death zone.

It turned out that Lobsang Jangbu had waited for Fischer on the summit, then descended with him. They were soon joined by Taiwanese team leader Makalu Gau. Below the South Summit, however, Fischer began to glissade down the wrong gully. He had to climb back up and join the main route where Lobsang and Makalu Gau were descending. Fischer's oxygen may have run out here, because he began to think and act irrationally, according to Lobsang, who struggled to keep him on a consistent downward course.

Fischer may have been developing cerebral edema, a potentially fatal swelling of the brain; irrationality is one early symptom. Both he and Gau slowed dramatically. As the light faded, Lobsang needed to physically help Fischer along, while Gau staggered behind them. Darkness and exhaustion overcame them on the Triangular Face, below the Southeast Ridge, and they sat down in a rocky area exposed to the wind. In good conditions, they were no more than an hour from Camp IV.

Lobsang tried to make a bivouac for Fischer and Gau, but between two and three o'clock in the morning, unable to do anything more for his close friend Fischer, he decided to descend to

Camp IV. Fischer was not responding, and he may have told Lobsang to save himself.

JUST BEFORE 5:00 A.M., on the eleventh of May, the radio in Hall's tent at ABC again sputtered to life. A Sherpa requested that David, Ed, and I come over to Hall's communication tent.

"Is someone coming to get me?" the voice crackled. It was Rob Hall. To our astonishment, he was still on the South Summit. Hall would need to move or he would die. Ed and David said they could picture the lonely, sheltered depression just beyond the South Summit where Hall had spent the night. And where was Hansen? He might have fallen from the narrow traverse between the Hillary Step and the South Summit, Ed figured, or possibly made it to Hall's snowy niche. If Hansen was alive, he would be in bad condition.

At ABC, several climbers had gathered at Hall's dining tent. Ed grabbed the radio and exhorted his old climbing friend Hall to stand up and descend. Hall's voice was weak and staticky. "Doug is gone," he said obscurely. Did he mean Hansen was dead, or had he been separated from Hall in the storm and darkness? Just as puzzling, Hall then asked where Andy Harris was. He said that Harris had been with him the previous night, although Jon Krakauer said he had seen Harris not far from Camp IV.

By ten o'clock that morning, we had gained a better picture of who was where on the mountain. A much-weakened and near-death Hall was still stranded on the South Summit, and Hansen was probably dead. Scott Fischer and Makalu Gau were last seen below the Southeast Ridge, and Base Camp had received an unconfirmed report that Fischer was dead. The bodies of Beck

Weathers and Yasuko Namba had been identified, lying near Camp IV. Andy Harris never arrived at the South Col.

At Base Camp and ABC, those who knew Hall were imploring him to turn his oxygen flow up, inhale a good dose of it for a boost of energy, and then get moving. Hall may have had ice on his mask and regulator, a common annoyance. I was surprised to hear others trying to reassure Hall over the radio that help would come soon, as if he didn't need to worry. I'd have been worried as hell in his situation. He may have been lulled into complacency, however, by the soporific effect of hypoxia and hypothermia. It would have been nearly impossible for an exhausted climber who had spent the night exposed to the elements at that altitude to simply stand up and start moving. Climbers talk about the moment when their hands become too cold to zip up their parkas or pull on their mittens as the turning point when things get worse before they get better. And in those conditions, sitting down can be the last move a climber ever makes.

Ed was fully absorbed by the radio. He told Hall not to wait for the Sherpas, stressing that he would run into them partway down the mountain. "Turn your oxygen all the way up; then crawl and pull your way up the rope to the South Summit," he said, almost shouting. From where Hall was sitting, he would have to climb up twenty feet and over this snow dome before he could descend. Hall replied that he was suffering from uncontrollable shakes, a sure sign that he was becoming hypothermic.

Veikka Gustafsson, a member of Mal Duff's British team and a close friend of Hall's, cried during the radio calls. He plainly wanted to speak to Hall but was simply unable to without breaking into tears. He had climbed with Hall before on Everest and

Dhaulagiri, and they had the kind of bond that forms between those who have survived life-threatening situations together. They were similar in some respects to what Himalayan Buddhists call *nedrogs*, companions in pilgrimage, those karmically linked on a spiritual quest.

Ed was also in tears, and he released the talk button on the radio so that Rob wouldn't hear him crying. When Dr. Jan Arnold, Hall's pregnant wife, was patched through to Rob from their home in New Zealand, everyone at ABC and Base Camp broke down. Sounding clear and strong when he spoke with her, Hall told his wife several times not to worry about him.

Then Hall said he would try to get up and depart. Everyone breathed a tentative sigh of relief.

A few hours later Hall radioed down again. Ed asked him how he was doing and how far he had reached. Hall hadn't moved at all. His hands were so badly frostbitten, he said, that he couldn't deal with the ropes. At that point we knew it was over for Hall. Rescue remained his only distant hope. Those of us at ABC shared looks of solemn despair.

DAVID BREASHEARS, ED VIESTURS, and I discussed where to best apply our efforts. It looked like a triage situation: should we sacrifice some still-living climbers in order to save those who were more easily rescued? Should a climber leave behind a breathing but unresponsive Scott Fischer, for instance, en route to retrieving Rob Hall? And even if climbers or Sherpas reached Hall, how would they get him down? Above the South Col, attending to one's own survival is hard enough. Plus, as this season was again proving, accidents usually occur when descending, and when least expected.

Our motivation would have to remain appropriate and consistent. For the time being at least, we gave up all thoughts of climbing and filming and dedicated ourselves to coordinating a rescue or providing help. We didn't want to see the Sherpas and other rescuers get strung out over the mountain, potentially making the situation worse. The Sherpas and veteran climbers were aware of cases in which rescuers took heroic measures and became victims themselves.

We would do all we could within our abilities and within the confines of safety. It was frustrating that, ultimately, those limitations left us with little that we could do.

The Taiwanese team leader Makalu Gau and the American Beck Weathers were evacuated by Lieutenant Colonel Madan K.C. in one of the highest helicopter rescues in history. I have never witnessed a depth of gratitude like Weathers's. He had lain outside at 26,000 feet for nearly twenty-two hours, was given up for dead, and then stood up and found his way to Camp IV.

6

A LESSON
IN
IMPERMANENCE

If the IMAX and other teams at Advance Base Camp were to help those higher on the mountain, we first needed to communicate with Camp IV. We knew that Rob Hall was stranded, Andy Harris and Doug Hansen were missing and probably dead, Scott Fischer and Makalu Gau were either dead or near death, and Beck Weathers and Yasuko Namba were dead. Others were still alive, but we didn't know their condition and whether clothing, food, oxygen, or physical rescue was needed most.

Jon Krakauer and his teammate Stuart Hutchison's radio batteries were dying, and theirs was the only working radio left on the South Col—except for the South Africans'. The South Africans had reached the South Col the same day as the other teams, but they were exhausted and had postponed their attempt by one day, to May 11. Their radio could pick up and transmit in all the frequencies used by the other teams.

Ian Woodall, the South African team leader, refused to give up their radio. The other teams heavily lobbied his brother Philip at Base Camp, but Woodall said that they had run out of food and supplies—a claim that seemed odd considering that they were still planning a summit attempt. The South Africans weren't exactly endearing themselves to the other expeditions. They were acting as if the predicament of the other climbers was not their fault and therefore not their problem. Why expend energy and resources to help people they didn't know? I wondered what response would greet them if they were to encounter trouble themselves.

A cache of batteries was sitting in our South Col tent, and over the radio David told Jon Krakauer to tear open the tent and take them. The Sherpas had insisted that the tent be locked in the wake of earlier thefts on the South Col.

Several climbers at ABC were urging the Sherpas on the South Col to head up and attempt to retrieve survivors, namely Fischer, Hall, and Makalu Gau. Wongchu, who was the sirdar for the Taiwanese team as well as ours, got on the radio and scolded the Taiwanese team Sherpas for not heading out earlier to find them. He barked sternly into the walkie-talkie, ordering them to get out of whatever sleeping bags they were lying around in, to leave their tents on the South Col, and to get moving up the mountain. "If you don't make an effort to rescue these guys," he shouted, "I will personally escort you to jail the moment you return to level ground."

The rescue—or search for survivors—haltingly swung into gear. Ang Dorje and Lhakpa Tshering, who had reached the summit the day before with the New Zealand team, departed the South Col shortly after daybreak. They inched slowly upward, carrying bottles of oxygen, headed for Rob Hall on the South Summit. The weather was miserable.

A little more than one thousand feet above camp they encountered Scott Fischer, resting on a narrow terrace. He was breathing, they said, though barely and with teeth clenched. He didn't respond when they tried to rouse him. They decided to continue on toward Hall, who they knew was alive and coherent.

Later that morning Ngawang Sakya, the father of Fischer's sirdar Lobsang Jangbu, also headed up the mountain, joined by the Taiwanese team Sherpas Nima Gombu and Ngawang Tenzing. They hoped to find and retrieve Fischer and Gau. Ngawang Sakya found Fischer to be dead, or nearly so; cold goggles held to his face didn't show any condensation. Nearby, Ngawang and Nima found Makalu Gau badly frostbitten and immobile. They shook him forcefully, then opened their vacuum flask and poured hot tea into his mouth. Slowly, he came back to life—just in time. Gau would probably have died soon thereafter. Haltingly and with great effort, they dragged him down to the South Col. His karma had prescribed that he would continue living.

Meanwhile, higher on the mountain, Ang Dorje and Lhakpa Tshering battled through wind and blowing snow. One thousand feet below the South Summit, unable to continue, they dropped the oxygen bottles and a ski pole, then turned around. They saw no sign of the New Zealand guide Andy Harris, who was still missing.

When they returned to the South Col, Ang Dorje cried almost uncontrollably as he described his and Lhakpa Tshering's attempt, fighting through ferocious winds, to rescue Hall.

The two Sherpas had placed themselves at considerable risk getting even that far. Nonetheless, some of the climbers at ABC continued to yell into the radio at the Sherpas on the South Col, indignant that they hadn't tried harder to find and evacuate the lost climbers—Hall and Fischer especially—though everyone could see that the mountain was still socked in and blowing. One climber berated Ang Dorje and Lhakpa Tshering, saying, "What the hell are these guys doing, thinking only of themselves?" I could understand their anger and frustration, but why were they sending only the Sherpas and not the guides? I held my tongue, but wanted to tell them to get up there and look for Hall and other survivors themselves.

When Hall learned over the radio that the Sherpas had turned around, he left his finger on the transmit button of his walkie-talkie, and we could hear him crying. He knew that he wouldn't last another night, even though some of his teammates at Base Camp said they would try again the next day.

The other Sherpas and I respected Hall as an accomplished climber, and it petrified us that he was stuck up there. As we sat around the kitchen tent, some conjectured that a driven and resourceful guy like him would figure out a way to survive. Others remarked that Hall had abused the privilege of climbing the mountain by doing so for personal gain, and this was a ripening of karma within this lifetime.

That evening, going into his second night on the South Summit, Hall again spoke with his wife. Then he turned off his radio for the last time. From my own experience with cold, I can affirm that freezing and hypothermia are not really painful. The extremities become numb, and the ability to feel and think slows. Hall must have simply drifted off into an endless sleep.

The night of the storm, members of Todd Burleson's guided American expedition were at Camp III. Later, Dr. Ken Kamler would say that the next morning, May 11, he was afraid their high-performance tents would get blown off the mountain. Burleson and Pete Athans, both highly respected guides, were the only ones to selflessly head up through the ferocious, blowing whiteout, toward Camp IV on the South Col.

Athans and Burleson found Camp IV largely in tatters.

Sherpas and climbers alike were still in their sleeping bags, too exhausted even to find nearby oxygen bottles. The two veteran guides learned that the bodies of Yasuko Namba and Beck Weathers were lying at the edge of the Kangshung Face, several hundred yards away.

They went to work. The first thing they needed was oxygen. Over the radio David instructed them to take whatever bottles they could find from our oxygen cache. We had no thought other than to provide help, but I remember noting that giving up our oxygen probably signified the end of our chances for the summit. My dream would remain nothing more than a dream, my passion nothing more than a suppressed urge.

Athans and Burleson delivered oxygen bottles to several tents, placed masks on the faces of sleeping climbers, fired up stoves to melt snow, and urged those who could walk to descend as soon as possible. The winds continued to howl at a consistent forty miles per hour, and a kilometer-long plume of ice crystals trailed from the Southeast Ridge. As far as Athans and Burleson could tell while on the Col, the South African team members never left their tents.

To assist the descending survivors if they needed it, David decided that an emergency relief tent should be set up at Camp III. I remained at ABC to coordinate the movement of the Sherpas and to help Dr. Kamler convert the New Zealand team's dining tent into a field hospital. Kamler asked Base Camp to send up medical supplies, while I collected medicines from all of the teams, except the South Africans.

David, Robert, Araceli, Ed, and several Sherpas climbed to Camp III, just in time to meet the first group of exhausted, shell-shocked climbers descending from the South Col, some of them breathing bottled oxygen. Our team and others at Camp III placed them in tents and fed them soup and cocoa, knowing that warmth and rehydration would be what they needed most, and perhaps all we could give them. David had already decided not to hold them there; the space at Camp III was too steep and narrow for treating anyone, and if climbers rest when exhausted they stiffen up, making it difficult to get moving again. Many had moderate frostbite on their fingers and faces. David and the others checked them out and sent them on their way downward.

When Charlotte Fox and Sandy Pittman arrived at ABC, Wongchu immediately guided Sandy, who had bruises and minor frostbite, into our kitchen tent, where I gave her some soup and tea. As Wongchu rubbed her hands, I rubbed her back to warm her. When she had relaxed somewhat, I gave her a radio, led her to her tent, and told her to call if she wanted anything.

THE DRAMA ON the South Col wasn't over. Around five o'clock in the afternoon, Todd Burleson stepped from his team's tent and in the distance saw a ghostlike figure stumbling toward Camp IV, walking straight into the blowing snow. At first he thought it was a man having difficulty urinating, but as the form tottered toward him, he could see that his arm was locked upright, parallel to his shoulder, "like a mummy from a cheap horror flick," in Pete's words. The man's pile jacket was open down to his stomach, his eyes were swollen shut, and his face was so badly frostbitten that he was unrecognizable. If it wasn't Fischer, it had to be Beck Weathers. Unbelievably, Weathers had arisen from the dead.

Astounded, and now galvanized into action, Pete and Todd quickly helped Weathers to Scott Fischer's tent, knowing, sadly, that Fischer was unlikely to return to it. They were mainly concerned that Beck could have a heart attack, which can occur when a deeply hypothermic person is rapidly rewarmed. Taking care not to warm him too abruptly, they got him into two sleeping bags, gave him oxygen, and worked on rehydrating him. Beck's right arm was frozen like a limb from a porcelain statue, and he appeared to be near death.

Anatoli Boukreev took one look at Beck and was convinced that his good friend Scott Fischer could still be alive after all. Though it was already late afternoon, Boukreev threw some gear together and headed up the mountain into the darkness.

Boukreev found that Fischer was in fact dead. He arranged some stones around the body to protect it, then returned to the South Col. As he descended, a terrifying wind picked up, and he became lost in a whiteout eerily similar to that of the night before. He didn't find the tents until 10:00 P.M., when he heard Beck Weathers's loud moans.

Few climbers at Camp IV were aware that Weathers was there, but it was presumed that he would not live through the night. A doctor at Base Camp radioed up saying that, under the extreme circumstances, it wasn't advisable to sacrifice scarce manpower and resources in trying to bring him down, unless he could walk on his own.

That night there was some confusion over who would be looking after Beck. As his arm thawed, it swelled, and his cheap plastic watchband began to cut off his circulation. He tried to gnaw the watchband off but was unable to. Severely dehydrated, he was also unable to open his water bottle for a drink. High winds had virtually flattened his tent on top of him and restricted the ability of those on the South Col to provide help.

Beck Weathers's ordeal reminded me of a shocking accident my father told me about that occurred with the Swiss on Kedarnath, in India, in 1947. An injured climber, Wangdi Sherpa, was left for two nights at a high camp while his companions left to get help. Wangdi thought he had been left to die, and to put himself out of his misery he tried to stab himself and slit his own throat—unsuccessfully. He was rescued two days later, but the experience was so profoundly disturbing that he never climbed again.

The next morning, May 12, Beck was still very much alive. After Athans and Burleson gave him some soup and water, he was able to get up and walk—with assistance, which included a shot of dexamethasone, a steroid that is beneficial for cerebral edema and believed to temporarily increase strength. Pete and Todd hadn't removed Beck's boots, figuring they would never get them back on once his feet thawed. He was wearing a new brand of high-tech mountaineering boots, and his feet were relatively fine.

Weathers was still virtually blind, however, so Pete and Todd had to either describe the terrain ahead or walk backward and place his feet for him.

By now Ed Viesturs and Robert Schauer were climbing upward from Camp III to help them across a nasty, rocky area of the Yellow Band, which Beck could not have negotiated on his own. A slip on the rock-hard ice would have been disastrous. Working together, they lowered Beck and rappelled beside him. It is difficult enough to climb this section alone, and from ABC I watched their progress through binoculars, amazed at how they continued to forge ahead, with wind and blowing snow whipping by them.

When they finally clipped into the fixed lines of the Lhotse

Face, Beck was able to down-climb, though his frozen arms interfered with his coordination and his useless hands simply couldn't hold the rope. David also arrived, and Robert grasped Beck by his harness with one hand while Ed and David descended directly in front of him, backward, carefully steadying his feet on the hard blue ice while Beck placed his hands on their shoulders. To negotiate everyone around the anchors of the fixed rope, they had to contort themselves to unclip everyone and then clip in again. At the bergschrund, Robert again rappelled alongside as Ed lowered Beck on another rope.

Beck plodded into ABC with rhythmic, short strides, applying all his energy to the simple but excruciating task of moving forward. When I saw him, I was awed and frightened at the same time. He had been reduced to near death, yet some inner force had revived and propelled him. Any one of us could end up like him, I thought. Or maybe we wouldn't be as fortunate.

Beck Weathers's return from the virtually dead was unprecedented. No one imagined that such a feat was possible following a night out at 26,000 feet, in those conditions. His unusual rejuvenation illustrates the difficulty of diagnosing death at high altitudes. "Someone isn't dead until they are warm and dead," Dr. Kamler said, reiterating a medical axiom, though clearly no one was in a position to drag Weathers's frozen form back to camp, warm him up, and see whether he came to life. In conditions of severe cold and duress, therefore, you just can't be sure.

So what level of effort should be made to rescue those stranded in extreme conditions? Weathers made the miraculous plausible. But this prospect raises more doubt than inspiration. A stranded climber's likelihood of survival becomes not so much a matter of medical judgment—which is virtually impossible to apply in such conditions—as of statistical probability. As a result, distressed relatives and friends may not easily relinquish their hope that even the most desperately "lost" climber could be alive, and they may prod rescuers to place themselves at greater risk.

Here at ABC, we were grateful to at least have Beck Weathers. He wasn't out of danger yet, but if he could make it this far, I felt certain we could find a way to get him safely to Base Camp.

SHORTLY BEFORE DARK on May 12, Makalu Gau also arrived at ABC, and he was carried into the medical tent on a stretcher. The look in his eyes spoke of his brush with death. His nose was coal black, and his hands and toes had been frozen, thawed, and refrozen. I could tell that he would live, but he needed intravenous fluids and care for his injuries. He told me he had wanted to try for the summit alongside our team and was disappointed when we turned back. After Chen Yu-Nan was fatally injured, Gau wanted to abandon his attempt altogether, but Wongchu urged him to continue on. At that point Gau would have been of little help to his team lower down, Wongchu reasoned, and he was Taiwan's only remaining hope for getting a climber on the summit that season. Gau did what he thought was right, and he paid a terrible price. I was simply thankful he was alive.

We stayed up late that night treating people, amid nearly unmanageable confusion. Too many climbers and Sherpas wanted to help, and after a point they got in Ken Kamler's way. Then David told us on the radio from Camp III that he wanted the survivors to descend to Base Camp as quickly as possible. That meant an early morning start.

I presumed that news of the tragedy was already hitting the world, and the media would probably be saying that a Japanese woman had died, referring to Yasuko Namba. Would they mention her name? With Sumiyo on our team, we didn't want people to worry that it was her. David made a good move by radioing Paula at Base Camp and asking her to phone all of our families to tell them we were all right.

That evening Hall's staff at Base Camp, along with Beck Weathers's wife in Dallas, asked the U.S. embassy to authorize a helicopter rescue for Beck. There is little lift for takeoff at high altitudes, however, and the climbers at ABC agreed that only an unusual helicopter pilot would try to land above the Icefall. The last helicopter that landed in the Western Cwm, chartered by the Italians in 1973, is still there now. Then Base Camp received a message that Lieutenant Colonel Madan K.C., a Royal Nepal Army pilot, would attempt the rescue in the morning.

At four A.M. the next day, we overheard a radio call saying that the Himalaya of eastern Nepal were too windy for a helicopter rescue. Nonetheless, at daybreak those of us at ABC guided Beck Weathers down in the direction of Camp I while several Sherpas dragged Makalu Gau in a makeshift sled. The body of Chen Yu-Nan accompanied us, too. The other Taiwanese had already returned to Base Camp.

Shortly after we left ABC, I was amazed to hear the distant sound of a chopper. Then we saw it—a small green object, like a flying insect—and I remarked immediately that it was flying at a very high altitude. It circled above Base Camp, then, as we stood watching in disbelief, it climbed its way toward us and circled above ABC, apparently trying to get the feel of the wind in the area. But then the chopper turned and departed down-valley, without landing.

Hurrying, we arrived at Camp I just as the helicopter returned. David spied a reasonably flat place to land, and we realized that we should mark out a landing spot. I thought of urinating on the snow just as Araceli reached into her rucksack and pulled out a bottle of Kool-Aid. Ed grabbed it and poured out a giant pink "X" on the snow. The helicopter almost didn't set down. On the first try it settled in very slowly and came within a few feet of the landing spot, then the tail rotor nearly hit the edge of a crevasse. Lieutenant Colonel K.C. quickly pulled the helicopter up, and we all thought that was it—the last and only attempt he would make. "His pants must be full now," Robert said, as impressed as I was that the pilot would even try such a landing.

The helicopter circled and tried again. For a windsock, Ed held a scarf tied to a pole, while David gave hand signals. Gently, from a slightly different angle, K.C. set the chopper down. We ran crouching to this magnificent metal aircraft and opened the door. Wearing his oxygen mask, K.C. vigorously motioned that he could take only one passenger.

Even though the chopper had been dispatched for Weathers, Beck said that he simply couldn't go before Makalu Gau. Makalu was unable to walk, and carrying him through the Icefall would have been extremely difficult. David, Pete Athans, and Jon Krakauer quickly loaded Gau into the chopper, and it took off. I respected Beck immensely for this generous act.

Fifteen minutes later, defying all of our best guesses, K.C. returned and landed as he had before. When we finally got Weathers into the back seat, everyone heaved a sigh of relief. It would later be called one of the highest helicopter rescues in history.

We had done our work. We wouldn't have to carry Gau or

Weathers through the Icefall, at great risk to all of us, and there was no one left to rescue. Rob Hall, Scott Fischer, and Yasuko Namba were dead. Doug Hansen and Andy Harris were missing and unlikely to be alive.

Five of the Taiwanese team's Sherpas carried Chen Yu-Nan's body down to Base Camp. When they realized that they wouldn't make it all the way that evening, they left his body in the Icefall and descended to Base Camp. The next morning they went back up and carried him the rest of the way out.

As for ourselves and our own hopes for the summit, we would have to regroup at Base Camp and think and talk about it, though with our diminished supplies and heavy hearts, another attempt looked unlikely.

THE EVEREST IMAX team arrived at Base Camp a day behind many of the survivors, and the moment we stepped out of the Icefall and onto the glacial till of Base Camp, Araceli, Sumiyo, and I broke into tears. Finally we, too, like all the teams, could decompress. The disciplined concentration that the mountain demands had served us well under the duress of the tragedy, but our emotions burst like a flood as we removed our crampons at the edge of the Icefall.

The river issuing from the mouth of the Khumbu Glacier was frozen when we first arrived at Base Camp, but the warmer weather of mid-May had now turned it into a small but aggressive torrent. The glacial ice that Base Camp sat atop had melted, and the rocks on its surface had been shrugged and shuffled about. The snow surrounding our camp had also melted and ablated away in the searing sunshine, leaving our tents perched on shaded platforms of ice that reached as high as our heads.

Around Base Camp, people were struggling to make sense of the dismal events on the mountain. It was easy to cast blame, but each time I stepped back and reviewed everyone's actions, I marveled at the extraordinary effort that most climbers and Sherpas had made to assist others. In particular, Klev Schoening and Anatoli Boukreev had helped six other climbers narrowly escape death when they guided them to safety from their huddle on the South Col. And the climb from Camp III to the South Col that Athans and Burleson made on the morning of the eleventh, through extremely high winds, was as heroic as any excursion made that week. They downplayed their effort, saying that the only real "rescue," technically speaking, had been made by Ngawang Tenzing, the Sherpa who brought Makalu Gau down from below the Southeast Ridge.

Mistakes were made. Some of the climbers had been lulled into the belief that Everest is a benign mountain. On rare occasions warm and calm conditions have been encountered on the summit. But with little warning, the wind can change, clouds can seemingly arise from nowhere, and climbers suddenly find themselves in a desperate fight for their lives.

Could more have been done to save the stranded? The day after the storm, the IMAX team and others were positioned at ABC and Camp III headed up. I wondered what Yasuko Namba's chances might have been, lying near Weathers on the South Col. That morning it was assumed that Namba, like Beck, was not alive, or not rescuable. But if she was alive, and if she had been dragged to a tent and stabilized, these climbers may have been able to assist her down from Camp IV, as they did for Beck.

Like Sumiyo, Namba represented great aspirations for the people of Japan. She was the first Japanese woman to reach Everest's summit in nearly twenty years, and she was also the first

Japanese—man or woman—to stand on top of the Seven Summits.

Many other "what-ifs" were offered up to explain the season's events. What if the storm hadn't come? What if there hadn't been a delay in placing the fixed ropes at the Hillary Step? What if there had been better radio communication?

There are satisfactory, though perhaps not convincing, responses to these and other speculations. The extreme conditions of the South Col are nearly impossible to imagine. Victims and rescuers alike function only with great difficulty at extreme altitudes because hypoxia and exhaustion rob them of their judgment. When struggling to survive, the circumstances of others around you grow less urgent. People reflexively turn selfish in frightening situations. Even on expeditions when there's no particular emergency I have seen climbers cache personal food stocks at Base Camp or ABC, anxious that supplies might run out.

Sherpas feel that the causes of mountain tragedies are complex. Planetary alignment, prophecies, and the ripening of karma accumulated over previous lifetimes converge in an unyielding destiny. But when the factor of judgment is added to the mix, the outcome can quickly change. I believe that fewer people would have died if the leaders had followed their own summit day strategies and given higher priority to guiding their clients than to bagging the summit. The victims that day weren't doomed by a single incident or decision, but rather by a compounding series of poor choices and unlucky events. And ultimately, of course, each climber had made the personal decision to be on the mountain that day.

Preparing for Everest physically is relatively easy. Mental preparation is more difficult. The climber must develop mindfulness and, most important, approach the mountain without hubris. For Sherpas, respect is the platform for each step we take. Most foreign climbers respect our beliefs and customs, and abide by them; of the ones who don't, we feel they are partly "excused" by the mountain's demons and deities—to the degree that they are unaware of the non-tangible processes at work around them.

We should always be prepared for atrocious conditions. The media-hyped "freak" storm of May 10 may not in fact have been that unusual. Unquestionably, on May 11 the Sherpas placed themselves at risk to rescue survivors. Some of the climbing Sherpas suggested, however, that if the dynamic had been different, Hall might have been rescued, Makalu Gau might have been retrieved sooner, and though saving Fischer would have been less likely, perhaps he could have been hauled down.

The Sherpas wouldn't have taken extraordinary measures for nothing. When I spoke with some Sherpas later, they said they were waiting for a member of Hall's or Fischer's teams to offer, over the radio, a sizable reward for retrieving these climbers, perhaps on the order of $5,000.

The Sherpas love the mountains and take pride in their work, but their primary motivation is financial. Assisting climbing expeditions is a job for them, not recreation. They have a strong professional allegiance to their climbing teams, but that sense of duty does not extend to unduly risking their own lives. Obtaining *sonam*—merit—by saving a life is a great motivator, but compassionate behavior is also expressed through respect for one's own life.

Sherpas do respond to incentive pay. Having already made the decision to enter what they know is a high-risk profession, they are willing to examine and consider additional risks and benefits. Having said that, I would also assume that Ang Dorje, who was very close to Rob Hall and involved in his business, gave his best shot to rescuing Hall, without regard to any incentive. He was genuinely distraught by Hall's death.

After Hall died on the mountain, some of the climbing Sherpas speculated that his demise was caused by having taken too much from the mountain without giving back. This observation may have been slightly unfair considering that Sherpas are also known for using the mountain for personal gain, though perhaps not in the same sense that the leaders of large commercial expeditions do. The Sherpas are on the mountain out of necessity. Moreover, Hall would have earned sonam—and a favorable rebirth—by staying with his client, Doug Hansen.

I was surprised to learn from one Sherpa that Hansen, who was struggling up the Southeast Ridge, was prepared on two occasions to turn around and retreat to the South Col. Hall, who was climbing ahead of Hansen, actually down-climbed the Hillary Step to encourage and help Hansen up. Bearing the burden of possibly having pushed Hansen beyond his capacity, Hall couldn't very well abandon him near the summit and allow him to die there. In the end, regardless of what one might say about his judgment and motives, Hall was a loyal friend and a true gentleman.

The press seems to have enjoyed playing up a mercenary scenario in which Hall and Fischer were competing against each other. I believe, however, that despite their tremendous ambition and drive, they were not rivals as such. Each simply wanted success for himself and his team. Each was competing with himself, in effect, hoping to establish a record that would attract future clients. As I learned in America, Western culture is performance-driven. The guides needed to perform—they needed to show that they could deliver.

This compulsive drive is what got Hall and Fischer into trouble. They shared a "go for it" attitude, which serves anyone well in controlled circumstances. Everest, however, is different. As Ed Viesturs put it, "You don't conquer Everest—you sneak up on it and then get the hell outta there." I might add that you do so with its permission.

In 1952 and 1953, many Sherpas were worried that if the mountain were finally climbed, there would be no more expeditions and Everest would become, literally, history. This worry translated into some mild resentment of my father's efforts—mostly before the first ascent. Ever practical, Rob Hall's sirdar Ang Tsering also feared that the deaths of the 1996 season might result in fewer climbing jobs for Sherpas. Soon after that season, however, guides and Sherpas were surprised when commercial guiding companies were inundated with Everest climbing requests. Putting one's life at risk must be the bar that foreigners keep coming to jump over. The higher that bar, the better.

The Sherpas don't greatly mind that foreigners take the glory and credit for successful ascents. Most Sherpas want to be paid well, ideally with a bonus, because their principal desire is to provide for their families and bring improvements to their villages. They do appreciate, however, fair treatment and personal acknowledgment.

I thought of what Trulshig Rimpoche had said about the hardship suffered many years ago by people in Chomolungma's vicinity, when the mountain was defiled and the goddess Miyolangsangma went neglected. The ignorance, anger, and greed of samsara, which forms the very axis of the Wheel of Life, is endless, and I was beginning to feel that we may have entered a new cycle of neglect and suffering, the cause and effect of collective karma.

FROM BASE CAMP, I called Soyang on the satellite phone and explained, as best I could, what had happened on the mountain. Our relatives had been calling her in a worried state, and her voice clearly conveyed their concern. She seemed fairly upbeat herself, I think because she assumed we would be leaving the mountain and I would be coming home soon. Without exactly saying that we might consider another attempt, I told her that we planned to hang out a few more days at Base Camp to reflect on our situation.

I was especially disturbed to hear the news, reported over the radio by United News of India, that three Sherpa climbers on an Indian expedition had also reached Everest's summit on May 10, from the north side. Tragically, all three of them were found dead by a Japanese expedition climbing from the same side. My mother's younger brother, Ang Tharkay, who had joined the India-Tibet Border Police on my father's urging, was on that expedition. Because the report didn't name those who were lost, another layer was added to my general anxiety.

The Indians were my countrymen, and I recalled my youthful aspiration to climb with the Indians in 1983, when they hoped to put the first Indian woman on the summit. My brother-in-law Lhatoo Dorjee reached the summit with that expedition.

India wasn't known for its mountaineers then, and it still has few recreational climbers. Today thirty-five graduates from the Himalayan Mountaineering Institute, which my father established, have climbed Everest. The Indians who climb are dedicated and energetic and have wholeheartedly adopted what I refer to as the "traditional" mountaineering spirit of noncompetitive camaraderie. In India climbers have nothing like the status of a cinema actor or an industrialist. They are motivated solely by a love for the mountains—and a sense of pilgrimage perhaps. The three Sherpas on the north side died for that love.

I later heard an account, which has not been fully clarified, that the Japanese had seen the Indian Sherpas in difficult shape—but alive—earlier that day as they passed them on their own way to the summit. It grieved me to think that they may have been in a position to provide help, and I wondered whether it was true that climbers could simply walk past others in distress. I was relieved to hear that my uncle was not among the missing, and also to hear that Matt Dickinson, who was climbing from the north side, felt that the Japanese were in no position to stage a rescue at that elevation and in those conditions.

ON THE FOURTEENTH of May, four days after the storm, Rob Hall's and Scott Fischer's distraught teammates convened an impromptu memorial service at their Base Camp lhap-so. This was the last time all the teams would be together. The first groups of climbers would begin to leave for home later that day.

The morning dawned cloudy, and a pall of gloom hung over the emotional, ad-hoc proceedings. The survivors stood silently, bandages covering their frostbite, as Sherpas ignited juniper branches at the base of the lhap-so's small rock altar. They kept it burning throughout the service, and as the fragrant smoke curled upward it led our eyes toward the mountain and the summit. I made a silent appeal to Miyolangsangma to forgive us all, and thanked her for allowing many to live.

Lobsang Jangbu and Ang Dorje, Fischer's and Hall's sirdars, prepared the ritual objects and offerings. One climber-monk sat cross-legged, reciting from Buddhist texts as Sherpas and foreign climbers placed candy bars and other offerings on the altar, arranging them around a photo of Fischer.

Taking turns to step forward, the climbers and Base Camp support staff paid their respects to the dead climbers. Neal Beidleman was the first to speak, and he fought back tears, then paused to weep. Some recited poems, and many cried, including Lobsang Jangbu, who had been like a brother—or a son—to Scott Fischer. Others exhumed memories of past adventures with the lost climbers, as if clinging to the vitality of those times, not wanting to let go.

While I prayed for a favorable rebirth for the dead climbers, I also prayed for my father. May 14 marked the tenth anniversary of his funeral. I thought of how I missed him, and how I wished we had spent more time together. Too often he was traveling, distracted, or otherwise unable to answer my questions about climbing, and life. And also about death. I now wanted him to be beside me and to tell me, from the grave, about the afterworld and the next life, to offer me guidance or understanding about this transition he had made—the transition that the climbers we were praying for were now making.

I was in the United States when my father died. The last time I saw him was nearly a year earlier at a government guest house in New Delhi, just prior to leaving for college on my first trip overseas. My father introduced me to the legendary Indian climbers Colonel Narendra "Bull" Kumar and Commander Jogindar Singh, two of his very old friends. They were colorful and successful chaps, but they seemed peripheral to me at the time. In fact, it was in Delhi that my father and I first spoke with each other about our lives and the future. He coached me on working hard, on being honest, and on being myself.

"I know that college will be a new and foreign place for you," he said, "but I have confidence that you can take care of yourself. What I really mean to say is that I have confidence in *you*." It was there in Delhi that I saw him as more than simply a father. He was a fellow traveler, a pilgrim—a nedrog, a companion on the path of life. Then I had an unexpected and uncomfortable feeling that I might not see him again. He must have sensed the same, for I think he had purposely selected that time to shed his mantle of father, anticipating that it would be forcefully shed before long. When we parted, I cried.

EVERY SHERPA AND climber on the mountain must have been aware of the risk of death on Everest, yet some of the Western climbers seemed genuinely surprised by the tragedy, as if it was something that couldn't and simply shouldn't have happened.

This is what Sherpa families go through all the time, I thought. It may sound unfair, but despite the crying and carrying on, I didn't sense a deeply sincere feeling of loss in many of the mourners. Some of them seemed relieved that it wasn't they who were killed, as if the tragedy had only tarnished their satisfaction of reaching the summit. Araceli thought that some people were offering excuses for what they had done on the mountain. Perhaps what tears they shed arose as much from tension as from grief. Confronting death can lead us to question ourselves and evaluate our lives, but were people following that lead?

After a death, Westerners tend to openly share remembrances and emotions as a form of catharsis. This is not an entirely satisfactory way to resolve a transition such as death, I believe. The Sherpas are as emotional about the death of loved ones as anyone else, but much of our grief and guilt are expressed through rituals and offerings, religious practice, and prayer. Talking and crying among friends aren't enough. We believe that relatives and lamas and prayers and propitiations are essential to guide the dead person to a favorable rebirth.

In the days after the May 10 tragedy, teachings about death crowded my mind—how death should be prepared for and faced, and what it means. Buddhists view death as a critical turning point on the Wheel of Life, the endless cycle of birth, death, and rebirth. Death is part of a continuum, one that Buddhists hope will result, after not too many millions of cycles, in enlightenment and liberation from the Wheel—for individuals and eventually for all sentient beings.

What determines all of this? The lamas say that the key factors in our rebirth are the merit and karma that we accumulate during our lifetime, our final thoughts at the moment of death, and our ability to navigate the frightening distractions of the after-death transition period of bardo. Buddhist practice trains us to remain aware during this disturbing and disorienting state and to recognize bardo's frightening visions and sounds as no more than illusory manifestations of our own untamed negative emotions.

I've noticed that Sherpas and other Nepalese and Indians tend to take life less seriously than Westerners do, perhaps because they recognize that this is only one of many lives. One might conclude that we are merely fatalistic—lightheartedly resigned to the inevitability that we will be reborn. But it is self-defeating to resign ourselves to being reborn into the samsaric existence to which we've become so attached. For one thing, if we have not accumulated an immense reserve of merit, we may not even be reborn as humans. "Precious human life" describes our mortal human rebirth, which is granted to only the most genuine and devoted of practitioners and believers, and those with good karma amassed from previous lives. It is either inspiring or depressing to think that, as the lamas say, a human rebirth is as unlikely as a turtle swimming somewhere in the world's oceans happening to surface into a single, randomly cast net.

This is why it is a shame to squander one's precious human rebirth. In the mountains I've seen Westerners take unusual risks. And in Kathmandu it is common to see the city youth racing their motorcycles or driving cars like maniacs at night with the headlights off. These people are either unaware of the risks or choose to flaunt them.

Buddhist teachings and beliefs were all I could find to guide me through the tragedy, and I could feel my faith in them growing. My emotions were a churning sea, and the lamas' words an island of dry land, a refuge. Indeed, the act of "taking refuge" in the three gems—the Buddha, the dharma teachings, and the community of practitioners—is at the core of Buddhism, and this is our first step in dedicating ourselves to a spiritual path.

Once we have taken and found refuge, we then take the Bodhisattva Vow, and pledge to act in all ways from a foundation of compassion, and to dedicate any merit that we gain to others.

Somehow, it sounded right to me, partly because it sounded so logical, like the laws of physics and thermodynamics that I studied at college in Wisconsin. In the case of Buddhism, at least, science and religion are compatible. Spiritual principles and explanations are brilliantly reflected in the laws of the physical universe. Even recent scientific discoveries reiterate what the

Buddha said, and what religious scholars observed, more than two millennia ago.

Karma, for instance, is really no more than the law of cause and effect. Just as each action has an equal and opposite reaction, all of our deeds have good and unfavorable consequences—with the same inevitability and precision of physical law. And reincarnation: matter (of the physical world) and consciousness (of the spiritual world) are neither created nor destroyed.

A version of the Big Bang Theory was predicted in Buddha's teachings. The universe forms, abides for eons, then collapses, only to be re-formed again. The lamas says that even the release of great powers by the splitting of the atom was long ago foreseen and characterized.

Buddhism doesn't demand allegiance. It quietly asks for investigation. It's simply an explanation for the cosmos, external as well as internal. Some understanding of these basic principles would be useful, I felt, now that I was trying to reconcile my inner self with the outer task of figuring out why we were here, and where we were going.

MOST OF THOSE gathered for the memorial service dispersed when it was over to pack up and depart. Many climbers went down-valley individually rather than as a team—as if the team were a useful construct for getting up the mountain but deserved no ongoing allegiance. "Once the stream is crossed, the stick is tossed," one of our proverbs says. I watched some of the climbers head out, then went over to our kitchen tent. The other Sherpas were hanging out in a depressed funk. Some of them hadn't gotten so much as a thank-you from the guided clients whom they assisted down the mountain, often after exceptional struggle. The clients simply disappeared, some without saying good-bye. We notice this kind of behavior.

For the first time on the mountain that season I felt a loneliness that I hadn't experienced since my time in the United States. When I arrived in America at age eighteen, I was impressed by the enormous measure of the place. Sherpa villagers—like my father before he began to travel—have images of modern, foreign countries fixed firmly, but vaguely, in their imaginations. Before we had schooling in geography, we simply lumped them all together: Hong Kong, Malaysia, Japan, the United States, and England were all provinces of the same modern world, located close to each other but very far away from us.

America is a young country with a dynamic and, one might say, immature or formative culture. In terms of technical and material progress, it is far ahead of the developing world. In terms of culture and tradition, it is less advanced. I felt that meaning and connection were missing from my life in the United States, as if the country were lacking a spiritual core. All momentum and no center.

Like many Sherpas, I assumed that America had become properous and developed by virtue of its spiritual progress. But those of us who have visited the country find ourselves asking where that sense of sacredness and spirituality has gone. Its absence, I can understand now, is the source of the restlessness, dissatisfaction, and confusion that I saw afflicting many Americans. Wealth and material possessions haven't eased their malaise. Perhaps they have only aggravated it.

I have been with Hindus from Nepal and India when they visit a metropolis such as New York City for the first time, and they are awed by the technology—the airplanes, bridges, and skyscrapers—to the point of being overwhelmed. Standing in the cement and steel canyons of the city, they feel petrified and insignificant. But because of our teachings in impermanence, Himalayan Buddhists are only fleetingly impressed by such man-made creations. We can peer up at all of it and know that before long—soon, in fact, by the reckoning of the eons and eras by which we measure time—it will all crumble and be gone.

I can understand why my own people, especially the young, are prepared to abandon their culture and values to chase dreams in foreign lands: they can usually earn enough money to send a portion of it back home. And the quality of public education throughout the Himalaya is pitiable. Still, it disheartens me that many of my countrymen may never attain the dreams they chase, and the dreams may not fully satisfy them if they do realize them. Will they be able to reclaim the culture of their birth someday when they wish to return and embrace it? Will they know where to find it? Will they have the discipline and patience to apply themselves and to open their hearts and minds to the teachings that have been developed in their homeland over the centuries?

In Khumbu, foreign visitors bemoan the loss of the traditional Sherpa way of life, and many blame themselves for having led the Sherpas' rush toward all things modern. Tourists, however, are not the primary reason for this shift, at least not directly, and I feel that they overestimate their impact on the culture. Trekkers and climbers have provided the Sherpas with the wealth needed to become materialistic consumers, but they have furnished little of the resulting style and content. Asian satellite television, the Hindi cinema, and the distractions of the capital city are, unfortunately, becoming our new cultural reference points. Westerners and Easterners alike presume that materialism is the easy path to human fulfillment, but in the long run it may not be very sustaining.

By and large, traditions are better maintained where there is no exposure to the outside world. But surprisingly, even with fifteen thousand relatively wealthy tourists passing through their villages each year, Khumbu Sherpas have maintained their traditions to a remarkable degree. Partially as a result of greater incomes, Sherpas have renewed their support for festivals and religious traditions, and begun to send more of their sons to the monasteries. Some Sherpas, in other words, are spending their money on being better Sherpas.

While in college, I constantly noticed differences between East and West. I listened carefully to the conversations and remarks of my peers and compared my own experience and background to theirs. Many of them were as ignorant of the larger world as the villagers of my father's generation. A common reaction when I introduced myself was "You're from Darjeeling? Cool, man, *excellent*"—followed by "Where's Darjeeling?"

I found America to be organized, prepared, and on schedule. I could easily reassure myself that I was doing something important there, though I grew to wonder what I was actually accomplishing. And what were the people around me achieving? Success was the universal holy grail, and my American classmates had begun to pursue it even before they graduated. What did they expect to gain from it? More leisure time? More material goods? America has countless time-saving appliances and conveniences, so why is it that Americans seem more pressed for time than those who don't have them?

One foreign aid worker calculated that subsistence farmers in the Himalaya have more leisure time than Westerners do. It's true that, in the absence of labor-saving devices, it takes us three hours to cook our evening meal and nearly that long to cook the morning meal. But we are together while we cook—there's activity, discussion, visitors, laughter, and learning. Much of our work doubles as leisure time, though we don't generally distinguish between work and play.

I saw television for the first time in Darjeeling only in the early 1980s, when I was an upperclassman at Saint Paul's, and I was warned to stay at least fifteen feet away from the set. In America I was surprised that many people believe that professional TV wrestling is real. Even the fighting is artificial there! And do people need all that stuff they advertise?

I wouldn't propose that Buddhism be taught as a compulsory subject, but it's a shame that Tibetan Buddhism's foundation, the Four Noble Truths, can't be conveyed in a simple way to the people who seem to have a desperate need for them:

1. All life is suffering.

2. Suffering is caused by desire.

3. The way to eliminate suffering is to reduce one's desire.

4. Buddhist practice is the pathway to the cessation of desire.

Intellectually, the Four Noble Truths are simple. The lamas say that understanding and applying them is even simpler. Amid the seductions of comfort and success, however, humans find them painfully difficult to put into practice. Unless we are willing to take a first step, this understanding will remain out of reach. It must be human nature to avoid giving up that which gives us pleasure and to avoid difficult work—though I think it's mainly the fear of work that limits us.

I saw people in the United States who were always on the lookout for shortcuts, for the condensed version of spirituality. Many in the West believe that they will go to heaven—which I consider to be the same as enlightenment, or nirvana—simply by saying they believe in God. I don't think it is that easy. Lamas view powerful "born again" or other mystical experiences as important and genuine reminders of the value of faith. But such spiritual adventures are only a beginning, not an end, for they don't guarantee entry into heaven or a favorable rebirth. They may not even provide exceptional insight or understanding. That's because all ordinary experience is *temporary*, the lamas say, including "born again" experiences—and the thrill of standing on top of the world's highest peak.

Buddhism teaches us how to make these thrilling, life-and-death-confirming experiences last longer, without having to do the mountain climbing part. Unfortunately for most, following Buddhist teachings may be more difficult than climbing. Lamas reiterate that the lessons are there in the palms of our hands, but, like so many people, I have found it difficult to learn them.

Ten people had died on the mountain, as far as we knew, and the words of Chatral Rimpoche once again echoed in my head: "Why do you want to do this thing?" Indeed, why did any of us want to do this thing? Was it worth the price these people had paid?

Returning to climb the mountain was a difficult decision, one that I could make only after consulting my wife, Soyang, our family lama, and the other team members. Perhaps Everest was telling us to go home.

7

A
DIFFICULT
DECISION

Within a day Base Camp was virtually abandoned. I felt unnerved and disheartened. Everest was no longer the mountain my father had climbed, and it was no longer my mountain. Should I accept that Chomolungma had changed irretrievably for me and reunite with my family in a less ominous, more generous world? Had Everest turned on the climbers and Sherpas for the remainder of the season?

Emotions circled in my head like a pack of animals chasing their tails. I was torn between conflicting elements of my Buddhist faith, my Sherpa beliefs and superstitions, my professionalism, my love for my family, and my abiding desire to climb the mountain.

Everest had been taken away from us all, and lives were taken from some. Those who had reached the summit and returned were grieving and miserable. And those of us considering another attempt were left with the prospect of walking over the bodies of our friends en route to the top of an angry peak. I continued to cling to the image of my father on the summit, and of Miyolangsangma, looking for hope in them, trying to take refuge in them. But they weren't always there for me, I couldn't always see them. At the moment they were shrouded in fog.

The thought of my wife, Soyang, who was pregnant and suffering from severe morning sickness, tugged at me and pulled me homeward. She was set against any return to the mountain, and so was Ed Viesturs's wife, Paula. As another new husband, I could relate to how divided Ed must have felt. He was already depressed by the loss of his friends Hall and Fischer, and he became even more worried when the South Africans announced their plan to try for the summit again.

Araceli said that she didn't want to climb on a route with dead bodies on it. Sumiyo was spooked especially by the death of Yasuko Namba. I began to envy those who had already departed: they wouldn't have to hang around to watch mistakes get made all over again.

To their credit, the producers at MacGillivray Freeman Films did not pressure us to make another attempt, though its $5 million movie was at stake and $1 million or more had already been spent. David made it clear that the decision of whether to try again or to go home would be ours. Greg MacGillivray said that if in David's and the team's collective judgment we felt it unsafe to climb, then he would fully support a decision to abandon the expedition.

Understandably, most of the climbing Sherpas were uneasy about trying again after having spent two months on the mountain already. Lounging about Base Camp, demoralized bands of Sherpas revived our game of *sho* dice gambling with new intensity. Some of them dropped in to see Dr. Jim Litch and other Base Camp doctors, complaining of ill health but with indefinite symptoms; Litch felt that they may have come looking mostly for a dose of hope and confidence. The season had been hexed, the Sherpas figured, and a number of them snarled at the idea of making another attempt or ignored the topic altogether. They were vaguely aware that the world's media had captured the story—the tragedy was about to break on the cover of *News-week*—and more of them began to worry that the deaths would turn climbers and clients away from Everest, meaning less work in the future. Moreover, they were just plain tired.

The Sherpas also weren't convinced that Chomolungma's period of bad luck had ended with the storm. While the mountain was being evacuated on the twelfth of May, another unsettling accident occurred on the Lhotse Face. Klev Schoening, climbing with Scott Fischer's expedition, was having trouble seeing out of one eye after it was frostbitten on the South Col. He was down-climbing closely behind Wangchuk Lama, the sirdar for the Nepalese Cleaning and Climbing Expedition, which was attached to Scott's team.

Out of the darkness, not far from where Chen Yu-Nan had died, rockfall rained down on them from Lhotse. Lama lay down to his right as Schoening lay down to his left. "Wangchuk got beaned with a rock," Schoening said, "and it sounded like he'd been hit with a baseball bat—a sickening sound. He went limp immediately and began sliding down the fixed line in front of me." This is always alarming, because in a fast fall a climber can "zipper" right through all the protection. "But I was able to jump in front of him and begin to arrest his slide. I watched what seemed like his last breath leave his lips, a gasping exhaust of death."

Then they began sliding together down the fixed ropes, and another rock hit Lama's rucksack. Finally they both came to a stop, perched precariously near the top of the bergschrund. Neal Beidleman reached them and tied them off, but Lama had stopped breathing. Fortunately, over the next fifteen minutes Lama gradually began to breathe and steadily became more alert, and some Sherpas arrived and gave him oxygen. Beidleman and a Sherpa helped him down the last couple of rope lengths, and at the bottom of the Lhotse Face he was able to walk.

Wangchuk hadn't been asked by his team to climb to Camp III. On his own, he had talked other Sherpas into climbing with him to Camp III to help with the rescue—another example of Sherpas volunteering to help. He was flown to Kathmandu, and though he eventually made a full recovery, people at Base Camp didn't learn of his progress until the end of the season.

Bijaya Manandhar, the IMAX team's Nepalese liaison officer, had become one of my good friends. We sat near the edge of the Icefall and shared a cigarette. "Nothing is feeling right," I confided. "I want to pack up and split along with everyone else."

"You're getting the opportunity of a lifetime," he said. "You were one in a billion people to be selected for this expedition, and you should be grateful to David for the opportunity." He reminded me of the importance of living up to one's dream. "Complete this project, climb this mountain—and come down, too. Simply deal with events and make decisions as problems arise. Hang in there."

His words were uncharacteristic for Hindus, who tend toward the fatalistic. All that will happen in this lifetime, they say, is written on our foreheads by a goddess named Baabi six days after we are born. Maybe Bijaya knew more about me than I did myself. He was acquainted with few people at Base Camp, and his opinions of events were uncluttered. The Nepalese tend to be nationalistic, but he never referred to my father's or my nationality. I was an Indian citizen, and my father had an Indian passport, but Bijaya considered us simply to be Nepalese and was proud of us. Anyone who speaks Nepali must be Nepalese on some level.

Then I remembered that my father had given up on Everest altogether following the second, bitterly cold, Swiss expedition of the fall of 1952. He was sick and drained. His recovery from malaria had lingered into the beginning of 1953. Then Major Wylie talked him into joining the British—not by offering any philosophical reflection or divination, but by simply reminding him of his dream. Wylie reassured my father from the beginning and supported him throughout the expedition, then guided him through the political ordeal that would beleaguer him after Everest.

Bijaya was my Major Wylie. If the rest of the team was determined to make another attempt, then I'd consider it, I decided privately.

Ed told David and me that he wanted to try again. He saw no reason why there should be a curse hanging over the mountain. "Everest is not a death sentence," he offered. Robert agreed. Araceli and Sumiyo said they would think about returning.

There was no logical reason not to try again. Putting the tragedy aside, there was no better time for us to head up. David felt that all we really had to confront was our own fears resulting from the unfortunate tragedy. The mountain hadn't changed, he emphasized. We would never be together again, most likely, nor in better physical condition. The camps were mostly stocked with supplies, and we were standing before a partially open weather window that could open even wider but would certainly close before long. In any event, our permits would expire on the first of June.

It wouldn't be possible unless the Sherpas were willing. And I would have to speak with Soyang, who would be difficult to convince. Each morning that I was on the mountain, Soyang and her mother lit butter lamps in their altar room, then climbed to the roof of their house to ignite piles of juniper incense and pray to Miyolangsangma. I half worried that the goddess would grow weary of their appeals.

I called Soyang on the satellite phone and told her we were thinking about going up again. I was prepared for her objections, which I didn't challenge. Perhaps she could have another audience with Geshé Rimpoche, I said, and explain to him all that had happened on the mountain. Then request another divination. A favorable forecast would put the Sherpas' minds at rest, too, and might be essential to get them to reconsider the mountain at all. I saw it as our only chance.

Conditions can change; in fact, they are constantly changing. I was now more afraid of the lama's reply than I was of the mountain, because I sensed it would determine the course of my future and again throw me at odds with my unfulfilled desire. I wrestled with the thought of telling Soyang not to ask him. No, the decision of whether to return to the mountain or not was too daunting to make on my own—harder than the blue ice of the Lhotse Face, harder perhaps than reaching the elusive summit itself. Mountaineering is hardship, but this was agony.

Soyang said that if the divination was favorable, she would relent.

I kept her on the phone while I worked over the phrasing for my question to Geshé Rimpoche: "There have been some deaths on Chomolungma. If we return to the mountain . . . and we make another attempt on the summit . . . will conditions be favorable, and will we return safely?"

It might have been unfair to ask whether we would reach the

summit, but the real reason one should not pose such a question is that the answer can affect one's psychological approach to the task. If we knew in advance that we would reach the summit, or that we would fail, I don't think any of us would apply as much effort. It is the *not-knowing* that keeps us moving forward.

The next morning when I called Soyang again, I immediately sensed a lightness in her voice. She said that Geshé Rimpoche had looked at the ritual dice and exclaimed, "Go! Go up!" In spite of all the deaths so far, he said, we would have very good weather and would do well. "And all will return safely," he assured her. He mentioned that at one place near the summit I would become frightened and that I should cast about some of the chaane, the blessed grains of rice and mandala sand that he had given me.

On the mountain, the storm clouds had lifted. I conveyed Geshé Rimpoche's findings to the Sherpas, who were still lolling dejectedly around Base Camp. The news aroused their interest, and they ruminated on it. Then over the next few hours I could see their moods lighten. They began to talk about the mountain and even to discuss what loads would have to be carried to which camps to restock it. Au Passang, the old man of few words, quietly said that he was ready to try again. This fortified the younger Sherpas, who respected his thirty years of expedition experience.

I turned to David and said, "Let's do it."

For me and the other team members, Beck Weathers's rejuvenation helped seal the decision. Beck had brought us hope, a ray of light and redemption in the midst of death and desperation. Though he wasn't an accomplished climber, Beck's epic tale of self-admitted folly, irrepressible resolve, immense gratitude, and possible divine intervention stirred me greatly. Had Beck been only another frozen corpse still lying on the South Col, I would be regarding the mountain very differently. No, Chomolungma wasn't cursed this season. Beck was the sign we were looking for, the sign that Miyolangsangma had done all she could, in the midst of chaos and misjudgment, to be merciful and forgiving.

One climbing Sherpa suggested that Beck Weathers revived when Rob Hall's departed spirit traveled down-slope from the South Summit and inhabited him. The timing didn't quite work for that to have happened, but the other Sherpas acknowledged the concept. Sherpas are loaded with accounts of visions and supernatural events that seem to occur most frequently at high altitudes, and especially on Chomolungma. Many of these visions are genuine, I believe, though others may be no more than mirages or hallucinations. My curiosity was piqued, however, when an American climber and filmmaker, Jeff Rhoads, had an unusual encounter with a goddess—or ghost—near the summit of Everest in 1998.

Rhoads and another American, Wally Berg, were approaching the Hillary Step from the South Summit behind two climbers they didn't know. The climber in front was quite slow, delaying the climber behind him, who seemed to be trying to pass. Like all summit climbers, they were wearing mounds of clothing and gear, but when they caught up with the second climber Rhoads recalls sensing that she was a woman. Rhoads admitted that he could have missed noting details carefully, due to hypoxia, and if Berg hadn't seen the second person, too, he might have been convinced that he simply imagined her.

"When the second climber, this woman, got around the slower one," Rhoads said, "she took off like I've never seen anyone climb at that altitude—as if she was walking down the sidewalk. But when Wally and I reached the top of the Hillary Step and continued on toward the summit, we could no longer see her ahead of us. Nor did we see her on the summit. In fact, we never saw her again. I was puzzled at the time, but began to think this was especially bizarre when we later learned that there weren't any women attempting the summit that day, no one was wearing a down suit of that color, and all the other climbers who reached the summit had been accounted for.

"A year earlier, my wife, Kelly, and I had been on Everest together, and when we returned home to Idaho a good friend who is a clairvoyant came to visit us. The moment she stepped inside she announced, 'You have a ghost in your house.' This startled us, as you can imagine, partly because it was a new house. We had just built it."

The clairvoyant told them they must have brought the ghost or spirit back with them from Everest. "Her spirit is definitely present," the clairvoyant said. "She's a woman, and with Asian features."

"How did she end up in our house?" Rhoads asked her.

"Well, there was a tragedy on the mountain, and this spirit is somehow connected to the deaths there." Indeed, Yasuko Namba and Passang Lhamu were two Asian woman who had died high on the mountain.

The clairvoyant described for them how to exorcise the spirit, so the Rhoadses burned some juniper branches and performed a small ritual in their house. And, before returning to attempt Everest again in 1998, they told the spirit that it couldn't stay, that it would have to climb into their luggage and return with them to the mountain. Apparently, it did, because it didn't appear in their house again.

This account confirmed for me that such experiences are not limited to Sherpas; they are not simply fabrications of our own clan. The Rhoadses said they constantly feel a powerful other-worldly, spiritual presence whenever they climb on Everest, and they don't feel this on other mountains. I know other foreign climbers who feel the same about Everest.

Sherpas climbing in 1997 tell the story of an American climber who retrieved Scott Fischer's wedding ring, which was on a string around his neck. After removing it he took two steps, then promptly fell 400 feet down the mountain. He wasn't seriously injured, but said he felt he had been pushed. The Sherpas said that it was Fischer's wandering spirit, his ghost, that had pushed him. But his friends in America consulted a Navajo shaman who said that it was not a ghostly spirit that had pushed him. It was a woman deity, a goddess.

I THOUGHT OF how difficult it would be to rebuild the motivation to climb to a point that we had already reached and then descended from. We also had to replace the twenty-eight oxygen bottles that had been used on the South Col. We gathered these mainly from Hall's and Fischer's teams and borrowed and bought the remainder, to bring our total back up to seventy. We would use oxygen only above Camp IV, beginning at 26,000 feet—except Ed, who would be climbing Everest a second time without bottled oxygen.

We commissioned a second puja—led by the same lama who was again summoned from the village of Pangboche—and we constructed a new lhap-so. Wongchu and the team said that this time no one was allowed to even think about roasting meat at Base Camp.

The route through the Icefall was deteriorating, and it required some repair before we could head through it again. Mal Duff's team, which had installed and maintained the ladders and fixed ropes, was leaving the mountain. Thankfully, he appointed two Sherpas to stay behind and continue to work on it.

By the time we struck out again into the Khumbu Icefall, on May 17, our commitment had grown and our faith had been renewed. From the top of the Icefall I again trudged through the solar collector of the Western Cwm, thankful that I would be making only one more trip through it. By now ABC was comfortable and familiar.

The weather high on the mountain wasn't cooperating, however, and we had heard no news from the meteorologist in London, who, at some expense to the expedition, was interpreting satellite weather data and relaying it to us over the satellite phone. The summit was still flying its signature pennant-like plume. That night—and then the following night—we lay in our tents listening to the malevolent roar of wind high on the mountain. The train was still running, the 747 endlessly trying to take off.

Todd Burleson's team had also arrived at ABC to make another attempt, but his clients were feeling unsure about the weather and the mountain. After a second night at ABC, they decided to return home. Even some of our Sherpas who had been encouraged by the favorable divination began to suspect that the weather wouldn't get any better, and one of them proposed that we turn around.

Patience. Again I invoked my father's teaching on patience. He had reached the top only on his seventh attempt. Seven is lucky for our family, and for the Sherpas. My grandmother Kinzom had seven sons, and my father had seven children. A party of seven is considered auspicious when traveling or working.

Despite the wind, I felt the tranquil form of Miyolangsangma sitting gracefully above us, protecting us all. Lying in the tent and praying, I felt that she knew why I had come; she understood my pilgrimage. Perhaps she recognized that I and others on the mountain were capable of a transformation like her own, and like that of the other Five Long-Life Sisters who inhabit five peaks within forty miles of Everest. Guru Rimpoche subdued and converted them all into defenders of the Buddhist faith, and they are now considered to be emanations of the Five Dakinis, the consorts of the Five Buddhas. They symbolize, in turn, the pure essences of the Five Elements—air, sky, earth, water, and fire.

One reason why people go into the mountains is to experience the purity of these elements—these goddesses—in their unobstructed form. In the mountains, worldly attachments are left behind, and in the absence of material distractions, we are opened up to spiritual thought. When we look out at the ocean or gaze at the sky and the clouds, or even the rock wall of a mountain, it is difficult for our minds to form labels. What is it really that we are looking at? There is no real thing there—just color and shape. And when we stop attaching labels to what we see, a sense of quietness flows in to fill the gap, bringing us a step closer to the understanding of emptiness.

When climbing, the presence of mind that one needs in dangerous situations makes one naturally undistracted, and that undistractedness is what generates awareness and a feeling of being completely alive. Every action becomes meaningful because each movement is a matter of life and death. As one rock climber reportedly said when asked why he climbed high and extremely difficult vertical cliffs solo, without a rope: "It helps my concentration."

In a sense, anyone who intentionally travels into the mountains is on a pilgrimage to Miyolangsangma and the other Five Long-Life Sisters. But theoretically, we shouldn't need to go to the mountains to visualize them and make offerings to them. We should be attempting to carry the spiritual experience of the mountains with us everywhere.

When we return to normal surroundings, the mundane can begin to feel like something of a meaningless state. We need to return to the mountains to feed that liberating experience, because we depend on external landscapes and events to aid our understanding. Rather than allowing the quality of being fully present, fully aware, to develop around us at all times—and in a safer environment—we become addicted to a certain quality of circumstance and experience. In effect, Buddhists suggest that climbers might focus on the substance of their pursuit—awareness and liberation—rather than on the setting they feel they need to be in for it to occur.

THE CLOUDS THAT FORMED below us a little bit earlier each day foreshadowed the approaching monsoon rains. Every summer tropical heat over the Indian Ocean produces a large mass of humid air that is drawn across the subcontinent toward the Himalaya by the convective currents generated above the five-kilometer-high Tibetan plateau. When the water-saturated air strikes the Himalaya and rises, it cools, and the moisture condenses as heavy rain that falls mainly on the south side of the range.

Hunkered in at ABC, I had time to speculate on why many Himalayan peaks might come to be regarded as goddesses: they are tall and imposing, certainly, but they also constitute an immense reservoir of snow and ice, the source water for irrigation in the plains, and for Nepal and north India's large theoretical hydroelectric potential.

Indeed, Miyolangsangma's "activity" is described as *inexhaustible giving*. She continually increases the longevity, wealth, and power of those who worship her. It is the power of Miyolangsangma, one Khumbu lama said, that has delivered us all the foreign tourists and their wealth. Faith is what she asks for in return.

Faith can even control the flow of water, as illustrated by the story that Namche Bazaar villagers tell about their spring, which flows from the middle of town. They say that some three decades ago the water in this spring stopped flowing completely—as if someone had turned off a tap. Not a drop flowed for three days, and the villagers had to fetch their water from a smaller spring that was a ten-minute walk away. Then they learned that the day before the spring had stopped its flow, a soldier posted at the nearby army camp had slaughtered a goat and cleaned out its intestines in the spring. This offended the *nagas*, the serpent spirits that oversee the quality and flow of the water, and the nagas fled, causing the spring to dry up. After the third day of no water, the Namche people hired a lama to ritually entice the nagas to return, and the water immediately began to flow full force.

I believe that the events of such stories happened much as the villagers describe them, though the epilogue of this one seems almost too predictable: infected sores soon covered the soldier's body, they say, and before long he died.

BY THE END of the second day at ABC, we were tired and discouraged, and the Sherpas were restive. Maybe the gods really

were sending us a message this year: don't come. My dream, however, was still alive and breathing. As David had said, the wind
that you hear in the distance is always worse than the wind you're
actually climbing in. He had also said that it's better to face the
mountain in your boots than lying in your tent thinking about
it—or as our proverb puts it: "The tiger of the mind is more
ferocious than the tiger of the jungle."

The morning of the third day we received confirmation from
our British meteorologist that the jet stream had moved to the
north. The window of good weather was opening, and we departed ABC in a buoyant mood. At the least, whether we reached
the summit or not, we would be heading home within a few days.

I took my time getting to Camp III, partly because the intensity of the midday sun there can make it uncomfortably hot, similar to conditions on the Western Cwm. It's no cooler in the tent,
and if there's no work to be done, we strip down to our T-shirts
and wait for the sun to set. When the sun goes behind the ridge,
it becomes cold very quickly.

At Camp III, I shared a tent with Sumiyo and Robert. Sumiyo
was between us, and after dark she began to cough almost constantly. Her wracking hacks eased somewhat when she was in a
sitting position, so she sat up the entire night. She didn't want
David to hear her from his nearby tent, knowing that he might
remove her from the summit team. I stayed up much of the night
myself, rubbing her back.

The next morning David agreed that Sumiyo should use a bottle of oxygen for the climb from Camp III to Camp IV on the
South Col. For me, the ascent to the South Col was one of the
most strenuous and draining parts of the climb, especially crossing
the Yellow Band and the Geneva Spur. The Yellow Band has one

tricky overhang, and because it is rock, not snow, crampons tend to slip, making it feel like roller-blading on an ice rink. Nonetheless, we shot a magazine of IMAX film in that dangerous area, taking time to anchor everything—the people as well as the camera.

From the top of the Geneva Spur, we dropped one hundred feet onto the South Col, and I soaked up the view, imagining what the Col had been like for my father. Wind was battering the place from the moment we arrived, just as it had in 1953—just as it nearly always does. My father told me of the extraordinary effort it had taken to form a single coherent thought at this elevation, and now I understood. I looked for the landmarks that I had seen in his photos, including one large hump of rock overlooking the Kangshung Face.

The South Col is a broad, rocky expanse, with Camp IV (Camp VIII of 1953) situated in its southwest corner, toward Lhotse. Its flatness makes the sheer drops to the east and west look like the edges of the earth. It's an austere, almost extraterrestrial world spinning at the margin of life, and the borders where colors intersect seem to vibrate. I felt grateful for the air I breathed, knowing its scarcity.

As I looked up at the mountain, a simple thought came to mind. *How the hell are we going to climb this thing?* The route upward looked impossibly steep. My father and the others who had climbed it ahead of me, I thought, had simply placed one foot ahead of the other—guided, in my father's case, by my stepmother Ang Lhamu and the prophecy that a Himalayan Buddhist would be the first to reach the top.

I surveyed the area around Camp IV—the garbage, the oxygen bottles, and, eighty feet from our camp, a perfectly preserved body, lying prone. Yasuko Namba's body would also be lying there, some four hundred yards away. It is difficult and risky to get bodies down from the South Col, and you can't bury them. The living can do little more than stand there and regard them; for me, they served as reminders of our own thin hold on life.

We erected four more tents next to our storage tents and anchored them with piles of large rocks and climbing ropes—not just one or two lines but four or five thrown over the top of each tent to keep them in place in the extreme winds. A gorak—raven—hopped about on the nearby scree, and I elected to take it as a favorable sign. It had come a long way to beg for food, and if I had had some on hand, I would have thrown it to the bird.

Camp IV is a way station, mostly, a place to rest and rehydrate. By the time we pitch camp (an exhausting chore at that altitude), make a meal that few of us eat, lie down without getting any sleep, then get up at 10:30 P.M. to prepare our gear and try to eat again, Camp IV hardly seems worth it. I couldn't imagine camping any higher than the South Col, but the belief in the early 1950s was that climbers could not reach the summit and return to the South Col in a day. In the 1950s a high camp, Camp IX, was hastily fashioned at 27,500 feet near the Balcony, the beginning of the Southeast Ridge.

Our logistical pyramid was in place, and we were positioned near its apex. For the summit push four Sherpas had been assigned to trade off carrying the camera, monopod, and film magazines, and two Sherpas were to carry oxygen for the others. Two additional Sherpas would be sent to the Southeast Ridge with oxygen to cache it for the returning climbers. If all went well, the summit team of eleven climbers and Sherpas would be on top no later than 11:00 A.M., and back on the South Col by 2:00 to 4:00 P.M., giving us a safety margin of a couple of hours before darkness.

Climbers who are persistent, patient, and motivated are generally the ones who summit, which may be one reason that slightly older climbers have a better record on endurance climbs such as Everest. But even when the weather is stable, only five or six climbers out of a team of ten can be expected to reach the summit. Anything can happen: illness, accidents, or other variables that are beyond a climber's control.

Sumiyo's cracked ribs had slowed her dramatically. We passed her above Camp III even though she had departed an hour ahead of us and was climbing on oxygen. Knowing that we simply couldn't risk having a sick or poorly performing climber above the South Col, David was forced to make the difficult decision to tell her to remain at Camp IV. The recent deaths had increased our already high level of caution, though it would have been prudent in any event for a team member to remain on the South Col for communications and safety.

Sumiyo must have suspected this decision, but she was heartbroken when David told her. She cried, and I did my best to comfort her. I could taste again my own tears and the panicked anger and frustration that ran through my veins when, as a boy of eighteen, I had asked my father for permission to join the Indian Everest expedition and he told me no. But my father, too, was nineteen years old in early 1933, when foreign climbers arrived in Darjeeling, and the town teemed with activity in preparation for the first British expedition since 1924. Just as I had been fearful of asking my father to help me, he had been terrified of presenting himself at the intimidating Planters' Club, where the sah'b Hugh Ruttledge, the expedition leader, sat up on the veranda while the Sherpas lined up to apply for work. My father had been rejected for being too young, and his Sherpa friends were powerless to influence the British.

Two years later, at the start of the 1935 British reconnaissance led by Eric Shipton, my father was almost left behind again. Shipton and Karma Pal, the local agent for the Sherpas, had selected the entire team from those with certificates showing expedition experience. My father wondered how he could ever be hired when he had never been hired before.

Then Shipton and his colleagues returned and announced that they needed two more Sherpas. My father borrowed some khaki shorts and a bush jacket and quickly jumped in line with twenty other candidates. They asked him for his certificate, and though he understood what they wanted, at the time he didn't know Hindi or English and couldn't respond. One of Shipton's colleagues told my father and another Sherpa to step aside. Dejected, my father began to leave, but they called him back— he had been selected, not de-selected. Ang Tshering was also chosen, the same Ang Tshering who was later killed on Nanga Parbat.

WHEN I CRAWLED into our South Col tent late that after-noon, Sumiyo was already inside, and I began to prepare my equipment. I wanted to pack things in the order I would need them, to get at them easily. The flags and other items to be left on the summit went on the bottom. In the middle I packed extra pairs of mittens, socks, sunglasses, goggles, and a small flask of tea and candies for energy. Water went on top, and I put extra batteries for my headlamp into my jacket pocket.

Sumiyo melted more water and began cooking, but the smell of the packaged food nauseated me, so I crawled out and went to

Dorje's tent. He is a good friend and a strong climber, and we cooked up some vermicelli noodles. Before I returned to our tent, we shared a cigarette, which momentarily eased my background altitude headache.

Anxiety about the summit kept me up praying for our safety and for good weather, just as my father had prayed. I could hear his prayers, and I quietly mouthed mine in unison.

My mother's prayers were also with me, and I felt I was absorbing her strong religious faith and meditative concentration. Shortly after I left for college in the United States, she undertook a retreat for several months in the chapel room on the top floor of our house. Her meals were passed through the door to her by Ai Lhakpa, the cook who has been with our family for the past thirty-five years.

Many can't afford the time for spiritual practice. They are needed to feed their families and care for their children, and then their grandchildren. My mother had completed that part of her life and was waiting for the grandchildren to be born. Over a period of several months, she did a *ngöndro*, a series of four "preliminary" ritual practices that act to clear obstacles to balanced and peaceful meditation and open the path to enlightenment. She created 100,000 mandalas out of grain and offered them to the deity. She recited the *Guru Yoga* mantra 100,000 times. She laid out a smooth flat board and did 100,000 full body prostrations (which is excellent exercise), and she recited the 100-syllable *Vajrasattva* mantra 100,000 times. This practice culminates by dedicating any merit that is gained to the enlightenment of all sentient beings—perfectly fitting my mother's generous nature.

She dedicated the comforts of our house to others as well.

The monks at the neighboring monastery frequently came to share our meals and to take showers and relax. At times I suspected that the monks were taking advantage of her, a feeling that may have contributed to my early cynicism about religious patronage. We have a saying: "In the same way that the more you work to warm yourself, the colder it seems, the more you respect monks, the more conceited they become." But the occasional laziness or ingratitude of the monks did not matter to my mother, because the purity of intention and the selfless act of giving brings merit to the giver.

Meditation formed the heart of my mother's ongoing practice, for this is one of the best techniques for understanding the Buddhist concepts of emptiness, impermanence, and compassion. In our tent on the South Col I sat up and meditated as best I could, drawing upon what my mother and the lamas had taught me. It may have been a shortage of oxygen reaching my brain, but I felt touched by a moment of serenity, as if both my parents had left for me a time capsule, filled with blessings, that I was to open and utilize at this time and place. I had my mother's ivory rosary with me, and I passed its 108 beads between my thumb and the crook of my forefinger, counting out scores of rounds. I then bunched the rosary and rolled it vigorously between my hands and pressed it against my eyes and face, visualizing Miyolangsangma, thanking her for all the fortune that had accrued, already, to me and my family. Thinking of my father's dedication and care, and my mother's devotion and awareness, I wished that the fruits of such Buddhist practice could be with me—at least for the summit climb and descent. Then I lay down and was able to sleep, without supplemental oxygen, but only briefly.

*Thillen and Lhakpa Dorje, two of our team's Sherpas, surmount the
treacherous Hillary Step amid a tangle of old fixed ropes.
From here we are less than an hour from the summit.
This view looks down onto the Kangshung Glacier, in Tibet,
more than 10,000 feet below.*

8

OBSTACLES
AND
BLESSINGS

8

OBSTACLES AND BLESSINGS

*L*ying in the tent on the South Col, I could feel my father's sense of anticipation as much as my own. At age thirty-nine, he had decided that his attempt with the British would be his last. He had risked his life enough times on this dangerous mountain, and his mother, Kinzom, had begged him to retire.

Two of the expedition's Brits, Charles Evans and Tom Bourdillon, had been selected for the first assault party. Their agreed-upon destination for that day was only the South Summit, with the option to make a try for the top if conditions were good. When they departed the South Col for the South Summit on May 26, carrying summit flags, my father was resigned to the possibility that they could reach the top. Colonel John Hunt had already selected my father and Edmund Hillary for the second summit team.

The Brits felt it was their last shot at the mountain, and were desperate for the expedition to succeed. As my father looked upward, he overheard Hunt and another climber talking about how splendid it would be if they reached the summit for the coming coronation of Queen Elizabeth II. He then understood why the team's Brits had been selected for the summit ahead of himself and the New Zealander Ed Hillary: conquering Everest would be the desired prize for Her Majesty. After all, the mountain itself had been renamed for a Brit, the nine-teenth-century surveyor Sir George Everest.

My father and the Sherpas felt pressured. Queen Elizabeth and the pride of England meant little to them. The United Kingdom had never controlled Nepal as it did India, and by 1953 India itself had been independent of the United Kingdom for six years. On the other hand, the chance that a Sherpa might reach the summit on a first ascent kept the Sherpas going; they recognized that it would confer honor on their people and on their Indian and Nepalese countrymen, and might even be of some value in monetary and career terms. My father no longer believed, as he and many other Sherpas did in the 1930s, that the primary reason the British wanted to get Sherpas to the summits of Himalayan peaks—beyond the obvious one of carrying loads—was to have witnesses for their achievements.

On the twenty-sixth of May, Dawa Namgyal and the leader, John Hunt, were also climbing high on the mountain, though they planned to carry loads only to Camp IX on the Southeast Ridge. They didn't quite reach their goal, and when they returned to the South Col, my father and Ed Hillary—who had just arrived on the South Col from lower down—went out to meet them. Hunt was having trouble with his closed-circuit oxygen system, and he collapsed for several minutes, completely exhausted. My father and Hillary helped him to his tent and gave him lemon juice, the Brits' staple beverage on Everest. Once Hunt and Dawa Namgyal were rested enough to speak, they described how they had reached 27,350 feet, about 200 feet below the site for Camp IX, and left the oxygen and supplies in the snow. My father brought Hunt some more lemon juice and was proud when Hunt told him that he would never forget his generosity.

Bourdillon and Evans were still high on the mountain, continuing upward. Their closed-circuit oxygen system was giving them problems, too, and gradually their pace slowed to a crawl. Then snow conditions worsened, and time ran out on them. They had no choice but to turn back, though they had reached the South Summit, the highest point to which humans had ever climbed. They had come within 280 vertical feet of the top.

Covered in snow and ice and in a state of near-collapse from exhaustion, Evans and Bourdillon arrived on the South Col. After they had relaxed and rehydrated, they answered all of the questions about the route put to them by my father and Hillary. For my father, their responses illustrated a common strength of mountaineers: their ability to share and to work as a team. Clearly, my father and Hillary would not have been standing on the South Col but for the sacrifice of these climbers and Sherpas who had forged the way.

Despite their defeat and disappointment, Evans and Bourdillon were not overly pessimistic about the obstacles higher up. Evans told my father that beyond the South Summit the route appeared long, steep, and possibly dangerous, but he was fairly confident that the one remaining section of ragged vertical rock could be overcome.

That night on the South Col the wind battered the British expedition's camp so ferociously that, in a hypoxic reverie, my father thought one of his dogs was attacking the tent, determined to rip it to shreds. Lying in his sleeping bag, he prayed for the wind to subside and the weather to improve.

The wind didn't diminish, forcing him and Hillary to spend a second night on the South Col. Wishing them luck and success, Hunt, Bourdillon, and Evans descended to ABC, leaving them on the South Col with Ang Nyima, Pemba, George Lowe, and Alf Gregory.

The five climbers lay in their tents for a second uncomfortable night, drinking large amounts of liquids and trying to keep warm, just as decades of climbers have since. Serenaded by the wind thrashing the walls of the tents, they forced themselves to eat a small amount of food.

I have taken dubious solace myself in the thought that for every person who has died on Everest, five have made the summit. Lying there in the darkness in 1953, however, my father was fully mindful that at that time, eighteen had died and none had made it.

I AROSE AT ten o'clock that evening and melted snow for tea, gagged down some food, and struggled into my down summit clothing. Despite the ordeal of performing even simple tasks at 26,000 feet, I felt I was working efficiently, as if it were coming to me by instinct. Again I checked my oxygen regulator and tank. None of us could afford to have problems with this critical life-line; oxygen system malfunctions had cost many strong climbers the summit—and some of them their lives.

The sky was clear and calm. I was ready. I sat for a moment, breathing deeply, praying to Miyolangsangma for extra strength.

Ed left Camp IV at 11:00 P.M. in order to get a head start, because he was climbing without bottled oxygen. At 11:30 P.M., David came by and rechecked the oxygen sets, then radioed Base Camp and told them we were departing and that all was in order. At Base Camp, Changba arose and walked out to the lhap-so and lit some boughs of juniper incense. He and the other Sherpas there would keep the juniper burning until we all returned to

Camp IV. David and Robert departed around midnight, along with Jangbu, Lhakpa, and Gombu, who was carrying the camera. Araceli, Dorje, and I left soon afterward, followed by Thillen and Muktu Lhakpa.

In darkness, we trudged across the plain of the South Col to the ice bulge, a tricky section of glare ice about one hundred meters across, like an ice rink tilted up at an angle. It usually has no fixed ropes, and our crampons barely bit—a dangerous situation when descending. From the ice bulge, a smooth, steep snowfield led to the base of the Triangular Face, where we clipped into the fixed rope left by the guided expeditions of two weeks earlier.

At extreme altitudes, physical performance decreases at an accelerating rate the higher one climbs. For the summit attempt, we had budgeted our oxygen to be used at the rate of three liters per minute, though I felt good enough to set my oxygen flow at half that rate. The extra oxygen would give me a margin of safety if I got into trouble.

Before we left camp, my stomach had been aching, and one bout of diarrhea had already struck. I now felt the pressure of another. Optimistically, I hoped the urge to crap might simply go away; sometimes such pressures abate for a while. Then I remembered Wongchu's high-altitude diarrhea story. He was in a doubly awkward place: if he didn't go soon he would crap in his pants, and if he did go he faced getting blown off the ridge. He said that he simply created a space there on the ridge to crap, and his feeling of relief afterward was so great that it gave him the boost of energy he had been missing for the past hour or two, and he shot up the mountain. I was in a relatively safe place and wasn't lagging behind, so I took the opportunity. Then I realized

I had no toilet paper. I asked every Sherpa if they had any. One of them gave me some wrapping paper.

It's a climb of about one thousand vertical feet up the fifty-degree snow slope of the Triangular Face, via couloirs and the Black Tower, to the Balcony. There the route meets the Southeast Ridge, at 27,600 feet. Below the Balcony there's only one short section of fixed rope and a lot of loose rock. If you fall, that's it. Your life depends on you, your crampons, and your ice ax.

My legs felt heavy from lack of sleep, and I had trouble with my gaiters, which were new and stiff but essential for keeping snow out of my boots. Placing each arduous step took five seconds—and that many full breaths. The summit is only a mile and a half from the South Col as the crow flies, but our speed averages out to a mere twelve feet—two body lengths—per minute. Babies crawl faster than that.

To make the tiring ascent manageable, I broke the day into segments, creating small objectives that would make up the whole. Above the South Col, I concentrated on the first goal: to reach the Southeast Ridge by dawn.

My visible world was limited to the cone of light shed by my headlamp, and the only sounds were my self-hypnotic recitation of mantras and the deep breathing echoing inside my oxygen mask. At first I had a problem with the mask, which was so large that I couldn't see my feet without twisting my head awkwardly. Fortunately, the oxygen bottle weighed only six pounds; I couldn't imagine carrying two twenty-pound bottles, as my father and the British and the Swiss had.

I wore thin polypropylene gloves—which I preferred because they gave me better control of my ice ax—and I now felt the cool touch of my mother's ivory rosary wrapped in coils around my wrist. On my other wrist was the Rolex watch that the Austrian adventurer Heinrich Harrer had given my father in memory of their times together in Lhasa in the 1940s. At the start of World War II, Harrer was captured by the British while climbing on Nanga Parbat, and was interred in a prison camp in northern India. He and another Austrian, Peter Aufschnaiter, escaped, and climbed over the Himalaya to Tibet, taking over a year to reach Lhasa. During my father's journey to Tibet with Professor Tucci, he ran into Harrer, and the two became friends. The watch had sat broken and idle for some years until I sent it to the Rolex company for repair. They fixed it and returned it to me free of charge, with a note stressing its historic value.

After climbing for about two hours, I glanced up and saw ahead of me what appeared to be colorful cloth material. At first I thought I had reached the Southeast Ridge and someone had set up a tent. Then my headlamp shone on a pair of climbing boots. They were connected to a corpse. It was Scott Fischer. He was sitting upright on the route, his upper body and face covered with snow. Another body, from years before, was lying nearby. Suddenly chilled, my heart racing, I chanted *Om Mane Padme Hum* several times and walked quickly around him, continuing on through the darkness and cold. I worked off my fear by climbing upward. And praying.

The higher I climbed, the more my heartbeats pulsed in my head, like an endless crescendo of lama's drums. I was constantly monitoring my body's functions and resources and watching the next six feet, placing my boots as solidly and efficiently as I could, anticipating the mini-surprises that the terrain always presents. If my foot slipped a few inches from where I had placed it, recovery would take half a dozen breaths. Where else would one expend that amount of energy in twenty hours? No one would hop onto an exercise machine for that long with no sleep, little food or water, and twenty pounds of gear and oxygen on his back. But they do it on Everest.

I caught up with Gombu, who seemed to be having trouble, and he told me he had vomited. I saw that the flow on his oxygen regulator was set at only half a liter per minute, so I cranked it up and helped him clear his mask.

Farther on, I reached the only resting point below the Southeast Ridge. Ed had created a depression in the snow on the steep slope, and others had sat and rested there—which is where I found Lhakpa Dorje, our climbing sirdar, who was carrying four bottles of oxygen. I was surprised to see that he wasn't breathing bottled oxygen himself, then realized that he had secretly planned to climb without it. Even more startling, he looked as if he was about to nod off to sleep. He was already very tired and clearly suffering some hypoxia.

I clapped my hands in front of his face, shook him, and pulled on his cheeks. He roused slightly and told me to go ahead, but I wanted to make sure he awoke fully. If he fell asleep, he would surely have tumbled forward into the Western Cwm. I sent him off ahead of me, then sat down for a moment myself. Again catching up with him, I goaded him upward, passing him only when I was certain he would reach the Southeast Ridge.

Surmounting a rocky area, I spotted some climbing equipment above me. This was the Balcony, the start of the Southeast Ridge, and I continued upward to the spot where David, Jangbu, Araceli, Robert, and Thillen were waiting. Thillen had the tripod, but Gombu was still well below us, climbing slowly with the camera. Meanwhile, Ed Viesturs hadn't waited for us; he had become cold and continued climbing upward.

David was as surprised as I to learn that Lhakpa Dorje was climbing without oxygen. Now our climbing sirdar would be unable to fully share the burden of carrying loads. Also, the camera hadn't arrived. I could feel David's frustration as we watched the gloriously textured sunrise disappear, as the sky grew brilliant.

He directed Jangbu, who was climbing strongly, to go down and retrieve the camera from Gombu. Jangbu swiftly descended nearly three hundred vertical feet—a significant elevation at this altitude.

The wait gave me a chance to rest and absorb one of the planet's most spectacular sunrises. The sun rose just behind Kangchenjunga, with Makalu to the southeast and Lhotse to our immediate south. Exhilarated at being high on the mountain, I watched the first glimmer on the horizon gradually grow brighter until it bathed the world in amber light.

I then gazed out over Khumbu, resting in the morning haze far below us, and spied the roof of the Tengboche monastery, the only visible sign of humans. Its placid form conjured up for me the sound of a monk blowing the morning conch shell from the courtyard cupola, the chanting of prayers, the rhythmic, haunting drumbeats, and anxious, high-pitched horns reverberating within the assembly hall.

In tracing the route we had come, I could see the difficulty my father and Raymond Lambert had faced in the spring of 1952. Immediately below the Balcony they had climbed to the east of our path and reached a dead end, forcing them to retrace their steps. They eventually found the line to the ridge that we use today.

SITTING ON THE Southeast Ridge, I never felt so alone and so at home at the same time. We were resting precisely on the small shelf where my father and Hillary had placed their last camp before the summit. I relived the story, imprinted in my mind, of their night here at Camp IX—their khaki-colored A-frame tent with oxygen bottles and supplies half-buried outside, and the two of them huddled inside.

George Lowe, Alf Gregory, and Ang Nyima had accompanied them here, taking the lead for much of the way, cutting steps with their ice axes. Toward midafternoon, just as all of them had grown weary, they reached the point a few hundred feet below the Balcony where Colonel Hunt and Dawa Namgyal had turned around. They had no choice but to pick up the food, tent, and oxygen tanks that had been dropped there and add them to their own loads. They continued upward carrying a staggering fifty to sixty pounds each.

At this small shelf, Hillary and my father said good-bye to Lowe, Gregory, and Ang Nyima—who had just enough time to reach the South Col before dark—and they began chipping away at the ice to make the site more level. Struggling with cold hands, they finally got their canvas tent erected just as darkness overtook them. They crawled in. Hillary had to balance on a narrow shelf about a foot higher than my father.

My father told me that while Hillary worked on preparing their oxygen systems, he fired up the tiny stove to melt snow. In need of rehydration, they drank coffee and lemon juice as fast as he could prepare it. They also ate biscuits, soup, sardines, and canned fruit. The fruit had frozen in the tin, and my father thawed it over the stove.

Leaving his clothes and boots on, my father crawled inside his sleeping bag. Hillary, to improve circulation in his feet, removed his boots and placed them next to his sleeping bag. They rolled over and leaned tightly against their respective sides of the canvas tent, using the weight of their bodies to further secure it against the tremendous gusts of wind that arose seemingly from nowhere and threatened, my father feared, to launch the tent off into space and down the Kangshung Face.

Surprisingly, my father was able to sleep, though he woke frequently. He was heartened and newly inspired when, shortly after midnight, the wind stopped altogether and they could hear only the sound of oxygen passing through their masks as they breathed. Here at the highest campsite in the world, Miyolangsangma was being kind to them.

Well before sunrise, my father again fired up the stove and melted snow for lemon juice and coffee, and they finished the food remaining from the night before. When they looked out from the tent, the sky was clear and calm, and faint light had appeared on the horizon. The valleys were still blanketed in darkness.

Hillary was alarmed to find that his boots had frozen stiff during the night and were as solid and immovable as cement. They spent an hour holding them over the stove, alternately scorching the leather and then working it vigorously. Hillary was concerned about the delay and afraid of frostbite. He didn't want to lose his toes, as Raymond Lambert had.

I could see them emerging from the tent. My father squinted far below toward the Tengboche monastery, sheltered in tranquil greenery, then pointed it out to Hillary. I turned also and could now pick out Tengboche's small gold spire in the gathering light, like an ethereal rocket poised for liftoff, and hear my father mouthing in unison with me, *Om Mane Padme Hum.* We stood there together, as close as we had ever been, and looked out and saw Everest's pyramidal shadow cast upon the western horizon, presiding over the misted valleys and lesser Himalayan peaks.

The next few hours would be the culmination of the 1953 British expedition, and its success or failure had been left entirely up to Hillary and Tenzing. They tied on their crampons, strapped on their forty-pound oxygen sets, and set off plodding upward.

I was not far behind.

JANGBU ARRIVED ON the Balcony for the second time, carrying the oversized camera. By now it had fully earned its nickname of "The Pig," descriptive of its large size and the prodigious amount of film it consumed. David and Robert set up the camera there on my father's tent site. They communicated in sign language, having lost their voices entirely. This happens frequently at high altitude from deeply inhaling cold, dry bottled oxygen, which contains no moisture.

To get the peak of Makalu into a shot he had envisioned, David motioned for Araceli and me to walk a bit off the route, toward the cornice of snow that hangs over the Kangshung Face and many thousands of feet of vertical drop. We were unroped, and Araceli generously let me go first to our turnaround point for the shot. When we turned and headed toward the camera, I was behind Araceli and obstructed by her, so David signaled for us to go back and redo it again—making it the highest "second take" in movie history. I was obliged to walk even closer to the cornice this time, and with each step I carefully checked the firmness of the snow with my ice ax.

Jangbu then took the camera and tied his own gear on top—at fifty pounds, an unheard-of load at that altitude—and continued up. Eventually, he handed the camera off to Thillen, until Thillen's strength began to flag higher on the mountain. Again Jangbu descended and ferried the camera upward.

The strength and stamina of Sherpas varies widely, even among those who are fit enough to carry loads above the South Col. Jangbu is in the exceptional category. I was touched when he told me that he had been fixated by my father's summit picture on the back of his fifth-grade social studies book. While walking the trail to school he would sing the song "Tenzing, Hero of Everest," which played on Radio Nepal. He, too, knew from a young age that he wanted to climb Everest, and I believe this early ambition contributed to his great strength at high altitudes. Jangbu is ten years younger than I am; he was born almost a quarter-century after the 1953 climb.

We plodded on toward the next landmark, the South Summit, 1,200 feet above us. Our route went to the right of the Southeast Ridge's rocky buttress, toward the East Face snow slopes, and much of it was in waist-deep snow. Ed was still ahead of us, breaking trail without bottled oxygen. Like Jangbu, the guy is a genuine force of nature.

Throughout the climb, I was enjoying the view and the exuberance of feeling my body in forward motion on a steep and exposed slope. At this altitude most climbers complain of being aware of little more than how much their head and body hurt. I set down my half-full oxygen bottle, which I could use on the return trip, and strapped on a full one. Another dose of energy surged through my body, and I felt as confident and strong as I ever have. Much of the time I didn't use oxygen at all, because I couldn't breathe comfortably through the mask and it fogged up my goggles. I probably could have climbed the mountain without it, but it wasn't a goal I had set for myself.

FROM THEIR HIGH camp on the Southeast Ridge, my father and Hillary set out upward. Hillary's boots were still stiff and his feet were cold, so my father led. They were climbing in radiant sunshine with little wind, a huge improvement over the bitter cold and gales that had slowed Raymond Lambert and my father a year earlier. Once Hillary's feet warmed, the two of them traded off leading, to share the work of breaking trail. In places, they were helped by Bourdillon's and Evans's footprints, though windblown snow had mostly filled them in and they had to kick or chop their own steps.

Near the top of the Southeast Ridge, they passed the point where my father and Lambert had turned back in the spring of 1952. At the South Summit they found the two bottles of oxygen that Bourdillon and Evans had left for them when they turned back, three days earlier. The gauges indicated that the bottles were full, so they could breathe a richer mixture from the bottles they were carrying, leaving the others for their descent.

THE EXPOSURE TO the east and west became more severe as we approached the South Summit, but my excitement at reaching that crux point in the climb motivated me to climb even harder. Then I encountered the same steep snow slope that had been so difficult for my father, and with every step I plunged into unstable snow nearly to my waist. Like him, I feared that as the angle steepened the hillside itself would slip away from beneath me and my safety would no longer be in my control. It was remarkable that my father and Hillary—and Ed Viesturs just ahead of us—were able to surmount this tiring section while breaking new trail. I stopped and turned up the oxygen flow on my tank to make sure I would be clear-headed, then took from my pocket some chaane, the blessed grains that Geshé Rimpoche had given me, and cast it in the area. This was surely the difficult section that Rimpoche had referred to in his divination. My legs were trembling, but I couldn't tell if it was from cold, exertion, or fear.

The rock section just below the South Summit again scared me. My heart pounded so hard that my eyeballs were throbbing in their sockets. We weren't roped, nor did we have the leisure to remove our crampons. A slip here on the smooth rock would lead to a fast and fatal slide down the Southwest Face.

When I finally rejoined the Southeast Ridge, I stepped atop the snowy dome of the South Summit and sat down, relieved. It was close to nine o'clock, the same time that my father had arrived here. We were pacing each other up the mountain.

From here I could see the summit ridge and the windswept overhang on the east side of the actual summit. I knew I would make it. Then I turned and looked into the depression on the far side of the South Summit, and I saw Rob Hall. He was in a sitting position, but leaning back, frozen. It looked as if he died in his sleep, and in a way he looked comfortable, dug into a nice corner, away from the wind, protected.

Many of the canisters abandoned on the South Summit would have had some oxygen remaining in them, and it was clear that Hall had been breathing from every oxygen bottle he could find. Now they were empty. Unable to get up or walk, Hall consigned himself to this snowy grave. Hall's wife, Jan, had asked that

David or Ed try to bring back something from his body, such as his ring, but both of them said that they couldn't steel themselves to do so. David even left Hall's ice ax behind.

What used to scare me most about Everest was the risk of freezing, of being helpless, like Rob Hall and Beck Weathers—scared of reaching the point when the lassitude and resignation of hypothermia take over, the course that leads quickly and quietly to death. The more gruesome part of seeing Hall was imagining what it would be like to speak to Soyang for the last time from this place; it made me sad for his wife. I also wondered about my cousin Lobsang Tsering. He had joined an Australian expedition, and he reached the summit on the record-setting day in 1993 when thirty-seven people made the top. Then he was lost. His body was later found below the Balcony, but it was difficult to determine what had killed him.

I looked up at the knife-edge ridge immediately beyond the South Summit, the traverse to the Hillary Step. To the east, cornices of snow hung out over the ten-thousand-foot drop to the Kangshung Glacier. To the southwest, the mountain fell away to the Western Cwm, eight thousand feet below, where we could now see the tiny tents of Advance Base Camp. The only possible route was atop a narrow, twisting line between the cornice and a sheer drop.

Bourdillon and Evans had warned my father and Hillary that this tricky traverse would be followed by a thirty-foot-high rocky pitch that is now called the Hillary Step. But at the South Summit my father's and Hillary's progress got a dual boost: the snow became firm for them, and they were able to dump two of their twenty-pound oxygen tanks.

Araceli and I passed Hall's body and headed one hundred meters along the undulating ridge to the base of the Hillary Step. The route isn't technically difficult, but as tired and hypoxic as we were at this altitude, we had to concentrate. Burying my ice ax just a couple of feet to my right, closer to the lip of the cornice, I withdrew it and looked through the hole and down onto the Kangshung Glacier, thousands of feet below. I would not have wanted to stand any closer to the edge, which could break off at any moment.

My father and Hillary took turns belaying each other across this section.

DRAPED DOWN THE rocks of the Hillary Step is a tangle of old ropes, most of which are untrustworthy and only make the climb more awkward. If anyone fell here, it would be from tripping on a rope. I could have free-climbed it, without being attached to a fixed rope, by simply grabbing a handful of lines and hauling myself up, though that's not exactly a sporting way to climb. Only one person can climb the Hillary Step at a time, as the climbers on May 10 had become uncomfortably aware.

A couple of veteran climbing Sherpas I spoke with referred to the Hillary Step as "Tenzing's Back," suggesting that Hillary might have started to lead up the section, but when he was foiled by the first move, he kneeled on my father's back and shoulders to get a boost. My father didn't tell me exactly how they made their first move here, and to climb this way would seem technically awkward and unnecessary. If this is what happened, however, the favor would have been returned by Hillary when he belayed my father, who followed him up the Step. They both jammed and wriggled their way to the top, gaining purchase by pressing their feet against the narrow gap between the rock and the inner side of the adjoining cornice.

For me the climb was fairly straightforward, perhaps because I knew I was walking on Tenzing's Back. He had hunched over for me, as he had so generously for hundreds of others ahead of me, regardless of nationality, inviting us upward to the final pitch. I had found my father's way. It felt like my way, and I was gaining strength as I gained altitude. We were sharing breaths from what he referred to as his "third lung," the extra reservoir of air that gave him more stamina even as he climbed higher on the mountain.

From the top of the Hillary Step, it's a long half-hour climb to the summit. The route flattens, though the precipitous drop on either side is a constant presence. A small fixed line follows part of the route, but none of us trusted it. I did slide one hand along it, however, for balance and psychological support. On the last stretch I took off my goggles because of the fogging caused by the oxygen, and every two minutes the oxygen mask itself would freeze up from condensation, creating icicles where the mask joins the supply tube. Despite the annoyances, I felt a glorious sense of peace.

Already on the summit for more than an hour, waiting for the camera, Ed had become cold and needed to get moving. Down was the only direction left for him to go. He passed Araceli and me as we approached the top, raised a thumb, and said, "You're there, man—this is it!" Then he gave me a hug.

For years my sleep had been filled with dreams of Chomolungma, all of them vivid, confident dreams. In them I was always with my father and older, more accomplished Sherpas. I would gradually gain altitude, finally be able to see the summit, then, just before reaching the top, I'd wake up.

Now I would see the ending, the part that even my dreams hadn't granted me. I began passing the "snowy humps" that my father referred to, consecutive waves of snow that occupied the upper horizon. Each appeared to be the summit, but as I reached them they revealed yet another hump farther on. Then, just as I was becoming used to the disappointment, the summit nearly surprised me.

Next to the survey mirrors and beneath a nest of kata scarves,
I placed photos of my mother and father and of His Holiness
the Dalai Lama. Then I prayed.

9

MEETING
MY FATHER

9

MEETING
MY FATHER

I could go no higher. Suddenly, I was looking down onto the brown ridges and rolling plains of Tibet. I caught my breath, but the panorama before me only seemed to take it away. David stood some feet from me, waving his hand to say, "Hey, over here." Dorje, Thillen, and Araceli were there also, smiling and animated. I went over to join them. Others of our team were approaching the summit, not far behind.

"Hey, Jam, you made it," David said hoarsely. We hugged.

"Thanks, David, for this opportunity," I told him. Then I cried briefly. I looked at my watch and it was only 11:30 A.M. We were ahead of schedule, despite the time we had spent filming and waiting for the camera.

It was clear in all directions, from the Tibetan plateau in the north to the blue pastel foothills of the south, merging with the Gangetic plain of India. From this perch I could see the white and brown obelisk of Makalu to the southeast, Lhotse and Lhotse Shar directly to the south, Cho Oyu nearby in the west, Manaslu, Annapurna, and Dhaulagiri in the distance to the west, and Kangchenjunga eighty miles to the east. With Everest, here were nine of the world's ten highest peaks. If not for the curvature of the earth and a bit of haze, I probably could have seen even more of the Great Himalayan Range. It was an unusual sensation to be looking downward at Himalayan giants that I had spent my life looking up at.

When the others arrived, nine of us stood on top together— Robert, David, Araceli, myself, Lhakpa, Muktu Lhakpa, Thillen, Dorje, and climbing sirdar Lhakpa Dorje. All of us were exuberant. David handed me the radio, and I spoke to Base Camp. "We're here—we're on the top, and it's great," I stammered. I wanted to say something more profound, something poetic maybe, but semi-hypoxia was retarding my ability to articulate. Base Camp responded gamely: "Great job! Congratulations!" Their excitement infected us as well.

I asked Paula to patch me through to my wife in Kathmandu. When Soyang came on the line, I said, "I'm at the top." She was caught by surprise, having assumed we were still at Camp II or III. "If my mother and I had known you were going for the summit today, we would have done more rituals and said more prayers," she said. Her surprise turned into cautious joy. "So now you don't have to go climb it again," she said with admonition. "Make sure you get down safely." My brother Dhamey was with her, and Soyang later said that he was tempted to announce the news to everyone. He called only my brother Norbu and sister Deki, however, not wanting to attract nerpa, the unfavorable influences of wandering ghosts, especially while I was still high on the mountain.

Once the camera arrived, it took some time for Robert and David to set it up. They had to feed the film through the gate with bare hands in order to align it properly and ensure that the opening was unobstructed by hairs or other minuscule objects, which would be magnified a thousand times on the screen, ruining the shot. "We have only one roll of film left," David said, "so we had better get it right." The camera worked perfectly, and we shot all ninety seconds of that one six-pound roll.

More acutely than before, I sensed my father's presence. He

was watching me, encouraging me, supporting me, proud of me. I was sharing with him the view that he and Hillary were the first people on earth to experience. I recalled his telling me how captivated Grandmother Kinzom was when he told her that while standing on this spot he could see both the Rongbuk and Tengboche monasteries—located on opposite sides of the Himalaya, many days' walk from each other.

I looked down on the ruins of the Rongbuk monastery, below the terminus of the Rongbuk Glacier, and panned over to the high pastures of Tibet's Kharta Valley, where my father chased yaks as a very young boy. Then I turned back and I saw him—my father.

He was right there behind me, off to the side where a patch of rocks meets the snow. Dressed in his 1953 feather jacket and woolens, his oxygen mask was pulled to one side and his goggles were lifted to his forehead. His face was shining, beaming—was he looking at me? Could he see me standing there, triumphant and exhausted, as he too had been? Or was it only I who could feel his presence?

I caught myself before I spoke aloud to him. Then I spoke to him anyway.

Both of our dreams have come true.

In clear tones I heard him respond, calmly, *Jamling, you didn't have to come so far; you didn't have to climb this mountain in order to speak with me and to be with me.*

He then told me he was pleased that a son of his had climbed Everest, and that he always knew that if anyone could do it, it was me. Later my uncle Tenzing Lotay told me that this was precisely the wish my father had shared with him in confidence years before. My uncle also told me of my father's conviction that I would have to make my own footsteps up the mountain.

I had done it on my own, but my father had been with me all along—ahead of me clearing the way, behind me with encouragement, and beside me with cautions of vigilance. Standing there on the summit, I felt I was touching his soul, his mind, his destiny, and his dreams. And I had received his blessings and approval. Perhaps I didn't really need to come so far to be near him and to understand him. But I had to make the trip in order to learn that his blessing was there all along.

The mountain itself came alive for me, as it had for him. He had waited and worked all his life for this moment, and the mountain rewarded him for his effort and patience: it changed from a lifeless, uncaring, and dangerous mound of rock—a rock that had with indifference taken the lives of so many—into a warm, friendly, and life-sustaining being. Miyolangsangma. I felt her embracing both of us.

In a similar way, my father had sensed his Swiss friend Raymond Lambert standing on the summit with him, and indeed he was wearing the red scarf that Lambert had given him. His boots were Swiss, too. His socks had been knitted by Ang Lhamu, and his balaclava had been given to him by Earl Denman in 1947, the year they made an attempt together from the north side.

Edmund Hillary took three photos of my father lifting his ice ax on the summit. Even a silhouette of the more famous of these photos is easily recognizable a half-century later. Then my father scooped out a depression in the snow and into it placed the red and blue stub of a pencil that his daughter, Nima, had given him, along with a small package of sweets—a traditional offering to loved ones. Hillary handed him a small black-and-white cloth cat that Colonel Hunt had given him for good luck, and my father placed that beside them. Finally, he recited a prayer and gave thanks to Miyolangsangma. He had reached the summit, finally, on his lucky seventh attempt.

On the summit I placed a picture of my parents neatly framed in a red vinyl wallet, a photograph of His Holiness the Dalai Lama, a kata scarf, and—as my father had done—a piece of candy as a form of offering. I also left an elephant-shaped rattle that my infant daughter had selected from a pile of toys, perhaps significant in light of Trulshig Rimpoche's translation of Cho-molungma: Unshakable Good Elephant Woman.

Araceli took out the *senyera,* the Catalan flag, while David and I photographed her. Over the radio she spoke with a reporter from Catalan television. Then I stepped up and assumed my father's historic pose for some photos. My pose, I saw later, was not identical to my father's, but its mirror image. My climb was similarly a reflection of my father's, reflecting his life and his values, yet distinctly my own.

My father knew before he ever set foot on the mountain that it had to be approached with respect and with love, the way a child climbs into the lap of its mother. Anyone who attacks the peak with aggression, like a soldier doing battle, will lose. Thus, there is but one appropriate response upon reaching the summit of Miyolangsangma's mountain: to express gratitude. Like my father, I placed my hands together and said *thu-chi-chay*—thank you—to Miyolangsangma and the mountain.

Then for several minutes I recited a prayer of refuge, brack-eted on each end with mantras.

Om Mane Padme Hum

Lama la gyapsong ché
Sanggye la gyapsong ché

Chö la gyapsong ché
Gedun la gyapsong ché
Om taare tutare ture svaha.

(Hail to the Jewel in the Lotus, I take refuge in the Guru, the Buddha, the
Dharma, and the Dharma Community, and ask the goddess Tara for
blessings for the enlightenment of all sentient beings.)

I opened the packet of blessed relics from high Tibetan lamas
that Geshé Rimpoche had given me and spread a handful around
the summit. Then I cast some chaane in the four cardinal directions
and unfurled the long prayer flag. I fastened one end of it to the
katas and other prayer flags that were draped on the survey stake
that had been anchored on the summit by a research expedition.

I SPENT NEARLY two hours on the summit before heading
down the mountain, feeling as lucky and satisfied as I know my
father had felt.

The highest bare ground on the mountain is located on a
rocky shelf about one hundred feet from the top. My father had
wondered idly whether anyone would ever pitch a tent and sleep
at this place, virtually on the summit. In fact, forty-six years later
Babu Chiri Sherpa did precisely that, spending nearly twenty
hours on the roof of the world, without supplemental oxygen.

Just after we left the top, we passed Göran Kropp and Jésus
Martinez on the summit ridge, and then "Ten Times" Ang
Rita—on his tenth ascent—who was climbing almost casually,
without bottled oxygen. I was descending a short distance
behind Araceli, at the same pace. Then below the South Summit,
I abruptly caught up with her. She was wobbling and unsteady,

and I shouted at her to stop. When I reached her, she had sat down and looked as if she didn't feel like going on, as if she had given up. I checked her oxygen tank. She hadn't been aware that it was empty. I pulled a half-full tank from my pack, cranked the flow to three liters per second, and gave it to her. She revived almost immediately, and we picked up speed quickly. For safety, we stayed together for the rest of the descent.

In the couloirs above the South Col, we sit-glissaded down several pitches of hard snow, gripping our ice axes in case we lost control and needed them for self-arrest. When we reached the level saddle of the Col, I was grateful that it was still light out. We walked slowly back to the tents. I drank some tea, took photos, and sat around feeling relaxed and happy, though utterly exhausted. Soon we were in our tents and asleep. We had been climbing above 26,000 feet for more than sixteen hours.

I awoke an hour or two later, unable to open my eyes—they were burning torturously, as if someone had thrown sand in them. I was snow-blind. Ultraviolet radiation from the sun, especially when reflected from bright snow at that altitude, can seriously irritate the cornea. It is extremely painful, but fortunately temporary. On an earlier climb in the Himalaya, my father lost his glacier goggles and suffered snow-blindness, and after that time he always carried two pairs of dark glasses, as I had. My oxygen mask had fogged my goggles, however, forcing me to remove them briefly on the final stretch to the summit.

Ed gave me some antibiotic eyedrops, which Sumiyo administered. Mainly, I was worried about being blind in the morning: if I were unable to descend, I would be in grave danger. Muktu Lhakpa had also been hit by snow-blindness, which came upon him at the South Summit. When he had arrived on the South

Col, crying and wailing, I never imagined that I would soon be sharing his experience.

In the morning I was still virtually blind. I had no choice but to embark on what became the most frightening part of the climb for me. I called Dorje and Thillen and asked if they could descend with me. They had their own gear to carry down but could walk with me in between them. I prepared everything with my eyes closed.

Dorje walked immediately in front of me, and we began our descent to Camp III. On the Lhotse Face, I could steal a quick and terribly painful look above me for anything dangerous, then similarly get a still-picture glimpse of the terrain below before taking several steps with my eyes closed. Then I'd have to stop and wait for nearly a minute for the pain to subside. Over and over I repeated the process, all the while praying and thinking of my father. And of Beck Weathers. I could begin to comprehend his agony, though I was suffering only a fraction of his ill fortune.

At Camp III, Kropp and Martinez, the Swede and Spaniard who were on the summit with us, gave me some juice, the fuel I needed to keep going. Martinez also gave me some extremely dark glacier goggles, which seemed to help.

It was only when I reached the bergschrund above Camp II that I became confident I would make it. I staggered into ABC and was grateful when the kitchen crew brought me tea and food. I ate some shyakpa Sherpa stew, and even though my eyes were in tremendous pain, I felt happy and safe.

Before reaching ABC, I had passed Ian Woodall and Bruce Herrod, the leader and photographer for the South African team, who were heading up. Woodall said nothing as he went by—rude as usual. Herrod was a gentleman, by contrast, and I had gotten on well with him at Base Camp. He said, "Congrats," and I thanked him.

The next morning at ABC I was fine, thankfully, but I still used two pairs of goggles. We decided to spend an extra day at ABC to complete some filming, pack up the camp, and clean the area. Rather than race down the mountain, as if escaping from it, the extra day helped us gather our thoughts in a relaxing limbo between the mountain and the workaday world of Base Camp.

Descending from ABC, we shared equal loads, eighty to one hundred pounds each. The late spring melting made the crossing of the longest ladder in the Icefall a dicey stunt, and David couldn't resist filming Araceli and me there. Wearing our full packs, we descended and then turned around and crossed the ladders again in an uphill direction.

ARRIVING AT BASE Camp was glorious. Finally, relief and celebration. We toasted with bottles of Coca-Cola and beer. I felt saturated with warmth, and some of the climbers and Base Camp staff were shedding tears of joy.

I quickly ducked away from the group of well-wishers and walked over to the lhap-so. Jangbu was there already, praying. I removed the sungwa amulet that Geshé Rimpoche had given me and placed it on one of the slate shelves that form the altar at the base of the lhap-so. Then I stepped back next to Jangbu. I tried to let all extraneous thoughts dissolve, and fixed Miyolangsangma and the protective and tutelary deities in my heart. I offered as sincere a measure of thanks as I have ever summoned, a level of gratitude that I vowed would stay with me forever. I can still feel that gratitude now. Miyolangsangma had allowed us to climb her. She had granted us safe passage.

For Araceli, the honor heaped upon her in Spain and Catalonia as the first Spanish woman to reach the summit was merely a by-product of the climb. She had joined us on Everest for the personal challenge and the joy of climbing. Nonetheless, I knew she would delight in the attention and celebrate wildly when she returned to Barcelona. The Catalans are known for their appetite for food, drink, and partying, and her parents run a gourmet restaurant. At Base Camp she quickly recovered her youthful, refreshed demeanor and looked as if she had never left level ground.

We stayed at Base Camp a couple of days for filming and packing up. On the twenty-ninth of May, the forty-third anniversary of my father's climb, we opened the remaining bottles of wine and drank abundantly, and Robert and I shared cigarettes. The tarpaulin roof of the kitchen was removed, signaling the end of the season for us. We felt like teenagers busting out of high school on the last day of the year.

Before departing, we gathered at the lhap-so to light juniper incense for the last time. Jangbu lowered the tharshing prayer flag pole, while a former monk read a prayer. For a long time I stood and prayed, this time partly for Bruce Herrod, the friendliest member of the South African team. We had just heard news that had quickly dampened our celebration: Herrod had apparently died on the mountain, two days after our ascent, on May 25. He had reached the summit behind two of his team members, at the startling time of 5:00 P.M., and never returned to the South Col.

Other than those on his own team, the IMAX team climbers were the last to see Herrod alive, when we passed him and Ian Woodall near the Yellow Band. We had also passed them two days before our own summit push, on the twenty-first, as we were heading up and the South African members were heading down.

At the time, we wondered why they were descending. Woodall and teammate Cathy Dowd said they were in poor shape and were low on supplemental oxygen. Herrod was in fine form, however, and I keep thinking that if he had turned around and tagged along with our team, he could have easily made it to the summit with us and returned safely. On the day when he reached the top, late in the afternoon, he was apparently in much poorer condition, which was ironic considering that Herrod was clearly a stronger climber than Woodall. His was the eleventh but not the final death of the 1996 season.

At Base Camp I didn't see anyone congratulating the South Africans for reaching the top. I feel that Ian Woodall's lack of experience was a contributing factor in Herrod's death. On our team, for example, Breashears would never have allowed a climber to go off alone, without a Sherpa, and well beyond a safe turnaround time. Woodall didn't seem to have learned anything from the earlier tragic events, which he hadn't paid much attention to anyway. The following year Anatoli Boukreev would encounter Herrod's body dangling from a rope at the bottom of the Hillary Step, with no indication as to how he fell—perhaps from being caught in the tangle of old ropes, the hazard I had feared most when on the Hillary Step myself.

Three weeks later that 1997 season, Pete Athans (climbing with David Breashears on David's fourth and Pete's fifth Everest ascents) retrieved Herrod's camera and then cut him from the rope. The film was developed, and clearly visible in Herrod's self-portrait on the summit, taken as he crouched alone in the approaching darkness, are the pictures of my father and mother and His Holiness the Dalai Lama that I had placed there two days earlier.

◆————————◆

WALKING OUT DOWN-VALLEY the other Sherpas and I were greeted by villagers with kata scarves who dragged us into their homes for chang and beer. We were properly drunk by the time we reached Pangboche, where a relative of mine begged us to spend the night. We carried onward, however, and well after dark reached Dewoche and joined the rest of the team. A similar reception continued through the next day.

In 1953 the British expedition faced a return march to Kathmandu of three weeks. We had to walk only two days to catch an hour-long helicopter flight from the Syangboche airstrip above Namche Bazaar. The monsoon had arrived, however, and we were stuck in cloudy weather at Syangboche for four days. Eager to greet us, Soyang and my in-laws brought fresh bread and fruit to the airport in Kathmandu each morning, and each day they returned to their house without me.

I felt that I was practically home as soon as I heard the Russian Mi-17 helicopter coming into the airstrip. We gratefully threw our bags in. I heaved a sigh of relief.

In Kathmandu a small crowd of reporters and friends met us, along with Soyang and her parents. I hugged our team members, who went off to the Hotel Yak and Yeti. We had become family, and I felt uncomfortable leaving them, as if returning to normal life would be disorienting without the camaraderie and network of support we had developed.

At Soyang's family house, I went immediately to the prayer room. Alone in the quiet, I did some prostrations and prayed. Miyolangsangma had been kind to us, and I thanked her again. I then stepped out of the room, slipped on my sandals, and renewed my promise to Soyang that this would be the last high Himalayan peak that I would attempt to climb.

◆————————◆

ON THE MORNING OF JUNE 2, 1953, three days after my father and Hillary reached the top, All India Radio announced that Great Britain's attempt had failed—likely referring to Evans's and Bourdillon's aborted try for the top. But James Morris, the *London Times* reporter who was attached to the expedition, had descended from Advance Base Camp at a virtual run. To get the news scoop to England before the rest of the world heard it, he sent the report in prearranged code through the police radio in Namche Bazaar to the British embassy in Kathmandu. From Kathmandu, Ambassador Summerhayes promptly relayed the message to London, then reportedly waited fifteen hours before releasing the news to the other press agencies in Kathmandu. This drew some criticism that he had used his diplomatic position in the agency of a private newspaper. The king of Nepal was also somewhat tardily informed, but, luckily for British diplomacy, His Majesty had not previously heard the news from another source, and didn't appear bothered.

In Darjeeling, the people of the city had resigned themselves to defeat. They patiently awaited news that the expedition would be returning to Kathmandu. My stepmother Ang Lhamu was relieved that Tenzing would finally be off the mountain—for the last time, she hoped.

Then late that night, June 2, the team's and Hillary's and my father's success was finally announced on the radio. My father's friend Mitra Babu heard it, and he rushed over to the family home in Toong Soong Busti and awoke Ang Lhamu. Others had heard, too. Lights came on, dogs barked, a clamor grew around the neighborhood, and relatives and friends quickly converged on their modest tin-roofed house. The town soon erupted in spontaneous celebration, and a school holiday was called for the following day. Pictures of Tenzing were plastered all over town, and government officials paid respectful visits to Ang Lhamu.

MY FATHER STAYED only one night at Base Camp on his way off the mountain, and in a single day he walked and jogged thirty-five miles down-valley to his home village of Thame to see his mother, Grandmother Kinzom. She was overjoyed to see him and pleased with his success. Then she looked him in the eyes—I'm certain with the look of loving seriousness that Soyang gave me—and said, "So now you don't have to climb it again." That's precisely what Soyang said to me over the radio when I was on the summit.

Even in the primitive communication era of 1953, my father received a cable from Sir Winston Churchill at Tengboche, and he was flooded with messages and greetings from then on. He and Hillary assumed that few people outside the circle of mountaineering enthusiasts would take notice of their experiences on Everest. Instead, the entire world quickly became spellbound by their victory. The public would not be so obsessed with Everest again until our season of 1996, when it was mainly the tragedy, not the triumph, that captivated the media.

I asked myself, as my father had of himself in the midst of some postpartum sadness following his climb, "Why, at long last, would Miyolangsangma allow a human to reach her summit? And why was I the one chosen to do so?" Chatral Rimpoche had told me that my father's success was not the result of prayer and practice when he was a monk, for he wasn't particularly pious, but it was clearly a product of the law of cause and effect, the fruitful ripening of merit he had earned in past lives.

Rimpoche added that part of my own success was due to the continued karmic effects of that substantial merit.

Numerous plans and counterplans were developed for my father even before the team returned to Kathmandu. Mitra Babu asked a poet named Dharma Raj Thapa to compose a sentimental song in Nepali with lyrics about my father and the mountain ("Our Tenzing Sherpa climbed to the top of the Himalay / He comforted Hillary and showed him the way / He must have slept at night lying on bare snow / While the iridescent Impeyan pheasant spread its wings in respectful show / This Son of the Himals has made proud Shiva's wives / People of the world know he'll have many long and favorable lives. . . ."). The tune was promptly aired on the radio throughout Nepal, India, and Tibet, and was soon hummed and sung by villagers across the Himalaya.

Now that the Nepalese had a new hero, they wanted a name for the world's highest peak, too. The mountain carried its traditional Tibetan/Sherpa name—Chomolungma—and since the 1850s it had also borne the English name of Everest. (I have heard that Sir George Everest pronounced his name with a long first vowel, as in "evening.") Historically, Everest the mountain held no particular religious significance for most Nepalese, so they selected "Sagarmatha" ("Brow of the Sky"), a name that had been proposed in the 1930s by the historian Baburam Acharya. Not many people realize that this title is a relatively recent patriotic invention.

It was after Everest that the real difficulties began for my father, trials much harder than the climb itself, he said. Politicians, bureaucrats, patriots, and the press in Nepal and India wanted him to make statements about the mountain, his nationality, and national politics. Before they were even off the mountain, Major Wylie had cautioned him that this would happen and had coached him on how to respond. My father spoke very little, but he found that people were quite capable of putting words in his mouth for him.

The politics began in full force at a town well outside of Kathmandu. A boisterous crowd of journalists and curious Nepalese nearly separated my father from his team. None of them wanted to hear about the climb or events on the mountain; they simply wanted him to say that he had reached the top ahead of Hillary and that he was Nepalese, not Indian. And while he was at it, what differences did he have with the British? He simply kept repeating that he, Hillary, the British, and the Sherpas should all be regarded as equal members of the expedition, and that they all deserved to share equally in the accomplishment. Continually, he attempted to remind them of the crucial role played by the other Sherpas. But Tenzing was the only hero who interested them.

A mild air of antagonism welled up around the British, which caught them off guard. At the roadhead town of Banepa, Hillary and Hunt were stuffed into the back of a jeep. Knowing how Westerners get nervous in the midst of teeming, excited crowds in foreign countries, I can understand why they would have shoved back vigorously at the masses trying to clamber onto the vehicle. I probably would have, too.

My father, meanwhile, was taken to the front of the jeep and propped up on the seats in a valiant stance, his upper body projecting through the open roof. Throngs of bystanders cast vermilion powder and flowers on the passengers and vehicle, and chanting rose up along the way of *Tenzing zindabad!* ("Long live Tenzing!"). They passed beneath flower-decked bamboo arches that spanned the road, some of which were wrapped in paper and painted with scenes—mostly of a triumphant Tenzing at the crest with a rope tied to his waist that led down one of the supports to a sprawling Caucasian figure, near ground level.

After the months of isolation on the mountain, the noise and crowding and airborne offerings were dreamlike for my father but stressful. He told me that he honestly would have preferred to return from Everest as another anonymous climber. He was embarrassed by the fuss the Nepalese made over him, the ambivalence they showed to the other Sherpas, and the indifferent reception they accorded the British.

On the road to Kathmandu, he made what he admitted was a foolish mistake. Even though he was illiterate at the time, a group of journalists or politicians (he didn't know which) pressured him into signing a statement that he had reached the summit before Hillary. This only exacerbated the nationalistic fervor among some Nepalese, and understandably irritated the British.

Ang Lhamu and my half-sisters, Pem Pem and Nima, had arrived in Kathmandu from Darjeeling, and they went out to greet him about three miles from the city. They embraced joyously. Ang Lhamu placed a silk kata around his neck (he was still wearing the red scarf that Raymond Lambert had given him), and the girls presented him with the flower garlands they had made for him. Then they nearly lost him in the crowd.

My father, his family, Colonel Hunt, and Edmund Hillary were transferred to a horse-drawn coach that was sent by King Tribhuvan, and it spirited them into the tiny capital city. My father, exhausted and overwhelmed, placed his hands together in salutation to all the admirers.

In Kathmandu they were taken directly to the Royal Palace, where the king awarded my father the Nepal Star medal, the highest possible distinction for a civilian, and bestowed other medals on Hillary and Hunt. All of them were still clad in their walking shorts and battered shoes; one of the Brits was in pajamas, the loose attire he had preferred for trekking in the heat, and he stood discreetly behind the others.

My father told His Majesty that he was grateful for the women who got him to Chomolungma's summit, referring to Ang Lhamu and the girls especially, but also of course to the goddess Miyolangsangma.

THE QUESTION OF WHO first stepped on Everest's summit has plagued my father and Edmund Hillary—and the spirit of the mountain—ever since the press converged on them during their return march. In Kathmandu, much of the Nepalese public and press categorically declared that Tenzing must have reached the top first, even if only inches or seconds ahead of Hillary. Others said that Hillary was first, or that only one of them had made it, or that neither of them had, or that one had dragged the other. The truth, it seemed, didn't matter, and my father was ashamed that Everest had been reduced to the level of nationalistic politics.

It was an unstable time in Nepalese politics to begin with. The hundred-year-old Rana regime, the ruling oligarchy, had been vanquished, and yet the multiparty democracy promised by King Tribhuvan hadn't exactly arrived. This left the nascent political parties vying with each other for power at the same time that anti-Indian sentiment was growing. Nepal had stepped out of isolation only three short years prior to 1953, and the country earnestly wanted a powerful icon to accompany the independent identity they were struggling to portray to the larger world.

In Kathmandu, emotions and exaggerations spread like a virus, aided by a small but feisty press. Some felt snubbed when it was believed that the original messages of felicitation sent by the Queen of England and the Duke of Edinburgh were sent only to the British. In fact, although the messages were delivered through the embassy, they were addressed to all members of the expedition. Then, when my father turned down an invitation to a reception at the British Embassy (for reasons that had nothing to do with the expedition), it only added more grist to the rumor mill.

Colonel Hunt reached a boiling point. At a press conference in Kathmandu where my father was being built up as a hero, Hunt stated that, far from being a hero, my father was simply an aide, that he had little technical mountaineering skill, and that Hillary had led all but a small part of the climb above 28,000 feet.

Fortunately for everyone, Hunt later retracted his statement, and my father withdrew his own, too, the one he had signed during the march out saying that he had reached the top first. To settle the issue—and everyone's nerves—my father and Hillary convened in the Prime Minister's office and signed a joint statement saying that they had reached the top "almost together."

This only fueled more speculation, however, as people stumbled over the word *almost*, demanding to know what it meant. It mattered little that the annals of mountaineering do not distinguish between members of the same rope team who arrive together on a summit, just as we don't differentiate the arrival times of passengers sitting in the front of an airliner from those sitting in the rear.

In his autobiography, my father admitted that Hillary reached the top a few seconds ahead of him. Years later, my father told me that he made this concession in the hope of finally ridding himself of the interminable questions, and to relieve the mountain and mountaineering from a growing political legacy. My father deserves credit for his public admission, for he would happily grant the summit to his friend and companion Hillary in order to resolve the issue. It was his final offering of respect for a mountain that he knew could never be conquered. Indeed, to claim that one had conquered it would be arrogant, if not sacrilegious. Humans are granted no more than an audience with Everest's summit, and then only rarely and for brief moments.

Indeed, the lamas counsel us to behave like the saintly Bodhisattvas: in keeping with the Bodhisattva vow of dedicating any merit accrued to the enlightenment of all sentient beings, we should offer victory and wealth to others and take loss and defeat for ourselves. My father was not a zealous Buddhist, but I believe his actions in daily life reflected these principles.

No one disputes that my father and Hillary were within a few feet of each other as they approached the summit. I am certain that my father had no thought of pushing Hillary aside and sprinting for the top to claim it as some sort of prize. I don't believe that Hillary did either. Both of them knew that two climbers roped together on a mountain are an extension of each other. On summit day they became one—a blend of Hillary's drive and technical skills and my father's spirit, tenacity, and experience. In effect, their complementary qualities merged into a single climber.

Nonetheless, the question of who was first didn't abate, and after my father's death people now turn to my siblings and me for a response. I may have been anticipating these queries when, a year before he died, I posed the question to him myself.

"Who was really first?" I asked. I was twenty years old, and it seemed funny to me at the time that I hadn't questioned him sooner.

"We climbed as a team, Jamling. We couldn't have made it without each other."

For me, that settled the issue, and I pressed him no further. If the exact chronology of summit day is ever clearly determined, it will provide neither Hillary nor my father with more status or power, nor take anything from either of them. Nothing is at stake here.

As for the ancient prophecy that a Himalayan Buddhist would be the first to reach the top: if one assumes Hillary preceded my father by some seconds, devout Sherpas are little bothered, for we have a well-developed sense of the figurative. Prophecies, however accurate, don't tend to dwell on details of a few feet or a few moments. Indeed, their metaphorical wording seems designed to confound the literal minded.

In the larger picture, the more people argue over this invented and trivial issue, the more they forget the others who were on the mountain before my father and Hillary—the Sherpas and climbers whose backs they basically climbed on to get there. Even before the 1953 climb, Colonel Hunt reiterated that the triumph of the first ascent party would have to be shared by all those who had preceded them, especially those who had died.

The Swiss in particular contributed to the British expedition's success. Aware that the Swiss had left some full oxygen bottles on the mountain, the British had regulators made to fit those bottles. They also consumed small amounts of food left by the Swiss on the South Col. But learning details of the mountain gleaned by the Swiss over two seasons was certainly of greater value to them, and much of that knowledge was conveyed to the British by my father. In 1953, the entire route above Base Camp was new to Hillary. My father had been above the South Col, on the Nepal side of the mountain, twice before, and he had reached within a thousand feet of the summit.

Yes, there were some personal differences in 1953, compounded by diverging national cultures. In the confusion that followed the expedition's return to Kathmandu, mistakes were made, and I may never be certain, in every case, where blame and acclaim should be conferred. Mostly, I feel empathy when I picture this international group of mountaineers, exhausted and homesick, being caught by surprise without a road map for handling the making of history. Along the way, they tumbled into a boiling, lumpy stew containing the vestiges of British colonialism, reawakened Nepalese nationalism, and an avaricious press.

Our Buddhist training, when applied, helps guide us through challenges such as these. It teaches us that egotism and arrogance are misguided, for it demonstrates that all we behold has no inherent existence, that the true nature of the mind is emptiness, and that the concept of a self as distinct from others is illusory. This knowledge can free us to apply our short human lives to do compassionate work.

MY FATHER WAS ADAMANT that Chomolungma was too big to sustain personal and nationalistic arguments, and the privilege of climbing Everest too great an honor to debase through

small-mindedness. Indeed, after a relationship with the mountain of nearly two decades, he felt defensive and proprietary in
the face of any talk that concerned the mountain, sensing that
Miyolangsangma could turn wrathful if people politicized her.
Climbers shun politics, and Buddhists say that political talk only
perpetuates ignorance, anger, and suffering. The mountain
itself is indifferent—an immutable fact that we would do well
to learn from.

The more my father continued to feel twisted and tugged on,
the more he wished to be left alone. Many wondered what political message he was trying to convey, for instance, in the order of
the flags that he held aloft on Everest. Tied to the top of his ice
ax was the United Nations flag, followed by the flags of Great
Britain, Nepal, and then India. The Nepalese were perturbed
that the British flag flew higher than theirs, but I assume they
were relieved that it was positioned above India's. My father had
no political intentions, however, when he arranged the flags,
other than to place the UN flag at the top. He liked to think of
their success as not strictly for themselves or the individual countries, but for people everywhere, for all mankind. It was also
important for him to acknowledge that this was a British-
sponsored expedition: the British had organized and paid for it,
and he wouldn't have made it without them. And if he had placed
the Indian or Nepalese flag at the top, with one necessarily above
the other, it would only have heightened the divisiveness between
those two countries.

For my own quiver of flags, I used the same logical order my
father did: all mankind, sponsor, homeland, nationality. I placed
the UN flag at the top, then the flags of the United States, Nepal,
and India. I included the Tibetan flag because Tibet represents the

cultural and ethnic roots of the Sherpas, and Tibet shares the mountain with Nepal. On the summit I held them up all together, as my father had, then Robert took photos of me holding each of them individually. I even strung them horizontally, though I imagine someone might find a problem with that orientation, too.

I was the first Sherpa or Tibetan to fly a Tibetan flag from Everest's summit, and it was that flag that brought me the most criticism—ironically, from Khumbu Sherpas. They are Nepalese citizens, and Nepal doesn't acknowledge Tibet as distinct from China. They felt that I had turned my back on them in a way, because Nepal would be officially displeased if they were to fly the Tibetan flag. But our Sherpa ancestors came from eastern Tibet, I pointed out. I would assume that the Khumbu Sherpas can empathize with the hardship the Tibetans have suffered as a result of the Chinese occupation of their country.

In 1953 the British and New Zealand climbers' stories and photos were tied up tightly by the *London Times*—further distancing them from the Nepalese and Indians. As a result, the local press focused its efforts on my father to learn what transpired on the mountain. They were desperate to label him, to define where he fit in. They questioned why he wore Western or Indian or Nepalese clothing, and why he spoke Hindi, Nepali, Tibetan, or Bengali.

My father was perplexed that no one had cared about his nationality before. He spoke about the newly elevated issue of his identity and nationality with Nepal's prime minister, and reiterated that he was born from the womb of Nepal—or at least moved there at a young age—and was brought up in the lap of India. He loved and was attached to Nepal, he said, then added that his children were being raised in India alongside the children of other prominent Nepalese. Sagarmatha, he maintained, does not belong to a single country, or even to two countries. It belongs to every country of the globe. He felt the same about himself.

To his relief, the prime minister and high-level government officials did not try to pressure him, as others of lower civil status had. They simply offered him a house and other benefits if he chose to stay in Nepal, and wished him happiness and good luck, wherever he decided to settle. But by then he had lived most of his adult life in India, and so he decided to return there. India, too, was in need of heroes.

I feel it was unfair for some Nepalese, and a handful of Sherpas, to say that Tenzing betrayed his Sherpa homeland. My father and other Khumbu Sherpas of his generation did not emigrate to Darjeeling for political reasons. Their move was strictly economic: foreign teams were excluded from climbing in Nepal, and Sherpas would not be able to find work again in Nepal's mountains until the country was opened in the 1950s. If Nepal were to be closed again, Solu and Khumbu Sherpas would again emigrate to Darjeeling for work.

The Indian government has even offered military and civil assignments to Jangbu and several other Sherpas. When Jangbu returned to his home village in Solu, at age twenty-four, he was extended the automatic rank of major in the Indian Army.

I have my own citizenship and identity issues, although they may be less complicated than my father's. I was born in India as an Indian citizen, and I remain an Indian to this day. My quandary mainly concerns cultural identity. I've decided that I belong to both cultures, East and West, and both belong to me.

Mainly as an unintended result of the Everest climb, I have rediscovered my faith in Buddhism and have renewed my respect for Eastern and Himalayan traditions—while I continue to engage the scrutiny and skepticism that I learned in the West. In fact, Tibetan Buddhism encourages skepticism. His Holiness the Dalai Lama says that we must not take someone's word for it— we should always question deeply, experience fully for ourselves, then decide on our own.

What makes Tibetan Buddhism work, in my mind, is that it contains an encyclopedic body of written works—its canon, commentaries, and revealed texts—which address virtually every metaphysical question ever raised. Buddhist teachings are a logical guide book to life, intricate yet simple, providing us with the intellectual basis for faith.

Eastern and Western views, though often divergent, are not contradictory. The "mystery" that Westerners have projected onto the East we see as little more than a simple and rather prosaic way of life. Conversely, the materialism of the West is an exotic wonder and enigma for us. Just as trekkers covet the simplicity and wholeness of our ancient lifestyles, Sherpas crave cars, clothes, and computers. Rather than pass each other going in opposite directions on the path of cultural evolution, I propose that we expand the healthy synergy that already exists—however latently—between the two hemispheres of thought.

I could not have climbed Everest without help from both the East and the West, and neither could my father. Even Sherpas rely on modern technology, such as the lightweight down pants and jackets, bottled oxygen, and front-point crampons that make climbing possible. We also need financing and organization from foreign sponsors. But just as important, we depend on the support of our extended families and the guidance of the three gems—the Buddha and protective deities, the religious teachings, and our community of lamas and devout believers.

The procession for my father's funeral was more than a mile long
as thousands came to Darjeeling to pay their respects. His three sons and
three of our cousins accompanied his bier to the cremation site at
the Himalayan Mountaineering Institute, which he founded.

10

FREEDOM FROM DESIRE

In early July 1953, my father and his family flew in King Tribhuvan's private plane from Kathmandu to India. At the West Bengal Governor's House in Calcutta there were more receptions and festivities. In the Calcutta film footage he is being exalted like a god, but you can clearly see him suffering from the stress.

In New Delhi he was summoned for an audience with "Panditji"—Prime Minister Jawaharlal Nehru. Panditji wanted to discuss my father's future and to offer him help. My father also wanted Nehru's advice. The British had invited my father to London, and he was thinking of declining, partly because the initial invitation had not included his family.

Nehru advised my father to go. Then he took him to his home, where he told him, "Listen, you can't see the queen of England in those khaki shorts and tired hiking shoes." He opened the doors to his wardrobe and gave my father five of his own suits—they wore the same size. He even gave my father some items that had belonged to his own father, and he presented gifts to Ang Lhamu and my half-sisters. My father sensed immediately that, aside from any position Nehru held as national leader, this was a friend he could trust. Panditji became like a father to him.

My father asked what he could do for him. Nehru spoke to him about the future of climbing in India and said, "I want you to produce a thousand Tenzings." This was the genesis of the Himalayan Mountaineering Institute in Darjeeling. Mountaineering had never been a part of Indian culture, and HMI was designed to instill mountaineering knowledge and skills, and love for the mountains, in Indians and other South Asians. The institute would also be of value to the military, and, indeed, it was organized under the army. My father was placed in charge of instruction, and the institute grew to become a widely recognized fixture within the Indian civil service.

From Delhi, Ang Lhamu, Pem Pem, Nima, and my father flew with Charles Wylie to London. In that era it took three days of travel by airplane from India to England, with each night stop falling in a different country. They carried both Indian and Nepalese passports, and at each stop Wylie had to fill out triplicate forms for each family member's passport.

They joined the British expedition members and their families for a lavish reception at Buckingham Palace. Wylie shepherded my father and family through the six thousand people gathered for their reception, all of them wanting his autograph. Wylie sometimes had to protect him and say no on his behalf. The Nepalese are proud of their hospitality, but the trappings, grandeur, and excitement of this royal event was like a dream compared to the modest welcome that the Nepalese had given to the British in Kathmandu.

The queen knighted John Hunt and Edmund Hillary and presented my father with the George Medal, the United Kingdom's foremost award below a knighthood and the highest honor, it is said, that can be bestowed on a foreigner. In view of

India's recent independence from the United Kingdom, India might not have much respected a knighthood for my father anyway. With keen interest, the queen questioned my father about the climb. He answered in basic English, declining Sir John Hunt's translation from Hindi.

The queen then asked Ang Lhamu what she had done when she heard the news of the successful ascent. "I went out and bought my husband a tin of milk," she replied. This was the automatic gesture that had come to her, symbolic of the time she had become acquainted with my father in the 1930s when he was delivering his landlord's milk to the wealthy people of the neighborhood where she worked.

At the reception, my father was pleased to meet up again with Eric Shipton, the leader of two previous British expeditions to Everest. He proudly reminded Shipton that he had given him his first expedition assignment, eighteen years earlier.

IN INDIA'S HIERARCHICAL society, caste mobility is almost inconceivable. Virtually no one from Tenzing's lowly stature had ever received the kind of overnight worldwide recognition that came to him. As a result, for hundreds of millions of Indians he became a powerful symbol of hope, and of national independence, especially emerging as he did in the twilight of British colonialism.

Every schoolchild in India and Nepal has read about Tenzing and Hillary on Everest. Even a half century after their climb, when I pass through immigration in Nepal or India—a generally demeaning experience—if I simply mention my name or speak about my father, some officers practically salute me. Gravely serious bureaucrats get a twinkle in their eye and respond with curiosity and wonder. Many high-level Indian civil servants have been through a program at the Himalayan Mountaineering Institute. The Nepalese, too, remain proud that Tenzing was one of their people.

No group respected my father or reveres his memory more than the people of India's state of West Bengal. Bengalis continue to visit Darjeeling by the thousands. The foreign and forbidding character of snow-covered mountains to these people from the sweltering plains must magnify the mystery and grandeur that they project onto my father.

What most captures the imaginations of the more adoring of the Bengalis, however, is the Hindu belief that Lord Shiva lives on top of Everest. After my father's climb, some Hindus asked him whether he saw Shiva at the summit. As if the nationalistic pressures weren't enough, pious Hindus prodded my father to claim that he had had spiritual revelations or visions while on the mountain.

Some Hindus literally worshiped my father, and some still do. Indeed, the more devout among them believe that only an actual manifestation of Shiva could have been the first to reach the top. When he was in the hospital in Delhi, strangers would enter his room and sit on the floor, touch his feet and cry. They arrived in endless pilgrimage at our door in Darjeeling, and I would sometimes see them standing on the road in front of the house, tearful, grateful to simply touch the front gate. From a young age we realized he wasn't an ordinary dad.

The adoration soon became a burden, and my father began to look for ways to evade it. Family and friends always got a chuckle to see Bengali tourists shout up to him from the street below when he was out gardening (an activity he loved), "Hey, gardener! Where's Tenzing Sah'b? Is he in the house?" And my father would respond, "No, I think he went into town." When he did leave, he often took a secret route, up through the grove of mountain bamboo behind the house and onto the high road above.

I don't think he was looking for Shiva on the summit. He was more interested in finding evidence that George Mallory and Andrew Irvine—the British pair who disappeared in 1924 while heading for the summit from the north side—had reached it before them. Mountaineering historians have figured that if Mallory's vest pocket camera could be found, it would contain exposed film that could be developed. If the two Brits had reached the summit, they certainly would have taken a summit shot to document their feat.

Mallory's body was discovered in the spring of 1999, seventy-five years to the week after their fated climb, but there was no camera with it, nor other clues about the summit. The search for Irvine's body and the camera continues.

AFTER THE CLIMB, Soyang and I spent a week in Kathmandu with her parents. Then with our daughter Deki we set off by car on the circuitous route that trends eastward to Darjeeling, two long days' drive away. Crossing the border into India, we were surprised by scores of relatives and friends who had come down from Darjeeling to greet us on the plains. They draped katas around my neck and offered us tea and biscuits, and I saw that banners had been stretched across the front of several cars, welcoming me home. When we reached Darjeeling, they assembled groups of well-wishers into an impromptu parade, and I was escorted to Ghang-la, our family home.

I couldn't get through the entrance gate for the crowd, mostly Sherpas, who were milling about in a disorganized fashion, still preparing for my arrival. Several people shouted, then they hastily leaped onto the sides of the path, forming a cordon along the cement stairs that lead up to the house, as if I were a high incarnate lama. I was guided over to three people who were standing beside the front gate, positioned to formally present the welcoming *sujhaang*, which blesses and confers good fortune on the arriving person, as is done for guests at a Sherpa wedding party.

The three sujhaang greeters do not have to be related, but they must come from intact families, with all parents and siblings still alive, so that their good luck will be transferred to the person being honored. One of them offered me chang, another offered milk, and the third held out *tsema*, a divided tray with tsampa and butter on one side and barley on the other. I stopped to take some of each item in my mouth, then flicked some into the air with the ring finger of my right hand, as an offering to the deities.

By the time I reached the top landing I could barely see out over the pile of katas. A hundred or more of them were mounded and draped around my neck like a massive yoke. One relative announced to the crowd that I had been the first to complete a Sherpa father-son team to reach the summit, but I believe there has been at least one such team ahead of my father and me.

Beer and chang flowed, and I was coerced into finishing an entire bottle of beer before I could even enter the house. A warm welcome quickly grew into a great party. But before the afternoon got out of hand, I slipped away to the chapel room and closed the door behind me. The thangka scroll painting of Miyolangsangma peered down at me from the altar, and I did three prostrations. I recited a prayer, not so much a concluding prayer as a prayer of new beginnings.

It was gratifying for the Sherpas that I had climbed Everest. They were pleased that I had shown respect for my parents in the best way possible—through achievements and noble actions, especially in a venture that the family specializes in. Many in our community have seen their brothers and sisters and sons and daughters leave the family home to seek their fortunes in the outside world. Not all of them return. Distressingly, many of those who have stayed in our homeland have been lost to the community, too. Virtually all Sherpa families have relatives who have died in climbing accidents.

As the second eldest son, I always ranked somewhere behind my brother Norbu, the studious one. At college in Wisconsin my grades were poor, and I got into a certain amount of trouble. When I walked alone down the small town streets, young guys would roll up beside me in a pickup, stick their head out the window, and call me "chink" and other names. I admit that at the time I enjoyed taking them on and generally beat the crap out of them, though this kind of response nearly got me thrown out of school.

I had a sponsor who supported me through college, and I regret the difficulties that I caused him and his family. Ten years later, however, I attended the premiere of the Everest IMAX film in Chicago, and from the podium I was able to thank them for their generosity. The family was in tears. Finally, I felt I had come full circle, and in a sense I felt I was thanking my father and mother at the same time.

It came as something of a surprise to many of our relatives, considering our schooling in America, that a child of Tenzing's would follow in his footsteps. I can't keep track of the hundreds in our massive joint family, but I think my relatives are pleased that I married a local woman and that I have contributed to the local community. My uncle who lives next door, Tenzing Lotay, said that both my parents predicted that I would be the one to remain in Darjeeling and take care of family affairs and carry on our traditions. Deki and Norbu married Westerners and live in the United States, and my brother Dhamey and his wife, the daughter of a Bhutanese ambassador, live in Hong Kong.

I'm encouraged that Norbu has been helping the Himalaya through his work with the American Himalayan Foundation. Also, Dhamey is now planning to come back and live in the region—possibly some of the time in Bhutan, where it is customary for the son-in-law to move in with the wife's family. It is unusual for a Bhutanese to marry a Sherpa, but their links to Chatral Rimpoche, guru and teacher to both families, overcame any ethnic incompatibility.

I FELT A sense of achievement when I reached the summit, but I also found it to be a first step, a beginning, just as the years after 1953 were the beginning of a new and different life for my father. Stepping on the summit of Everest freed me from the confinement of my ambitions. And it freed me from following my father, from searching for him. It has launched me onto my own path. Perhaps this path will someday lead to a place of even greater understanding, compassion, and peace of mind.

Thousands of people visit the Himalaya each year, and hundreds promise to help the local people. But only a few of them actually return to do something. My father and Ed Hillary are two who did, and I'm committed to joining them. The Sherpas have become recognized worldwide partly as a result of my father's later work, and I realize that I, too, am an ambassador for the Sherpa people. My goal is to educate people about the Sherpas and our culture and to seek out support for them so that they can enter the twenty-first century with access to decent education, health care, and a basic standard of living, and have the skills and motivation to plan their own future.

When devout climbing Sherpas visit the lhap-so at Base Camp, before setting foot on the mountain, they take Miyolangsangma into their hearts and pray to her with undivided devotion. It's while standing there that some of them vow to perform a charitable deed if they can be granted safe passage and success on their climb. Over the years, many Sherpas, including Jangbu and Wongchu, have returned to their villages and installed drinking water and small hydroelectrical systems, built schools, donated money and labor to restore the village monasteries, and become the patrons for rituals that benefit the entire village.

I have vowed to take this path as well, and that is one reason I sought the blessings of His Holiness the Dalai Lama. In December 1996, I joined 350,000 other devout Buddhists in Salugara, West Bengal, for a three-day Kalachakra ("Wheel of Time") initiation given by His Holiness. Soyang and I and our daughter Deki were given VIP seats next to His Holiness, but Soyang felt shy about sitting up above the gathering. At one point between sessions during the weeklong event, we were granted an audience with him. It was the first time I had been in his presence since I was a young boy. He was pleased that I had climbed Everest, and grateful that I had displayed the Tibetan flag on the summit. He then placed his hand on our heads and blessed us. His blessing may have contributed to our fortune of having twins, whom Soyang gave birth to a year and a half later.

◆━━━━━◆

BAD LUCK SEEMED to follow many of those who were on Everest in the spring of 1996. Lobsang Jangbu, the hotshot sirdar and close friend of Scott Fischer, was invited to climb Everest in the fall of 1996 with a Japanese expedition. Sherpa friends of his tried to talk him out of it, mainly because the fall season is much colder and considered more dangerous. Lobsang himself had decided, partly in response to pleas from his pregnant wife, that he would abandon Himalayan climbing altogether after that season. He had already made arrangements to move to the United States part-time to develop his trekking and commercial guiding business.

Lobsang was also a follower of Geshé Rimpoche, and before every climb he religiously went to Rimpoche for a divination and a blessing. Before the spring climbing season, we intersected in Rimpoche's quarters at one point, both of us seeking blessings.

Tragically for those of us who followed and respected him, Geshé Rimpoche passed away in July, shortly after our spring climb.

Lobsang knew that he would need to consult a lama before approaching the mountain, so on his way up to Base Camp in the fall season he asked the Tengboche Lama for a divination. Disturbingly, Tengboche Rimpoche said that the divination was quite clearly *unfavorable*, and he urged Lobsang not to climb that season.

Lobsang had already been hired as a sirdar, and he was being paid handsomely as a result of his excellent performance in the spring. He had climbed Everest five times before and felt confident in his abilities.

Lobsang was climbing above Camp III when a massive

avalanche of snow and ice released from the steep Lhotse Face and roared down to the floor of the Western Cwm. En route it swept over a Japanese climber and several Sherpas, but miraculously left them uninjured. Climbers on an exposed section above the Yellow Band weren't so lucky, and a Frenchman and two Sherpas—all from different expeditions—were swept away by the awesome torrent of snow. One of them was Lobsang Jangbu.

A shock of his hair is all that was ever found. His wife gave birth to their first child, a boy, one month after his death.

It was the first time Lobsang had climbed without Geshé Rimpoche's blessing and benediction, and he did so even after the Tengboche Lama's unfavorable divination. Coincidence? Who knows, but I tend to think not. One Sherpa suggested that Scott Fischer's wandering ghost, his *shrindi*, pulled Lobsang off the mountain because the two of them had bonded so closely. Lobsang had regarded Fischer like a father, he said, and when two people's spirits and karma are intertwined in this manner— such as between a husband and wife or father and son—so, too, is their fate and their luck. With that kind of karmic link to Fischer, Lobsang Jangbu might have died that season even if he hadn't been climbing.

I believe that the averages would confirm that those who defy the words of a high lama, especially when the lama has done a divination, are putting themselves at grave risk. Sherpas occasionally climb, travel, or engage in activities that their lamas advise them against, and in most cases that I'm aware of they have met with misfortune. With such a high correlation between poor divinations and bad luck, I don't think that our caution in such matters can be ascribed to mere superstition.

To many families, bad luck comes in clusters. Ngawang Topgay, the Sherpa on Scott Fischer's team who was airlifted out at the beginning of the season with suspected pulmonary edema, was Lobsang Jangbu's uncle. He died in Kathmandu before the beginning of the monsoon. His was the twelfth and last death of the spring 1996 season.

When people die an accidental or "untimely" death, their ghosts can wander, awaiting dispatch to heaven or to one of several hell realms. Some of these shrindi are merely lost, unaware that they have died, and they learn that they are dead only when they don't see their shadows or their footprints in the sand. Other shrindi are more needy and malignant, and these are the ones that can cause sickness and trouble. Village shamans can sometimes recognize their presence when a relative or acquaintance of the deceased acquires the same sickness that killed the dead person. For instance, if a person dies during bouts of nausea, or from an injury to the face, acquaintances who become nauseated or are wounded in the face are believed to be infected with the dead person's shrindi.

For these cases, the shaman enters a trance and can determine what it is the shrindi wants. Once those demands are met and the shrindi is placated, the afflicted person often quickly recovers. I found it curious when I learned that the Navajo word for these wandering ghosts is *chindi.*

In the fall of 1996, Dawa Sherpa, a top sirdar who was on Everest in the spring, was killed while climbing with the Koreans. His daughter was born on the day he was killed. He came from a wealthy family, and his relatives chartered a helicopter to fly his body to his home village in Solu for cremation.

In the winter of 1997, Anatoli Boukreev, another force of

nature like Ed Viesturs, and arguably the world's strongest climber at the time, was lost in an avalanche while climbing Annapurna I. I was especially saddened to hear of the death, in the spring of 1998, of Ngawang Tenzing. He was the Sherpa who, the day after he had reached the summit without oxygen, had hiked up and revived Makalu Gau above the South Col and carried him down to camp. In 1998 Ngawang, who had been a well-respected monk from Thame, my father's village, was climbing with Todd Burleson's group and was lost in a storm on the South Col. It is thought that he wandered off the Kangshung Face.

The Taiwanese team leader Makalu Gau visited Nepal in 1999, and he cried when he heard the news about Ngawang Tenzing.

WHILE IN COLLEGE, before my father passed away, I had a series of disturbing dreams in which I was attending his funeral. These were so upsetting that I called Norbu to talk about them. Norbu said that during his last visit to Darjeeling a respected Hindu saddhu had read his palm and told him he would soon face some family complications that would cause him to come home.

In the spring of 1986, our father made a trip to Switzerland, where he had a check-up and was found to be in good health. A few weeks after he returned to Darjeeling, he arose early one morning to use the toilet. He returned to bed in some pain, and very quickly died, our mother said. He had suffered a brain hemorrhage. He was seventy-two years old.

Dhamey was at the family home, but Norbu was in New Hampshire, I was in Wisconsin, and Deki was in Michigan. Norbu received a call from our cousin Phinjo, who said that our father had "gone away." Phinjo was too upset himself to state directly that he had died.

It was as if he didn't really need to tell us. That afternoon when I was at work, as close to his time of death as I can calculate, I suddenly became startled and lost my train of thought. Something was telling me that there had been a change in our family—that's how I would describe the sensation—and the only thing that immediately fit together was that our father had died. I couldn't focus for the rest of the afternoon. I had been waiting for Phinjo's phone call.

The three of us who were in the United States gathered in New York City and flew together, in tears, to Delhi and Bagdogra, West Bengal. Darjeeling District had been closed to visitors owing to the "Gorkhaland" succession movement, and demonstrations had been planned for that day. The strike was formally suspended to allow people, but no cars, to move freely through the city for the funeral, although relatives and mourners arriving from Nepal were halted at the border and not allowed to proceed.

Sir Edmund Hillary, who was New Zealand's ambassador to India at the time, was on our flight to Bagdogra, along with Lady June Hillary. They joined us in a small army jeep convoy that escorted us across the plains and up the steep switchbacks to Darjeeling. Ours were the only vehicles on the highway, which has since been renamed Tenzing Norgay Road.

We had planned to cremate him near the vegetable garden at Ghang-la, in the courtyard at the side of the house. But when it became evident that people would be arriving by the thousands, we decided to cremate him at the Himalayan Mountaineering Institute climbing school. Tenzing Norgay Sherpa, we again realized, was as much a citizen of Darjeeling, India, and the world as a member of our family.

The house and grounds at Ghang-la were thronged with relatives who were running about busy and agitated—and worried, they said, that we had lost our father when we were so young. Hundreds of people filed through the house to view his body.

Six sons and nephews carried the corpse, which was arranged on a bier. We negotiated the bier down the winding staircase and through the door and then circuited the house three times. We then descended to the front gate and placed the bier on an army truck decorated in flower garlands and wreaths.

The procession was led by a car draped in katas and marigolds, with a thangka of the Wheel of Life propped on the hood. As the car led us through town, well-wishers threw on more flowers and katas. The students of Saint Joseph's, Darjeeling's other large private school, stood in uniform lining both sides of the road at intervals along the procession route. Standing on the truck bed beside the bier, I nodded to those I knew in the crowd. I could visualize my father passing these same people, riding in the HMI jeep on this very road, placing both hands together in a brief greeting of "Namaste" to the people who saluted or recognized him.

By the time we reached the grounds of the Himalayan Mountaineering Institute, the procession had grown to nearly a kilometer and a half in length, and the truck and lead car were blanketed in marigolds, like orange snow.

All the high lamas of Darjeeling attended, including Chatral Rimpoche and his monks. Dignitaries from West Bengal came, along with the queen of England's envoy to India, bearing a message of condolence from Her Majesty. Thousands of well-wishers packed the area, including hundreds of beggars, as always.

They can generally find food, and people tend to be charitable when they are grieving.

His cremation site was on the top of a hillock next to the coffee shop that he enjoyed retreating to in the afternoons. A pyre was fashioned out of brick, with an empty space in the center. Monks ran back and forth, piling it up with wood, juniper boughs, incense, and blessed objects. Relatives and close friends wrote words on pieces of paper and added them to the pyre, along with countless flowers. Sir Edmund Hillary dedicated his written eulogy, "To a friend dearly missed."

Then a remarkable thing happened. A small cloud appeared directly overhead in an otherwise perfectly blue sky. A few drops of rain fell on us, which quickly built into a downpour that lasted about one minute. It subsided as quickly as it had come. Even the monks stopped chanting momentarily, partly to protect their texts from the water, but more to witness it all. At cremations, unusual celestial events are considered highly favorable. At the time, Halley's Comet was also making its appearance after seventy-six years.

Army soldiers fired off a twenty-one-gun salute, then my two brothers and I and my cousin Lobsang (who would die on Everest seven years later) lit the pyre simultaneously from the four cardinal directions. We then poured ghee on it to help it burst into flame. The monks and several family elders took over, feeding wood into the holes of the pyre.

Finally there was a loud pop, which was my father's skull cracking. This is believed to be the moment when the soul—which in Buddhism is really the consciousness, or the life-force—is released from the body. For Sherpas, this life-force can dwell within an individual at the same time that it resides within the natural features of the region. One's fortune depends on maintaining a healthy body and mind, but also on protecting the health of the local environment. Truly, my father shared his soul with that of the community and the natural world around him.

Three days later, Norbu and I went to collect his ashes, accompanied by three monks. The cremation site had been cordoned off and guarded around the clock, and the pyre had been covered with roofing tin to protect it from the elements. We removed the tin, and the monks looked carefully at the configuration of the bones and ashes, from which some details of his next incarnation can be determined. They were especially intrigued by what looked like bird footprints through the fine ash dust. One monk studied them carefully, finally declaring that it was clear that our father would reincarnate in the direction that the miniature foot steps led.

We collected all of the remains and returned to Ghang-la, where the monks asked Norbu to initiate the grinding of them into powder. They finished the process for him, and we watched them knead the powdery mixture with clay and other ingredients, then impress hundreds of small *tsa-tsas*—votive tablets in the shape of miniature stupas. These have found their way to various sacred sites in South Asia, including the monasteries at Thame and Tengboche and the flanks of Tibet's sacred Mount Kailash. The remaining ashes were poured into the Teesta River, which defines the border between Darjeeling District and Sikkim. On our father's behalf, Chatral Rimpoche traveled with seven of his monks to holy sites across northern India, making offerings and distributing alms and clothing to the poor.

We stayed home at Ghang-la for forty-nine days and answered telegrams and letters. This was when I realized the extent to which my father had helped put Sherpas on the map of the world. Already a Swiss company had produced a "Sherpa Tensing"–brand sun lotion and lip balm; there were also Sherpa-brand shoes and even a model of car sold in New Zealand called the Sherpa—a compact car probably too small for the towering Ed Hillary, who was seen in an advertisement for it. The term *sherpa* seems to have entered the English lexicon, thankfully with the connotation of guide as much as porter, as in "the sherpas of Wall Street."

Our mother served tea and food to the endless stream of mourning guests, as is expected after the death of a husband. She broke from her chores to take long retreats in the chapel room on the top floor, for prayer, and sat next to the monks from Chatral Rimpoche's monastery. The monks were conducting the forty-nine-day Tibetan Book of the Dead ceremony, nonstop, day and night. The purpose of the ritual is to direct the soul away from this human life and into the next stage, as if declaring, "You no longer belong to this earth—you need to move on." The ritual provides the deceased with the needed direction and motivation to get there.

It is essential during this time that the monks be paid well, so the best of foods are prepared for the monks and mourners, at great cost. We needed donations from within the extended family to meet these costs, and we kept an account book in which all the donations were recorded. When we go to funerals, weddings, or New Year celebrations, we refer to this list and generally try to double the original donation in return.

On the forty-ninth day after my father's death, people in the community arrived for the concluding ceremony. And for five years a ceremony was held on each anniversary of his death. After the fifth anniversary, we, the survivors, are expected to have severed our connection to the deceased, for they have fully departed, while we remain with the living.

I must have missed that part, because my own powerful attachment to my father lingered for another nine years—until I climbed Everest. I feel that I released him on the summit. The respect and the love and the memories remain today—but not the attachment, the push and pull of father and son, the compulsion to please and impress him, or the stinging desire to have him back.

WHEN I RETURNED to the United States, I cried even more than I had in Darjeeling, and even though I felt I had been preparing for his death from a young age. He was nearly old enough to be my grandfather, and had lived a full life before my birth. I wrote him a letter after he died and asked him why he left; I wanted him to return so that he could see me as an adult. And I simply wanted to be with him.

His death left a hole in our lives, and it brought out some intense emotions and anger in me. I became depressed for nearly two years, and in college I consulted a psychiatrist. My dreams became fiercely vivid, and for a long time simply walking down the street was emotionally draining for me. Deki was sick for much of that period, and she fell into a coma for eight days. When she awoke from the coma, all that she recalled dreaming was that her mother, father, and *yidam*, her tutelary deity, came to her bedside to say good-bye to her. In fact, her reverie could be considered a favorable premonitory dream, as dreams of death and sickness generally are, Sherpas say.

In April 1997, a twenty-foot-high statue of my father was cast, and it was erected at the Himalayan Mountaineering Institute next to his cremation site, which also bears a memorial plaque. A quarter of a million people walk past these monuments each year. I am proud of the statue, but it also reminds me of the fame that took him away from us when we were children.

The warmth of his spirit and the love he gave to his children were immensely larger and more meaningful than his public image could ever convey. More than anything, he wanted us to become good members of the community, and to appreciate how lucky we were. His humility humbled me, by association. Whether he was hiking with a barefoot porter or speaking with the queen of England, he treated everyone equally. And ultimately, he never fully understood what all the hype and fuss about Everest were about. To him, Everest and mountaineering meant teamwork, respect, and sharing the joy of the mountains with friends. Learning these values was the blessing I received from him, and they continue to guide me.

After my father passed away, I grew closer to my mother. My sister and brothers and I needed to rely on her strength as an axis, like a prayer wheel, to help us deal with his passing. And we needed her resilience to manage the pressures put on us by the extended family and the Tenzing legacy.

After I climbed Everest, some in the Darjeeling community became envious of me, including a few within our sprawling extended family. My father's celebrity, combined with his incorrigible generosity, attracted relatives, friends, and strangers to Ghang-la, and they were all searching for something; many of his siblings and their children and grandchildren—of whom there were at least one hundred of us—wanted to claim a part of him for themselves. That may be one reason he traveled overseas so much.

My father had become friends with Lars Eric Lindblad, who had walked up to Ghang-la and introduced himself. Soon he had a new career, leading trips for Lindblad to Africa, Antarctica, Egypt, China, and every part of the world he had heard of or hoped to see. In the meantime, my mother learned to drive a car, even though Sherpa women didn't do that in those days. And having witnessed my father's success, she decided to start her own travel company, Tenzing Norgay Adventures. I now oversee its operations in Darjeeling and have opened a branch in Kathmandu. I consider this work a tribute to my parents, for it allowed them to send all of their children to college in the United States, for which I am grateful.

Seven years after my father's death, at Norbu's wedding, I saw my mother for the last time. When she died, the resentful, samsaric part of me wanted to say to some of the people in the community, "Okay, are you happy now? You've always wanted to see us fall apart or screw up, and now they're both dead." But our mother was the one who was finally relieved—of the burden of the community's expectations and gossip.

I believe that my mother has had a favorable reincarnation, the fruit of her unfailing charity and devotion. I missed her cremation in Darjeeling by a matter of hours as a result of an Indian Airlines cancellation. A monk told me when I arrived that a rainbow had appeared during the ceremony, a highly propitious event.

WHAT IS THE meaning of the few brief instants in human history when people have stood atop Everest? The answer depends on the motivation of the person standing there. Those prepared to truly see and listen will find something different, and greater, than what they were seeking. They will find that the spirit and blessings of the mountains can be found, ultimately, within all of us. And for those who have faith, Miyolangsangma, the omniscient and bountiful goddess of Everest, has another message: you will be protected.

Some climbers are driven by personal achievement and the desire for a trophy. Others are drawn to the mountains by something more mysterious, something more deeply personal. Perhaps they are motivated by a need for understanding, by a desire to gain freedom from the Wheel of Life, the cycle of birth, death, and rebirth. I feel that these climbers are nedrogs; they are sharing my pilgrimage. "Life in the mountains draws out the character of those who journey there," said the Pheriche clinic doctor Jim Litch, whom I met several times at Base Camp. "Maybe this is one of the many reasons we climb—to see ourselves at the core, not packaged and contained as we are when living within the constraints of technology and consumerism."

What have people learned from the tragic spring 1996 season on Everest? Dr. Tom Hornbein, who reached the top via the West Ridge on the 1963 American Everest expedition, was a good friend of my father's. "Mountains are hazardous, and there will be deaths," he confirms. "And as the crowding increases, it's like setting up more pins at the end of the bowling alley: there are more to knock down."

Dr. David Shlim, another friend from Nepal who understands the trap of second-guessing events, as we saw in 1996, agrees. "Drawing conclusions is difficult," he says. "The only thing that we can say for certain, after years of watching people attempt this mountain, is that climbing Everest remains really dangerous."

When I see climbers displaying arrogance in the lap of their great teacher, I feel they are putting themselves at risk. Ambition and aspiration alone are insufficient on Everest, as in life, for a goal can never be reached through force. But anyone motivated by compassion and a desire to help others will see the fruits of their efforts—though perhaps not in this lifetime. One should be diligent and persistent, but not impatient.

What I learned most—from both my father and the mountain—was humility. They both demanded it. At the end of six previous attempts to climb Chomolungma my father retreated, he said, not in defeat but in reverence. He told me that he was finally able to reach her summit in 1953—as a visitor on pilgrimage—only by virtue of respect for Miyolangsangma.

It was not until I reached the summit of Everest that I learned that I didn't need to climb the mountain to acquire my father's blessings. Nor did I need to climb it to make offerings to the goddess who resides there. Like a mother, she understands, guides, and protects regardless of where in the universe we find ourselves.

It is in our nature to strive, and to challenge ourselves in the physical world. Perhaps it is this struggle, and eventual mastery, that gives our lives meaning—a throwback to the time not so long ago when life's challenges revolved around the simple but dangerous and arduous job of survival.

I intend to keep my promise to Soyang to not climb any more large Himalayan peaks. Nonetheless, I still wistfully recall sitting alone in the Western Cwm and looking up, drawn to the jagged Nuptse-Lhotse Ridge, wondering whether it might be possible to do a full traverse along that ridgeline. Perhaps she'll consent if the lamas allow?

BEFORE SOYANG AND I departed Kathmandu for Darjeeling, we went to visit Geshé Rimpoche. I wanted to thank him especially for his divinations, prayers, and rituals on my behalf, and for the ritual objects that I carried with me. Again we arrived with fruit, katas, and some rupees. We entered his simple quarters, did three prostrations, then lowered our heads as we extended the offerings. He seemed happy, and was pleased that I had reached the summit and returned safely.

One month later Geshé Rimpoche passed away. On the day of his death he summoned his personal attendant, told him that he would be leaving his body that evening, and asked the attendant to prepare. He then gave the attendant some indications about his next incarnation. "In five years, come to the Gelugpa monastery in Mysore, and a small boy will approach you and tug on your robe. That will be me." He then assumed a meditative posture and remained in that position through his death.

Over one thousand people attended his cremation in the courtyard of the Samden Ling monastery, next to the Great Stupa of Boudhanath. When I left the cremation, I did several circuits of the stupa. Chanting the sacred syllables *Om Ah Hung,* I lit butter lamps, thanking the deities and the Buddha for granting me a human rebirth, and for doing so in a time and place and state of mind in which I could be open to accept the guidance of teachers such as Geshé Rimpoche, Chatral Rimpoche, Trulshig Rimpoche, and Tengboche Rimpoche. Hopefully, the lighting of the lamps would begin to supplant the darkness of my ignorance with illumination, allowing me to see more clearly in the remainder of this life, and into the next.

In 1997 I returned to Khumbu with some friends and made a beeline to the village of Thame to visit Grandfather Gaga. I didn't announce our visit to him, and this time we seemed to have genuinely surprised him. He busied himself making tea, while showing me things, changing into new clothes right before us to be presentable—trying to do everything at once.

Once we had sat down and teacups had been filled, I handed him a photo of myself standing on the summit. He looked at it and nodded knowingly, "Yes, I thought that's what you were doing up there. A Sherpa girl who lives nearby came down from Base Camp and told me she saw you there. So I prayed for you every day, for your safety and well-being."

Before the climb, I had sought Gaga's blessings without even telling him, for we say that simply visiting and listening to older relatives confers good fortune, the way a lama's teachings do, and that their touch is a blessing. I explained to him that the season had been unfavorable, that people had made mistakes that multiplied into tragedy and death, and that I had given up climbing high Himalayan peaks. Now, I told him, I had committed myself to bringing education, medical care, and other help to the Sherpas, to whatever degree this might be possible.

He smiled, happy with my choice, it seemed, and perhaps proud of me, the way I hoped my father would have been. As I left, he repeated a Sherpa Buddhist aphorism that captured my experience on Everest, and perhaps my future.

"We shouldn't believe that small wrongdoing can do no harm, because even a small spark can ignite a giant pile of hay. Similarly, the value of the smallest good deeds should not be underestimated, for even tiny flakes of snow, falling one atop another, can blanket the tallest mountains in pure whiteness."

Helping the Himalaya

MANY PEOPLE HAVE approached me asking how they might help the Sherpas, Tibetans, and other people of the Himalaya, and how they can contribute to protecting the fragile environment of the high valleys and plateaus in the vicinity of Mount Everest.

I inherited from my father the desire to climb, but also his concern for our community. After Everest, he started a trust to care for widows of Sherpas killed while climbing. To build upon his important efforts, I have been working with the American Himalayan Foundation (AHF), a compassionate and efficient nonprofit organization based in San Francisco and Kathmandu.

AHF began two decades ago by sending Sherpa children to school. Since then, they have supported schools, hospitals, and clinics of the Everest area; planted a million trees; and restored the jewel of Sherpa culture—Tengboche monastery. AHF has grown to embrace many other remote valleys of the Himalaya, building schools and hospitals, preventing young girls from being sold into prostitution, and restoring sacred monuments. For Tibetans inside Tibet and in exile, AHF offers emergency medical care to new refugees, scholarships for children, and the dignity of shelter for elders.

I am a son of the mountains, but I know many of you regard them as your spiritual home. I hope you share my love and desire to help this special part of the world, the Himalaya. Your gift will find its true reward through AHF. You can contact them at:

The American Himalayan Foundation
909 Montgomery Street, Suite 400
San Francisco, California 94132
USA

Phone: (415) 288–7245
E-mail: ahf@himalayan-foundation.org
Web site: www.himalayan-foundation.org

acknowledgments

DURING DIFFICULT AS well as fortunate times, most followers of Tibetan Buddhism place His Holiness the Dalai Lama in the forefronts of their minds. I feel that his guidance, blessings, and visualizations were instrumental in my safe ascent of Mount Everest and return to my family, and for what little understanding I may have gained en route.

In equal measure, I am deeply grateful to Trulshig Rimpoche, Chatral Rimpoche, Tengboche Rimpoche, and the late Geshé Sonam Rinchen Rimpoche for their divinations, prayers, and blessings before, during, and after the 1996 Everest IMAX Filming Expedition.

My wife, Soyang, deserves special thanks. She was patient with my dream, and ultimately she had faith in it. I could feel her prayers, blessings, and support throughout, as I do now. I also want to thank Soyang's parents, Metok Yangchen and Namgyal Dorjee, for their faith, prayers, assistance, and guidance.

My brother Dhamey Tenzing; my brother-in-law Tsedo; and my sisters, Deki Tenzing, Pem Pem Tshering, and Nima Galang, provided moral support and important background for this book. My eldest brother, Norbu Tenzing, was of indispensable support throughout, and I am especially appreciative of his help and commitment to this project.

Special thanks go to our editor, Doug Abrams, for approaching me and giving me the opportunity to share my story. Doug had confidence in me, and he was dedicated to the book throughout. His insightful editorial guidance and collaboration were instrumental in bringing this book to fruition.

I would also like to extend my sincere thanks to Stephen Hanselman, Margery Buchanan, Calla Devlin, Terri Leonard, Lisa Zuniga, Renée Sedliar, Jim Warner, Joe Rutt, and all those at HarperSanFrancisco who have worked with such dedication on this book. Further, I am grateful to Sally Uhlmann for inspiring and urging me to write this book, and for the important questions she raised. I am grateful to Bob Hoffman for encouraging me throughout the preparations for the 1996 season, and for introducing me to David Breashears. In particular, I am indebted to David Breashears for having faith in me. He gave me the opportunity to fulfill my lifelong dream, and I feel he deserves credit for our team's success, and for our safety. Thanks, David.

—*J.T.N.*

IN THE PREPARATION OF NOTES and text for this book, numerous people gave generously of their time. To varying degrees, they patiently submitted to interviews, provided background information and clarification, and reviewed the manuscript. We apologize if deserving persons are missing from the following list of friends, relatives, and advisors, to whom we say thank you and *tu-che-chay:*

Martin Adams, Matthew Akester, Robert Anderson, Stan Armington, Pete Athans, Brent Bishop, Richard Blum, Iwona Boretti, Peter Bro, Dr. Barbara Brower, Jennifer Carroll, Rapten Chazotsang, Jim Clash, the late Ani Chö-e, Scott Darsney, Rinchen Dharlo, Tsering Wangmo Dhompa, Kellie Erwin-Rhoads, Dr. James Fisher, Mary Gerty, Nawang Gombu, Alana Guarnieri, Elizabeth Hawley, Thomas Hornbein, M.D., Frances Howland, the late Dr. Richard J. Kohn, Vassi Koutsaftis, Jon Krakauer, Wendy Lama, Jim Lester, Jim Litch, M.D., Steve Matous, Zubin Medora, Sue Muncaster, Bob Peirce, Paul J. Pugliese, Pamela Putney, Jennifer Read, Jeff Rhoads, the late Gil Roberts, M.D., Bo Ross, Audrey Salkeld, Robert Schauer, Erik Pema Schmidt, Jeremy Schmidt, Marcia Binder Schmidt, Klev Schoening, Araceli Segarra, Ai Lhakpa Sherpa, Jangbu Sherpa, Nima Sherpa, Phurba Sonam Sherpa, Tenzing Lotay Sherpa, Wongchu Sherpa, David Shlim, M.D., Rajendra Shrestha, Warren Smith, Erica Stone, Deepak Thapa, Sue Thompson, Clark Trainor, Ed Viesturs, Gelong Wangdu, Ed Webster, Lt. Col. Charles Wylie (Ret'd), and Karen Zakrison.

Nepalese scholar and publisher Kanak Dixit provided help and inspiration, and Jeff Long offered inspired direction and illumination. On the mountain, Jangbu Sherpa climbed with almost superhuman strength and judgment, and later clarified the chronology and details of events. Greg MacGillivray, Steve Judson, and the staff of MacGillivray-Freeman Films are also to be thanked for their support and guidance. Our agents, Heide Lange and Sarah Lazin, have been dedicated and extremely helpful. Broughton Coburn is especially indebted to his wife, Didi, and to their children, Phoebe and Tenzing, for their help, love, and patience.

—*J.T.N.*
—*B.C.*

Photo Credits

GRATEFUL ACKNOWLEDGMENT is given to the following individuals and organizations for the photographs that appear in this book.

First photo insert
Miyolangsangma, the Everest goddess: Tenzing Collection; village of Thame, Rongbuk monastery, and Tenzing Norgay as a young man: Tenzing Collection; Tenzing with mother and stepmother, Tenzing with Jamling and Norbu, Jamling's wedding day: Tenzing Collection; Tenzing with the Dalai Lama: Tenzing Collection; Jamling with the Dalai Lama: courtesy of Vassi Koutsaftis; Chatral Rimpoche and Trulshik Rimpoche: Tenzing Collection; Great Stupa of Boudhanath; courtesy of David Breashears/MacGillivray Freeman Films; family portrait and Jamling with his grandfather: Tenzing Collection; Jamling lighting butter lamps: courtesy of David Breashears/ Macgillivray Freeman Films; memorial site Chukpö Laré: courtesy of Scott Darsney/Mountainworld Images; Tenzing with Raymond Lambert: The Swiss Foundation for Alpine Research; Edmund Hillary with Tenzing: George Band/Royal Geographical Society; Tenzing with Edmund Hillary: Alfred Gregory/Royal Geographical Society

Second photo insert
Sherpas at Camp IV, 1953: Alfred Gregory/Royal Geographical Society; IMAX Sherpas, 1996: Tenzing Collection; IMAX members: courtesy of David Breashears/MacGillivray Freeman Films; Khumbu Icefall, 1953: Alfred Gregory/Royal Geographical Society; Jamling ascending vertical wall

of ice: Tenzing Collection; climber on aluminum ladder: courtesy of Scott Darsney/Mountainworld Images; Western Cwm: courtesy of Robert Schauer; Tenzing on Lhontse Face, 1953: George Lowe/Royal Geographical Society; Jamling on Lhotse Face: Tenzing Collection; Chen Yu-Nan rescue: courtesy of Robert Schauer; climbers between the South Summit and the Hillary Step: Scott Fischer/Woodfin Camp; Base Camp shrine: courtesy of David Breashearsr/MacGillivray Freeman Films; approaching the Yellow Band: courtesy of Araceli Segarra; summit day and Southeast Ridge: Tenzing Collection; tricky traverse from the South Summit: courtesy of Robert Schauer (also used as chapter ornament); Tenzing on the summit: Edmund Hillary/Royal Geographical Society; Jamling on the summit: Tenzing Collection; Tenzing's funeral, Jamling with his siblings, and Jamling's daughters: Tenzing Collection

Chapter opening photographs

Chapter one, Geshe Rimpoche: Tenzing Collection; chapter two, Tengboche monastery: courtesy of Ed Viesturs; chapter three, ice axes: courtesy of Sumiyo Tsuzuki; chapter four, Camp I: courtesy of Robert Schauer; chapter five, Camp II: courtesy of Robert Schauer; chapter six, helicopter rescue: courtesy of Robert Schauer; chapter seven, decision to return: courtesy of Robert Schauer; chapter eight, Sherpas: courtesy of Araceli Segarra; chapter nine, Jamling on the summit: Tenzing Collection; chapter 10, funeral procession: Tenzing Collection